ISBN 978-0-483-14801-7
PIBN 10463480

This book is a reproduction of an important historical work. Forgotten Books uses state-of-the-art technology to digitally reconstruct the work, preserving the original format whilst repairing imperfections present in the aged copy. In rare cases, an imperfection in the original, such as a blemish or missing page, may be replicated in our edition. We do, however, repair the vast majority of imperfections successfully; any imperfections that remain are intentionally left to preserve the state of such historical works.

WORKS,

IN

VERSE and PROSE,

Of the Late RIGHT HONOURABLE

JOSEPH ADDISON, Esq;

With some Account of the LIFE and
WRITINGS of the AUTHOR,

By Mr. TICKELL.

VOLUME *the* SECOND.

DUBLIN:

Printed by R. REILLY, on *Cork-Hill*,
For GEORGE RISK, GEORGE EWING, and
WILLIAM SMITH, Booksellers in *Dame-
Street*, MDCCXXXV.

THE
DRUMMER:

OR, THE

HAUNTED HOUSE.

·A

COMEDY.

As it is Acted at the

Theatre-Royal in *Drury-Lane.*

BY

His MAJESTY's Servants.

———*Falſis terroribus implet*
Ut magus——————   HOR.

Printed in the YEAR M,DCC,XXXV,

THE

PREFACE.

HAVING recommended this Play to the Town, and delivered the Copy of it to the Bookfeller, I think myfelf obliged to give fome Account of it.

It had been fome Years in the Hands of the Author, and falling under my Perufal, I thought fo well of it, that I perfuaded him to make fome Additions and Alterations to it, and let it appear upon the Stage. I own I was very highly pleafed with it, and lik'd it the better, for the want of thofe ftudied Similes and Repartees, which we, who have writ before him, have thrown into our Plays, to indulge and gain upon a falfe Tafte

that

that has prevailed for many Years in the *Britiſh* Theatre. I believe the Author would have condeſcended to fall into this way a little more than he has, had he before the writing of it been often preſent at Theatrical Repreſentations. I was confirmed in my thoughts of the Play, by the Opinion of better Judges to whom it was communicated, who obſerved that the Scenes were drawn after *Moliere*'s Manner, and that an eaſy and natural Vein of Humour ran through the whole.

I do not queſtion but the Reader will diſcover this, and ſee many Beauties that eſcaped the Audience; the Touches being too delicate for every Taſte in a Popular Aſſembly. My Brother-ſharers were of opinion, at the firſt reading of it, that it was like a Picture in which the Strokes were not ſtrong enough to appear at a diſtance. As it is not in the common way of writing, the Approbation was at firſt doubtful, but has riſen every time it has been Acted, and has given an Opportunity in ſeveral of its Parts for as juſt and good Action as ever I ſaw on the Stage.

The

The Reader will confider that I fpeak here, not as the Author, but as the Patentee. Which is, perhaps, the Reafon why I am not diffufe in the Praifes of the Play, left I fhould feem like a Man who cries up his own Wares only to draw in Cuftomers

Richard Steele.

PRO-

PROLOGUE.

*I*N this grave Age, when Comedies are few,
   We crave your Patronage for one that's New;
Tho' 'twere poor Stuff, yet bid the Author fair,
And let the Scarceness recommend the Ware.
Long have your Ears been fill'd with tragick Parts,
Blood and Blank-verse have harden'd all your Hearts;
If e'er you smile, 'tis at some Party Stroaks,
Round-heads and Wooden-shoes are standing Jokes;
The same Conceit gives Claps and Hisses Birth,.
You're grown such Politicians in your Mirth!
For once we try (tho' tis, I own, unsafe,)
To please you All, and make both Parties laugh.

   Our Author, anxious for his Fame to-night,
And bashful in his first Attempt to write,
Lies cautiously obscure and unreveal'd,
Like antient Actors in a Masque conceal'd.
Censure, when no Man knows who writes the Play,
Were much good Malice meerly thrown away.
The mighty Criticks will not blast, for shame,.
A raw young Thing, who dares not tell his Name:
Good-natur'd Judges will th' Unknown defend,
And fear to blame, lest they shou'd hurt a Friend:

Each

PROLOGUE.

Each Wit may praise it, for his own dear Sake,
And hint he writ it, if the Thing shou'd take.
But if you're rough, and use him like a Dog,
Depend upon it———He'll remain Incog.
If you shou'd hiss, he swears he'll hiss as high,
And like a Culprit, join the Hue-and-Cry.

If cruel Men are still averse to spare
These Scenes, they fly for refuge to the Fair.
Tho' with a Ghost our Comedy be heighten'd,
Ladies, upon my word, you shan't be frighten'd;
O, 'tis a Ghost that scorns to be uncivil,
A well-spread, lusty, Jointure-hunting Devil:
An am'rous Ghost, that's faithful, fond and true,
Made up of Flesh and Blood———as much as you.
Then every Evening come in Flocks, undaunted,
We never think this House is too much Haunted.

A 5   Dramatis

Dramatis Personæ.

Sir George Truman,	Mr. *Wilks.*
Tinfel,	Mr. *Ciber.*
Fantome *the Drummer*,	Mr. *Mills.*
Vellum, *Sir* George Truman's Steward,	} Mr. *Johnfon.*
Butler,	Mr. *Penketham.*
Coachman,	Mr. *Miller.*
Gardiner,	Mr. *Morris.*
Lady Truman,	Mrs. *Oldfield.*
Abigal,	Mrs. *Saunders.*

THE

THE
DRUMMER:
OR, THE
HAUNTED-HOUSE.

❈❈❈❈❈❈❈❈❈❈❈❈❈❈❈❈❈❈❈❈❈

ACT I. SCENE I.

A Great Hall.

Enter the Butler, Coachman, *and* Gardiner.

BUTLER.

THERE came another Coach to Town laſt Night, that brought a Gentleman to enquire about the ſtrange Noiſe, we hear in the Houſe. This Spirit will bring a Power of Cuſtom to the *George*——If ſo be he continues his Pranks, I deſign to ſell a Pot of Ale, and ſet up the Sign of the Drum.

Coach,

Coach. I'll give Madam warning, that's flat——I've always liv'd in sober Families. I'll not disparage my self to be a Servant in a House that is haunted.

Gard. I'll e'en marry *Nell*, and rent a bit of Ground of my own, if both of you leave Madam; not but that Madam's a very good Woman——if Mrs. *Abigal* did not spoil her——come, here's her Health.

Butl. It's a very hard thing to be a Butler in a House, that is disturb'd. He made such a Racket in the Cellar last Night, that I'm afraid he'll sour all the Beer in my Barrels.

Coach. Why then, *John*, we ought to take it off as fast as we can. Here's to you——He rattled so loud under the Tiles last Night, that I verily thought the House wou'd have fallen over our Heads. I durst not go up into the Cock-loft this Morning, if I had not got one of the Maids to go along with me.

Gard. I thought I heard him in one of my Bed-posts —I marvel, *John*, how he gets into the House when all the Gates are shut.

Butl. Why look ye, *Peter*, your Spirit will creep you into an Augre-hole :——he'll whisk ye through a Key-hole, without so much as justling against one of the Wards.

Coach. Poor Madam is mainly frighted, that's certain, and verily believes 'tis my Master that was kill'd in the last Campaign.

Butl. Out of all manner of question, *Robin*, 'tis Sir *George*. Mrs. *Abigal* is of Opinion it can be none but his Honour; he always lov'd the Wars, and you know was mightily pleas'd from a Child with the Musick of a Drum.

Gard. I wonder his Body was never found after the Battle.

Butl. Found ! Why, you fool, is not his Body here about the House ? Dost thou think he can beat his Drum without Hands and Arms ?

Coach. 'Tis Master as sure as I stand here alive, and I verily believe I saw him last Night in the Town-close.

Gard. Ay ! how did he appear ?

Coach.

Coach. Like a white Horſe.

Butl. Pho, *Robin*, I tell ye he has never appear'd yet but in the Shape of the Sound of a Drum.

Coach. This makes one almoſt afraid of one's own Shadow. As I was walking from the Stable t'other Night without my Lanthorn, I fell acroſs a Beam that lay in my way, and faith my Heart was in my Mouth ——I thought I had ſtumbled over a Spirit.

Butl. Thou might'ſt as well have ſtumbled over a Straw, why, a Spirit is ſuch a little little Thing, that I have heard a Man, who was a great Scholar, ſay, that he'll dance ye a *Lancaſhire* Horn-pipe upon the point of a Needle——As I ſat in the Pantry laſt Night, counting my Spoons, the Candle methought burnt blue, and the ſpay'd Bitch look'd as if ſhe ſaw ſomething.

Coach. Ay poor Cur, ſhe's aimoſt frighten'd out of her Wits.

Gard. Ay I warrant ye, ſhe hears him many a time and often when we don't.

Butl. My Lady muſt have him laid, that's certain, whatever it coſt her.

Gard. I fancy, when one goes to market, one might hear of ſomebody that can make a ſpell.

Coach. Why may not the Parſon of our Pariſh lay him?

Butl. No, no, no, our Parſon cannot lay him.

Coach. Why not he as well as another man?

Butl. Why, ye fool, he is not qualified——He has not taken the oaths.

Gard. Why, d'ye think *John*, that the Spirit wou'd take the law of him?——faith, I cou'd tell you one way to drive him off.

Coach. How's that?

Gard. I'll tell you immediately [*drinks.*]——I fancy Mrs. *Abigal* might ſcold him out of the houſe.

Coach. Ay, ſhe has a tongue that would drown his Drum, if any thing cou'd.

Butl. Pugh, this is all froth! you underſtand nothing of the matter————the next time it makes a noiſe, I tell you what ought to be done,——I would have the ſteward ſpeak *Latin* to it. *Coach.*

Coach. Ay, that wou'd do, if the ſteward had but courage.

Gard. There you have it———He's a fearful man. If I had as much learning as he, and I met the ghoſt, I'd, tell him his own! but alack what can one of us poor men do with a Spirit, that can neither write nor read?

Butl. Thou art always cracking and boaſting, *Peter;* thou doſt not know what miſchief it might do thee, if ſuch a ſilly dog as thee ſhould offer to ſpeak to it. For ought I know, he might flea thee alive, and make parchment of thy ſkin to cover his Drum with.

Gard. A fiddleſtick! tell not me———I fear nothing; not I! I never did harm in my life, I never committed murder.

Butl. I verily believe thee, keep thy temper, *Peter;* after ſupper we'll drink each of us a double mug, and then let come what will.

Gard. Why that's well ſaid *John,* an honeſt man that is not quite ſober, has nothing to fear———Here's to ye— why how if he ſhou'd come this minute, here wou'd I ſtand. Ha! what noiſe is that?

Butl. and *Coach.* Ha! where?

Gard. The devil! the devil! Oh no, 'tis Mrs *Abigal.*

Butl. Ay faith! 'tis ſhe; 'tis Mrs. *Abigal!* a good miſtake! 'tis Mrs. *Abigal.*

Enter A B I G A L.

Ab. Here are your drunken ſots for you! Is this a time to be guzling, when gentry are come to the houſe! why don't you lay your cloth? How came you out of the ſtables? Why are not you at work in your garden?

Gard. Why, yonder's the fine *Londoner* and Madam fetching a walk together, and methought they look'd as if they ſhould ſay they had rather have my room than my company.

Butl. And ſo forſooth being all three met together, we are doing our endeavours to drink this ſame Drummer out of our heads.

Gard. For you muſt know, Mrs. *Abigal,* we are all of opinion, that one can't be a match for him, unleſs one be as drunk as a Drum.

Coach.

Coach. I am refolved to give Madam warning to hire herfelf another coachman; for I came to ferve my Mafter, d'ye fee, while he was alive, but do fuppofe that he has no further occafion for a coach, now he walks.

Butl. Truly, Mrs. *Abigal*, I muft needs fay, that this fame Spirit is a very odd fort of a body, after all, to fright Madam and his old fervants at this rate.

Gard. And truly, Mrs. *Abigal*, I muft needs fay, I ferv'd my Mafter contentedly, while he was living; but I will ferve no Man living (that is, no Man that is not living) without double wages.

Ab. Ay, 'tis fuch cowards as you that go about with idle ftories, to difgrace the houfe, and bring fo many Strangers about it; you firft frighten your felves, and then your neighbours.

Gard. Frighten'd! I fcorn your words. Frighten'd quoth-a!

Ab. What you fot! are you grown pot-valiant?

Gard. Frighten'd with a Drum! that's a good one! it will do us no harm, I'll anfwer for it. It will bring no bloodfhed along with it, take my word. It founds as like a train-band Drum as ever I heard in my life.

Butl. Pr'ythee, *Peter*, don't be fo prefumptuous.

Ab. Well, thefe drunken rogues take it as I could wifh. [*Afide.*

Gard. I fcorn to be frightned, now I am in for't; if old *Dub-a-dub* fhou'd come into the room, I wou'd take him————

Butl. Pr'ythee hold thy tongue.

Gard. I would take him—[*The Drum beats, the* Gard. *endeavours to get off, and falls.*

Butl. and *Coach.* Speak to it Mrs. *Abigal.*

Gard. Spare my life, and take all I have.

Coach. Make off, make off, good Butler, and let us go hide ourfelves in the cellar. [*They all run off.*

Abigal *fola.*

Ab. So, now the coaft is clear, I may venture to call out my Drummer.————But firft let me fhut the door,

left we be furpriz'd. Mr. *Fantome*, Mr. *Fantome!* [*He beats.*] Nay, nay, pray come out, the enemy's fled——— I muft fpeak with you immediately———don't ftay to beat a parley.   [*The back Scene opens, and difcovers*
                                 Fantome *with a Drum.*

Fant. Dear Mrs. *Nabby*, I have overheard all that has been faid, and find thou haft manag'd the thing fo well, that I could take thee in my arms, and kifs thee— if my Drum did not ftand in my way.

Ab. Well, O'my confcience, you are the merrieft ghoft! and the very picture of Sir *George Trueman.*

Fant. There you flatter me, Mrs *Abigal;* Sir *George* had that frefhnefs in his looks, that we Men of the town cannot come up to.

Ab. Oh! Death may have alter'd you, you know——— befides, you muft confider, you loft a great deal of blood in the battle.

Fant. Ay, that's right ; let me look never fo pale, this cut crofs my forehead will keep me in countenance.

Ab. 'Tis juft fuch a one as my mafter receiv'd from a curfed *French* trooper, as my Lady's letter inform'd her.

Fant. It happens luckily that this fuit of cloaths of Sir *George's* fits me fo well———I think I can't fail hitting the air of a Man with whom I was fo long acquainted.

Ab. You are the very Man———I vow I almoft ftart when I look upon you.

Fant. But what good will this do me, if I muft remain invifible ?

Ab. Pray what good did your being vifible do you ? The fair Mr. *Fantome* thought no woman cou'd withftand him ———But when you were feen by my Lady in your pro-per perfon, after fhe had taken a full furvey of you, and heard all the pretty things you could fay, fhe very civilly difmifs'd you for the fake of this empty, noify creature *Tinfel.* She fancies you have been gone from hence this fortnight.

Fant. Why really I love thy Lady fo well, that tho' I had no hopes of gaining her for my felf, I cou'd not bear to fee her given to another, efpecially fuch a wretch as *Tinfel.*

                                                          Ab.

Ab. Well, tell me truly Mr. *Fantome*, have not you a great opinion of my fidelity to my dear Lady, that I would not ſuffer her to be deluded in this manner, for leſs than a thouſand pound?

Fant. Thou art always reminding me of my promiſe—thou ſhalt have it, if thou canſt bring our project to bear; do'ſt not know that ſtories of ghoſts and apparitions gene-rally end in a pot of money?

Ab. Why, truly now Mr. *Fantome*, I ſhou'd think my ſeif a very bad Woman, if I had done what I do, for a farthing leſs.

Fant. Dear *Abigal*, how I admire thy virtue!

Ab. No, no, Mr. *Fantome*, I defy the worſt of my enemies to ſay I love miſchief for miſchief ſake.

Fant. But is thy Lady perſuaded that I am the ghoſt of her deceaſed huſband?

Ab. I endeavour to make her believe ſo, and tell her every time your Drum rattles, that her husband is chiding her for entertaining this new lover.

Fant. Pr'ythee make uſe of all thy art, for I am tir'd to death with ſtrowling round this wide old houſe like a rat behind a wainſcot.

Ab. Did not I tell you, 'twas the pureſt place in the world for you to play your tricks in? there's none of the family that knows every hole and corner in it, beſides my-ſelf.

Fant. Ah Mrs. *Abigal!* you have had your intrigues—

Ab. For you muſt know, when I was a romping young girl, I was a mighty lover of *hide and ſeek*.

Fant. I believe, by this time, I am as well acquainted with the houſe as yourſelf.

Ab. You are very much miſtaken, Mr. *Fantome*; but no matter for that; here is to be your ſtation to-night. This is the place unknown to any one living beſides my ſelf, ſince the death of the joyner; who, you muſt under-ſtand, being a lover of mine, contriv'd the wainſcot to move to and fro, in the manner that you find it. I deſign'd it for a wardrobe for my lady's caſt cloaths. Oh! the ſto-machers, ſtays, petticoats, commodes, lac'd ſhoes, and good things that I have had in it!——pray take care you
don't

don't break the cherry-brandy bottle that ſtands up in the corner.

Fant. Well, Mrs. *Abigal,* I hire your cloſet of you but for this one night—a thouſand pound you know is a very good rent.

Ab. Well, get you gone; you have ſuch a way with you, there's no denying you any thing!

Fant. I'm a thinking how *Tinſel* will ſtare when he ſees me come out of the wall: for I am reſolved to make my appearance to-night.

Ab Get you in, get you in, my Lady's at the door.

Fan. Pray take care ſhe does not keep me up ſo late as ſhe did laſt night, or depend upon it I'll beat the Tattoo.

Ab. I'm undone, I'm undone—— [*As he is going in*] Mr. *Fantome,* Mr. *Fantome,* you have put the thouſand pound bond into my brother's hands.

Fant. Thou ſhalt have it, I tell thee, thou ſhalt have it.
                                        [Fantome *goes in.*

Ab. No more words———vaniſh, vaniſh.

Enter Lady.

Ab. [*opening the door.*] Oh, dear Madam, was it you that made ſuch a knocking? my heart does ſo beat—— I vow you have frighted me to death——I thought verily it had been the Drummer.

Lady. I have been ſhowing the garden to Mr. *Tinſel;* he's moſt inſufferably witty upon us about this ſtory of the Drum.

Ab. Indeed, Madam, he's a very looſe man! I'm a-fraid 'tis he that hinders my poor maſter from reſting in his grave,

Lady. Well! an *Infidel* is ſuch a novelty in the country, that I am reſolv'd to divert my ſelf a day or two at leaſt with the oddneſs of his converſation.

Ab. Ah! Madam! the Drum began to beat in the houſe as ſoon as ever this creature was admitted to viſit you. All the while Mr. *Fantome* made his addreſſes to you, there was not a mouſe ſtirring in the family more than us'd to be———

Lady. This baggage has ſome deſign upon me, more
                                        than

than I can yet diſcover. [*Aſide.*]——Mr. *Fantome* was always thy favourite.

Ab. Ay, and ſhou'd have been yours too, by my conſent! Mr. *Fantome* was not ſuch a ſlight fantaſtick thing as this is.———Mr. *Fantome* was the beſt-built man one ſhou'd ſee in a ſummer's day! Mr. *Fantome* was a Man of Honour, and lov'd you! Poor ſoul! how has he ſigh'd when he has talk'd to me of my hard-hearted Lady.—— Well! I had as lief as a thouſand pounds you would marry Mr. *Fantome!*

Lady. To tell thee truly, I lov'd him well enough till I found he lov'd me ſo much. But Mr. *Tinſel* makes his court to me with ſo much neglect and indifference; and with ſuch an agreeable ſaucineſs.———Not that I ſay I'll marry him.

Ab. Marry him, quoth-a! no, if you ſhould, you'll be awaken'd ſooner than marry'd couples generally are— You'll quickly have a Drum at your window.

Lady. I'll hide my contempt of *Tinſel* for once, if it be but to ſee what this wench drives at. [*Aſide.*

Ab. Why, ſuppoſe your husband, after this fair warning he has given you, ſhou'd found you an alarm at Midnight; then open your Curtains with a Face as pale as my apron, and cry out with a hollow voice, What doſt thou do in Bed with this ſpindle-ſhank'd Fellow?

Lady. Why wilt thou needs have it to be my Husband? he never had any reaſon to be offended at me. I always lov'd him while he was living, and ſhould prefer him to any Man, were he ſo ſtill. Mr. *Tinſel* is indeed very idle in his Talk, but I fancy, *Abigal,* a diſcreet Woman might reform him.

Ab. That's a likely matter indeed! did you ever hear of a Woman who had power over a Man, when ſhe was his Wife, that had none while ſhe was his Miſtreſs! Oh! there's nothing in the world improves a Man in his Complaiſance like Marriage!

Lady. He is indeed, at preſent, too familiar in his Converſation.

Ab. Familiar! Madam, in troth, he's downright rude.

Lady. But that you know, *Abigal,* ſhows he has no

Diffi-

Diffimulation in him———Then he is apt to jeft a little too
much upon grave Subjects.

Ab. Grave Subjects! he jefts upon the Church.

Lady. But that you know, *Abigal,* may be only to fhew
his Wit———Then it muft be own'd, he is extreamly
talkative.

Ab. Talkative d'ye call it! he's downright impertinent.

Lady. But that you know, *Abigal,* is a fign he has been
us'd to good Company———Then indeed he is very pofitive.

Ab. Pofitive! Why he contradicts you in every thing
you fay.

Lady. But then you know, *Abigal,* he has been educated at the Inns of Court.

Ab. A bleffed Education indeed! it has made him forget his Catechifm!

Lady. You talk as if you hated him.

Ab. You talk as if you lov'd him.

Lady. Hold your tongue! here he comes.

Enter Tinfel.

Tinf. My dear Widow!

Ab. My dear Widdow! marry come up! *Afide.*

Lady. Let him alone, *Abigal,* fo long as he does not
call me My dear Wife, there's no harm done.

Tinf. I have been moft ridiculoufly diverted fince I left
you———your fervants have made a convert of my
booby. His head is fo filled with this foolifh ftory of a
Drummer, that I expect the rogue will be afraid hereafter
to go upon a meffage by moon-light.

Lady. Ah, Mr. *Tinfel,* what a lofs of billet-doux would
that be to many a fine lady!

Ab. Then you ftill believe this to be a foolifh ftory? I
thought my Lady had told you, that fhe had heard it
herfelf.

Tin. Ha, ha, ha!

Ab. Why, you would not perfuade us out of our fenfes?

Tinf. Ha, ha, ha!

Ab. There's manners for you, Madam. *Afide.*

Lady. Admirably rally'd! that laugh is unanfwerable!
now I'll be hang'd if you could forbear being witty upon

me,

me, if I ſhould tell.you I heard it no longer ago than laſt
night.

Tinſ. Fancy!

Lady. But what if I ſhould tell you my maid was
with me!

Tinſ. Vapours! vapours! pray my dear Widow, will
you anſwer me one queſtion?————had you ever this
noiſe of a Drum in your head, all the while your huſband
was living?

Lady. And pray, Mr. *Tinſel,* will you let me aſk you
another queſtion; do you think we can hear in the country, as well as you do in town?

Tinſ. Believe me, Madam, I could preſcribe you a cure
for theſe imaginations.

Ab. Don't tell my Lady of imaginations, Sir, I have
heard it my ſelf.

Tinſ. Hark thee, child——art thou not an old maid?

Ab. Sir, if I am, it is my own fault.

Tinſ. Whims! freaks! megrims! indeed Mrs. *Abigal.*

Ab. Marry, Sir, by your talk one would believe you
thought every thing that was good is a megrim.

Lady. Why truly I don't very well underſtand what
you meant by your doctrine to me in the garden juſt now,
that every thing we ſaw was made by chance.

Ab. A very pretty ſubject indeed for a lover to divert
his miſtreſs with.

Lady. But I ſuppoſe that was only a taſte of the converſation you would entertain me with after marriage.

Tinſ. Oh, I ſhall then have time to read you ſuch
lectures of motions, atoms, and nature—that you ſhall
learn to think as freely as the beſt of us, and be convinced in leſs than a month, that all about us is chance-
work.

—*Lady.* You are a very complaiſant perſon indeed, and
ſo you would make your court to me, by perſuading me
that I was made by chance!

Tinſ. Ha, ha, ha! well ſaid, my dear! why, faith,
thou wert a very lucky hit, that's certain!

Lady. Pray, Mr. *Tinſel,* where did you learn this odd
way of talking?

Tinſ.

Tinf. Ah, Widow, 'tis your country innocence makes you think it an odd way of talking.

Lady. Tho' you give no credit to ftories of apparitions, I hope you believe there are fuch things as fpirits!

Tinf. Simplicity!

Ab. I fancy you don't believe women have Souls, d'ye Sir?

Tinf. Foolifh enough!

Lady. I vow, Mr. *Tinfel,* I'm afraid malicious people will fay I'm in love with an Atheift.

Tinf. Oh, my dear, that's an old-fafhion'd word—— I'm a Free-thinker, child.

Ab. I am fure you are a free-fpeaker.

Lady. Really, Mr. *Tinfel,* confidering that you are fo fine a Gentleman, I'm amaz'd where you got all this learning! I wonder it has not fpoil'd your breeding.

Tinf. To tell you the truth, I have not time look into thefe dry matters myfelf, but I am convinc'd by four or five learned men, whom I fometimes over-hear at a Coffee-houfe I frequent, that our fore-fathers were a pack of affes, that the world has been in an error for fome thoufands of years, and that all the People upon earth, excepting thofe two or three worthy Gentlemen, are impos'd upon, cheated, bubbled, abus'd, bamboozl'd——

Ab. Madam, how can you hear fuch a profligate? he talks like the *London* prodigal.

Lady, Why really, I'm a thinking, if there be no fuch things as fpirits, a woman has no occafion for marrying———fhe need not be afraid to lie by herfelf.

Tinf. Ah! my dear! are hufbands good for nothing but to frighten away fpirits? doft thou think I could not inftruct thee in feveral other comforts of matrimony?

Lady. Ah! but you are a man of fo much knowledge that you would always be laughing at my ignorance——— you learned men are fo apt to defpife one!

Tinf. No, Child, I'd teach thee my principles, thou fhould'ft be as wife as I am———in a week's time.

Lady. Do you think your principles would make a woman the better wife?

Tinf. Pr'ythee, Widow don't be queer.

Lady.

Lady.. I love a gay temper, but I would not have you
rally things that are ferious.

Tinf. Well enough faith! where's the jeft of rallying
any thing elfe!

Ab. Ah, Madam, did you ever hear Mr. *Fantome* talk
at this rate?   [*Afide.*

Tinf. But where's this ghoft! the fon of a whore of a
Drummer? I'd fain hear him methinks.

Ab. Pray, Madam, don't fuffer him to give the Ghoft
fuch ill language, efpecially when you have reafon to believe it is my mafter.

Tinf. That's well enough faith, *Nab*; doft thou think
thy mafter is fo unreafonable, as to continue his claim to
his Relict after his bones are laid? Pray, Widow, remember the words of your contract, you have fulfill'd
them to a tittle————did not you marry Sir *George* to
the tune of, *'till death us do part?*

Lady. I muft not hear Sir *George*'s memory treated in
fo flight a manner ————this fellow muft have been a
fome pains to make himfelf fuch a finifh'd coxcomb.
                                                 [*Afide.*

Tinf. Give me but poffeffion of your perfon, and I'l
whirl you up to town for a winter, and cure you at once.
Oh! I have known many a country Lady come to *London* with frightful ftories of the hall houfe being haunted,
of fairies, fpirits, and witches; that by the time fhe
had feen a Comedy, play'd at an Affembly, and ambled
in a Ball or two, has been fo little afraid of bugbears,
that fhe has ventur'd home in a chair at all hours of the
night.

Ab. Hum————fauce-box.   *Afide.*

Tinf. 'Tis the folitude of the country that creates thefe
whimfies; there was never fuch a thing as a Ghoft heard
of at *London*, except in the play houfe—Oh we'd pafs
all our time in *London*. 'Tis the fcene of pleafure and
diverfions, where there's fomething to amufe you every
hour of the day. Life's not life in the country.

Lady. Well then, you have an opportunity of fhowing
the fincerity of that love to me which you profefs. You
                                                    may

may give a proof that you have an affection to my perfon, not my jointure.

Tinf. Your jointure! how can you think me fuch a
dog! but child, wont your jointure be the fame thing in
London as in the country?

Lady. No, you're deceiv'd! you muft know it is fettled
on me by marriage-articles, on condition that I live in
this old manfion-houfe, and keep it up in repair.

Tinf. How!

Ab. That's well put, Madam.

Tinf. Why faith I have been looking upon this houfe,
and think it is the prettieft habitation I. ever faw in my
life.

Lady. Ay, but then this cruel Drum!

Tinf. Something fo venerable in it!

Lady. Ay, but the Drum!

Tinf. For my part, I like this *Gothick* way of building
better than any of your new orders————it would be a
thoufand pities it fhould fall to ruin.

Lady. Ay, but the Drum!

Tinf. How pleafantly we two could pafs our time in this
delicious fituation. Our lives wou'd be a continu'd dream
of happinefs. Come, faith, Widow, let's go upon the
leads, and take a view of the country.

Lady. Ay, but the Drum! the Drum!

Tinf. My dear, take my word for't 'tis all fancy: befides, fhou'd he drum in thy very bed-chamber, I fhould
only hug thee the clofer.

Clafp'd in the folds of love, I'd meet my doom,
And act my joys, tho' thunder fhook the room.

ACT

ACT II. SCENE I.

SCENE opens, and difcovers Vellum *in his Office, and a Letter in his hand.*

VELLUM.

THIS Letter aftonifheth; may I believe my own eyes——or rather my fpectacles——*To* Humphrey Vellum, *Efq; Steward to the Lady* Truman.

> Vellum,
>
> I Doubt not but you will be glad to hear your mafter is alive, and defigns to be with you in half an hour. The report of my being flain in the Netherlands, has, I find, produced fome diforders in my family. I am now at the George-Inn: If an old man with a grey beard, in a black cloak, enquires after you, give him admittance. He paffes for a Conjurer, but is really
>
> Your faithful Friend,
> G. Trueman.
>
> P. S. Let this be a fecret, and you fhall find your account in it.

This amazeth me! and yet the reafons why I fhould believe he is ftill living are manifold——Firft, becaufe this has often been the cafe of other military adventures.

Secondly, becaufe the news of his death was firft publifh'd in *Dier's Letter.*

Thirdly, becaufe this letter can be written by none but himfelf——I know his hand, and manner of fpelling.

Fourthly,——

Enter BUTLER.

Butl. Sir, here's a ftrange old Gentleman that asks for you; he fays he's a Conjurer, but he looks very fufpicious; I wifh he ben't a Jefuit.

Vel. Admit him immediately.

Butl. I wish he ben't a Jesuit; but he says he's nothing but a Conjurer.

Vel. He says right——he is no more than a Conjurer, bring him in and withdraw.   [*Exit* Butler.

And Fourthly, as I was saying, because——

Enter B U T L E R *with Sir* G E O R G E.

Butl. Sir, here is the Conjurer——what a devilish long beard he has! I warrant it has been growing these hundred years.   [*Aside. Exit.*

Sir Geo. Dear *Vellum,* you have receiv'd my Letter: but before we proceed lock the door.

Vel. It is his voice.   [*Shuts the door.*

Sir Geo. In the next place help me off with this cumbersome Cloak.

Vel. It is his shape.

Sir Geo. So now lay my beard upon the table.

Vel. [*After having look'd on Sir* George *thro' his spectacles.*] It is his face, every lineament!

Sir Geo. Well, now I have put off the Conjurer and the old man, I can talk to thee more at my ease.

Vel. Believe me, my good master, I am as much rejoiced to see you alive, as I was upon the day you were born. Your name was, in all the news papers, in the list of those that were slain.

Sir Geo. We have not time to be particular. I shall only tell thee in general, that I was taken prisoner in the battle, and was under close confinement for several months. Upon my release, I was resolv'd to surprize my wife with the news of my being alive. I know, *Vellum,* you are a person of so much penetration, that I need not use any further arguments to convince you that I am so.

Vel. I am——and moreover, I question not but your good Lady will likewise be convinced of it. Her honour is a discerning Lady.

Sir Geo. I'm only afraid she shou'd be convinc'd of it to her sorrow. Is not she pleas'd with her imaginary Widow-hood? Tell me truly, was she afflicted at the report of my death?

Vel. Sorely.

                                          Sir Geo.

Sir Geo. How long did her grief laſt?

Vel. Longer than I have known any Widow's——at leaſt three days.

Sir Geo. Three days, ſay'ſt thou? three whole days? I'm afraid thou flattereſt me!——O woman! woman!

Vel. Grief is twofold.

Sir Geo. This blockhead is as methodical as ever—— but I know he's honeſt. [*Aſide.*

Vel. There is a real grief, and there is a methodical grief; ſhe was drown'd in tears till ſuch time as the Taylor had made her Widow's weeds——indeed they became her.

Sir Geo. Became her! and was that her comfort? truly a moſt ſeaſonable conſolation!

Vel. But I muſt needs ſay ſhe paid a due regard to your memory, and could not forbear weeping when ſhe ſaw company.

Sir Geo. That was kind indeed! I find ſhe griev'd with a great deal of good-breeding. But how comes this gang of lovers about her?

Vel. Her jointure is conſiderable.

Sir Geo. How this fool torments me! [*Aſide.*

Vel. Her perſon is amiable——

Sir Geo. Death! [*Aſide.*

Vel. But her character is unblemiſh'd. She has been as virtuous in your abſence as a *Penelope*————

Sir Geo. And has had as many ſuitors.

Vel. Several have made their overtures.

Sir Geo. Several!

Vel. But ſhe has rejected all.

Sir Geo. There thou reviv'ſt me——but what means this *Tinſel?* Are his viſits acceptable?

Vel. He is young.

Sir Geo. Does ſhe liſten to him?

Vel. He is gay.

Sir Geo. Sure ſhe could never entertain a thought of marrying ſuch a coxcomb!

Vel. He is not ill made.

Sir Geo. Are the vows and proteſtations that paſt between us come to this! I can't bear the thought of it! is *Tinsel* the man design'd for my worthy successor ?

Vel. You do not consider that you have been dead these fourteen months———

Sir Geo. Was there ever such a dog ?   [*Aside.*

Vel. And I have often heard her say, that she must never expect to find a second Sir *George Truman*———meaning your ho-nour.

Sir Geo. I think she lov'd me; but I must search into this story of the *Drummer* before I discover my self to her. I have put on this habit of a Conjurer, in order to introduce my self. It must be your business to recommend me as a most profound person, that by my great knowledge in the curious arts can silence the *Drummer*, and dispossess the house.

Vel. I am going to lay my accounts before my Lady, and I will endeavour to prevail upon her Ho-nour to admit the tryal of your art.

Sir Geo. I have scarce heard of any of these stories that did not arise from a love-intrigue———Amours raise as many ghosts as murders.

Vel. Mrs. *Abigal* endeavours to persuade us, that 'tis your ho-nour who troubles the house.

Sir Geo. That convinces me 'tis a cheat, for I think, *Vellum*, I may be pretty well assur'd it is not me.

Vel. I am apt to think so truly. Ha—ha—ha!

Sir Geo. *Abigal* had always an ascendant over her Lady, and if there is a trick in this matter, depend upon it she is at the bottom of it. I'll be hang'd if this ghost be not one of *Abigal's* familiars.

Vel. Mrs. *Abigal* has of late been very mysterious.

Sir Geo. I fancy, *Vellum*, thou could'st worm it out of her. I know formerly there was an amour between you.

Vel. Mrs. *Abigal* hath her allurements, and she knows I have pick'd up a competency in your Ho-nour's service.

Sir Geo. If thou hast, all I ask of thee in return is, that thou would'st immediately renew thy addresses to her. Coax her up. Thou hast such a silver tongue, *Vellum*, as 'twill be impossible for her to withstand. Besides, she is

ſo very a Woman, that ſhe'll like thee the better for giving her the pleaſure of telling a ſecret. In ſhort, whee-
dle her out of it, and I ſhall act by the Advice which thou
giveſt me.

Vel. Mrs. *Abigal* was never deaf to me, when I talk'd
upon that ſubject. I will take an opportunity of addreſſing my ſelf to her in the moſt pathetick manner.

Sir Geo. In the mean time lock me up in your office,
and bring me word what ſucceſs you have——Well, ſure
I am the firſt that ever was employ'd to lay himſelf.

Vel. You act indeed a threefold part in this houſe, you
are a Ghoſt, a Conjurer, and my ho-noured Maſter Sir
George Truman; he, he, he! You will pardon me for being jocular.

Sir Geo. O, Mr. *Vellnm*, with all my heart. You
know I love you Men of wit and humour. Be as merry as thou pleaſeſt, ſo thou do'ſt thy buſineſs. [*Mimicking
him.*] You will remember *Vellum*, your commiſſion is two
fold, firſt to gain admiſſion for me to your Lady, and ſecondly to get the Secret out of *Abigal*.

Vel. It ſufficeth. [*The Scene ſhuts.*

Enter L A D Y, *ſola.*

Lady. Women who have been happy in a firſt marriage,
are the moſt apt to venture upon a ſecond. But for my
part; I had a husband ſo every way ſuited to my Inclinations, that I muſt entirely forget him, before I can like
another Man. I have now been a widow but fourteen
Months, and have had twice as many lovers, all of 'em
profeſt admirers of my perſon; but paſſionately in love
with my jointure. I think it is a revenge I owe my ſex
to make an example of this worthleſs tribe of fellows,
who grow impudent, dreſs themſelves fine, and fancy we
are oblig'd to provide for 'em. But of all my captives,
Mr. *Tinſel* is the moſt extraordinary in his kind. I hope
the diverſion I give my ſeif with him is unblameable. I'm
ſure 'tis neceſſary to turn my thoughts off from the memory of that dear Man, who has been the greateſt happineſs
and affliction of my life. My heart would be a prey to
melancholy, if I did not find theſe innocent methods of re-
lieving it. But here comes *Abigal.* I muſt teaze the

B 3 baggage

baggage, for I find she has taken it into her head that I am entirely at her disposal.

Enter ABIGAL.

Ab. Madam! Madam! yonder's Mr. *Tinsel* has as good as taken possession of your house.. Marry, he says, he must have Sir *George's* apartment. enlarg'd ; for truly, says he, I hate to be straiten'd. Nay, he was so impudent as to shew me the chamber where he intends to consummate, as he calls it.

Lady. Well! he's a wild fellow.

Ab. Indeed he's a very sad man, Madam.

Lady. He's young, *Abigal;* 'tis a thousand pities he should be lost ; I should be mighty glad to reform him.

Ab. Reform him! marry hang him!

Lady.. Has not he a great deal of life ?

Ab. Ay, enough to make your heart ake.

Lady. I dare say thou think'st him a very agreeable Fellow.

Ab. He thinks himself so, I'll answer for him.

Lady. He's very good-natur'd!

Ab. He ought to be so, for he's very silly..

Lady. Dost thou think he loves me ?

Ab. Mr. *Fantome,* did I am sure.

Lady. With what raptures he talk'd!

Ab. Yes, but 'twas in praise of your jointure-house.

Lady. He has kept bad Company.

Ab. They must be very bad indeed, if they were worse than himself.

Lady. I have a strong fancy a good woman might reform him.

Ab. It would be a fine experiment, if it shou'd not succeed.

Lady. Well, *Abigal,* we'll talk of that another time ; here comes the Steward, I have no further occasion for you at present.   -   [*Exit* Abigal,

Enter VELLUM.

Vel. Madam, is your Ho-nour at leisure to look into the accounts of the last week ? They rise very high—— house-keeping is chargeable in a house that is haunted.

Lady.

Lady. How comes that to pafs? I hope the Drum neither eats nor drinks? But read your account, *Vellum.*

Vel. [*putting on and off his fpectacles in this Scene*] A hogfhead and a half of ale—it is not for the ghoft's drinking—But your Ho-nour's fervants fay they muft have fomething to keep up their courage againft this ftrange noife. They tell me they expect a double quantity of malt in their fmall-beer, fo long as the houfe continues in this condition.

Lady. At this rate they'll take care to be frighten'd all the year round, I'll anfwer for 'em. But go on.

Vel. *Item,* Two fheep, and a—Where is the ox?—Oh, I have him—and an ox—your Ho-nour muft always have a piece of cold beef in the houfe for the entertainment of fo many ftrangers, who come from all parts to hear this Drum. *Item,* Bread, ten peck-loaves—They cannot eat beef without bread—*Item,* three barrels of table beer—They muft have drink with their meat.

Lady. Sure no Woman in *England* has a Steward that makes fuch ingenious comments on his works. [*Afide.*

Vel, *Item,* To Mr. *Tinfel's* fervants five bottles of port wine—it was by your Ho-nour's order—*Item,* three bottles of fack for the ufe of Mrs. *Abigal.*

Lady. I fuppofe that was by your own order.

Vel. We have been long friends, we are your Ho-nour's ancient fervants; fack is an innocent cordial, and gives her fpirit to chide the fervants, when they are tardy in their bus'nefs; he, he, he! pardon me for being jocular.

Lady. Well, I fee you'll come together at laft.

Vel. *Item,* A dozen pound of watch-lights for the ufe of the fervants.

Lady. For the ufe of the fervants! What, are the rogues afraid of fleeping in the dark? What an unfortunate Woman am I! This is fuch a particular diftrefs, it puts me to my wits end. *Vellum,* what wou'd you advife me to do?

Vel. Madam, your Ho-nour has two points to confider. *Imprimis,* To retrench thefe extravagant expences, which fo many ftrangers bring upon you—*Secondly,* To clear the houfe of this invifible Drummer,

Lady.

Lady. This learned divifion leaves me juft as wife as I was. But how muft we bring thefe two points to bear ?

Vel. I befeech your Ho-nour to give me the hearing.

Lady. I do. But pr'ythee take pity on me, and be not tedious.

Vel. I will be concife. There is a certain perfon arrived this morning, an aged man of a venerable afpect, and of a long hoary beard, that reacheth down to his girdle. The common people call him a wizard, a white-witch, a con-jurer, a cunning-man, a necromancer, a——

Lady. No matter for his titles. But what of all this ?

Vel. Give me the hearing, good my Lady. He pre-tends to great skill in the occult fciences, and is come hither upon the rumour of this *Drum*. If one may be-lieve him, he knows the fecret of laying ghofts, or of quieting houfes that are haunted.

Lady. Pho, thefe are idle ftories to amufe the country people, this can do us no good.

Vel. It can do us no harm, my Lady.

Lady. I dare fay thou doft not believe there is any thing in it thy felf.

Vel. I cannot fay, I do ; there is no danger however in the experiment. Let him try his skill ; if it fhou'd fucceed, we are rid of the Drum ; if it fhou'd not, we may tell the world that it has, and by that means at leaft get out of this expenfive way of living ; fo that it muft turn to your advantage one way or another.

Lady. I think you argue very rightly. But where is the Man ? I would fain fee him. He muft be a curi-ofity.

Vel. I have already difcours'd him, and he is to be with me, in my office, half an hour hence. He asks nothing for his pains, till he has done his work,—no cure, no money.

Lady. That circumftance, I muft confefs, would make one believe there is more in his art than one wou'd ima-gine. Pray *Vellum* go and fetch him hither immedi-ately.

Vel. I am gone. He fhall be forth-coming forthwith.

[*Exeunt.*

Enter

Enter B U T L E R,. C O A C H M A N, *and*
G A R D I N E R.

Butl. Rare news, my lads, rare news!

Gard. What's the matter? haſt thou got any more
vales for us?

Butl. No, 'tis better than that.

Coach. Is there another ſtranger come to the houſe?

Butl. Ay, ſuch a ſtranger as will make all our lives
eaſy.

Gard. What! is he a Lord?

Butl. A Lord! no, nothing like it,——He's a Conjurer.

Coach. A Conjurer! what, is he come a wooing to my
Lady.

Butl. No, no, you fool, he's come a purpoſe to lay
the Spirit.

Coach. Ay marry, that's good news indeed; but
where is he?

Butl. He's lock'd up with the Steward in his office,
they are laying their heads together very cloſe. I fancy
they are caſting a figure.

Gard. Pr'ythee *John* what ſort of a creature is a Conjurer.

Butl. Why he's made much as other men are, if it was
not for his long grey beard.

Coach. Look ye *Peter*, it ſtands with reaſon, that a
Conjurer ſhou'd have a long grey beard——for did ye
ever know a Witch that was not an old Woman?

Gard. Why! I remember a Conjurer once at a fair,
that to my thinking was a very ſmock-fac'd man, and yet
he ſpew'd out fifty yards of green ferret. I fancy, *John,*
if thou'dſt get him into the pantry and give him a cup of
ale, he'd ſhew us a few tricks. Do'ſt think we cou'd not
perſuade him to ſwallow one of thy caſe-knives for his
diverſion? he'll certainly bring it up again.

Butl. *Peter*, thou art ſuch a wiſe-acre! thou do'ſt not
know the difference between a Conjurer and a Jugler.
This man muſt be a very great maſter of his trade. His
beard is at leaſt half a yard long, he's dreſs'd in a ſtrange

dark

dark cloak, as black as a coal. Your Conjurer always goes in mourning.

Gard. Is he a gentleman? had he a fword by his fide?

Butl. No, no, he's too grave a Man for that, a Conjurer is as grave as a Judge——but he had a long white wand in his hand.

Coach. You may be fure there's a good deal of virtue in that wand——I fancy 'tis made out of witch-elm.

Gard. I warrant you if the Ghoft appears, he'll whisk ye that wand before his eyes, and ftrike you the drum-ftick out of his hand.

Butl. No; the wand, look ye, is to make a circle, and if he once gets the Ghoft in a circle, then he has him ——let him get out again if he can. A circle, you muft know, is a Conjurer's trap.

Coach. But what will he do with him, when he has him there?

Butl. Why then he'll overpower him with his learning.

Gard. If he can once compafs him, and get him in lobs-pound, he'll make nothing of him, but fpeak a few hard words to him, and perhaps bind him over to his good behaviour for a thoufand years.

Coach. Ay, ay, he'll fend him packing to his grave again with a flea in his ear, I warrant him.

Butl. No, no, I would advife Madam to fpare no coft. If the Conjurer be but well paid, he'll take pains upon the Ghoft, and lay him, look ye, in the red fea—— and then he's laid for ever.

Coach. Ay marry, that wou'd fpoil his Drum for him.

Gard. Why *John*, there muft be a power of fpirits in that fame red-fea——I warrant ye they are as plenty as fifh.

Coach. Well, I wifh after all that he may not be too hard for the Conjurer; I'm afraid he'll find a tough bit of work on't.

Gard. I wifh the Spirit may not carry a corner of the houfe off with him.

Butl. As for that, *Peter*, you may be fure that the Steward has made his bargain with the cunning-man beforehand, that he fhall ftand to all cofts and damages——

but

but hark! yonder's Mrs: *Abigal*, we fhall have her with
us immediately, if we do not get off.

Gard. .Ay lads! if we could get Mrs. *Abigal* well laid
too—we fhould lead merry lives.

> *For to a man like me that's ftout and bold,*
> *A Ghoft is not fo dreadful as a Scold.*

A C T III. S C E N E I.

S C E N E *opens, and difcovers* Sir George *in* Vellum's *Office.*

Sir G E O R G E.

I Wonder I don't hear of *Vellum* yet. But I know his
Wifdom will do nothing rafhly. The fellow has been
fo us'd to form in bufinefs, that it has infected his whole
converfation. But I muft not find fault with that punctu-
al and exact behaviour, which has been of fo much ufe to
me; my eftate is the better for it.

Enter V E L L U M.

Well *Vellum*, I'm impatient to hear your fuccefs.

Vel. Firft, let me lock the door.

Sir Geo. Will your Lady admit me?

Vel. If this lock is not mended foon, it will be quite
fpoiled.

Sir Geo. Pr'ythee let the lock alone at prefent, and
anfwer me.

Vel. Delays in bufinefs are dangerous—I muft fend for
the fmith next week—and in the mean time will take a
minute of it.

Sir Geo. What fays your Lady?

Vel. This Pen is naught, and wants mending———
My Lady did you fay ?

Sir Geo. Does fhe admit me ?

Vel. I have gain'd admiffion for you as a Conjurer.

Sir Geo. That's enough! I'll gain admiffion for myfelf
as a Hufband. Does fhe believe there is any thing in my
art ?

Vel. It is hard to know what a woman believes.

Sir Geo. Did fhe afk no queftions about me ?

Vel. Sundry———fhe defires to talk with you herfelf,
before you enter upon your bufinefs.

Sir Geo. But when?

Vel. Immediately. This inftant.

Sir Geo. Pugh. What haft thou been doing all this
while ! Why didft not tell me fo ? Give me my cloak——
have you yet met with *Abigal ?*

Vel, I have not yet had an opportunity of talking with
her. But we have interchanged fome languifhing glances.

Sir Geo. Let thee alone for that, *Vellum,* I have formerly feen thee ogle her through thy fpectacles. Well !
this is a moft venerable cloak. After the bufinefs of this
day is over, I'll make thee a prefent of it. 'Twill become
thee mightily.

Vel. He, he, he ! wou'd you make a Conjurer of your
Steward ?

Sir Geo. Pr'ythee don't be jocular, I'm in hafte. Help
me on with my beard.

Vel. And what will your Ho--nour do with your caft
beard ?

Sir Geo. Why, faith, thy gravity wants only fuch a
beard to it; if thou would'ft wear it with the cloak, thou
would'ft make a moft compleat heathen philofopher. But
where's my wand ?

Vel. A fine taper ftick ! it is well chofen. I will keep
this till you are fheriff of the county. It is not my cuftom
to let any thing be loft.

Sir Geo. Come *Vellum,* lead the way. You muft introduce me to your Lady. Thou'rt the fitteft Fellow in
the world to be Mafter of the ceremonies to a Conjurer.

[*Exeunt.*

Enter

Enter Abigal *croſſing the ſtage,* Tinſel *following.*

Tin. *Naby, Naby,* whither ſo faſt child ?

Ab. Keep your hands to yourſelf. I'm going to call the Steward to my Lady.

Tinſ. What ? Goodman *two-fold ?* I met him walking with a ſtrange old fellow yonder. I ſuppoſe he belongs to the family too. He looks very antique. He muſt be ſome of the furniture of this old manſion-houſe.

Ab. What does the man mean ? Don't think to palm me, as you do my lady.

Tinſ. Pr'ythee, *Nabby,* tell me one thing ; what's the reaſon thou art my Enemy ?

Ab. Marry, becauſe I'm a friend to my Lady.

Tinſ. Doſt thou ſee any thing about me thou doſt not like ? Come hither, huſſy, give me a kiſs ; don't be ill-natur'd.

Ab. Sir, I know how to be civil. [*Kiſſes her.*]——— this rogue will carry off my Lady, if I don't take care.
[*Aſide.*

Tinſ. Thy lips are as ſoft as velvet, *Abigal,* I muſt get thee a huſband.

Ab. Ay, now you don't ſpeak idly, I can talk to you.

Tinſ. I have one in my eye for thee. Doſt thou love a young luſty ſon of a whore ?

Ab. Laud, how you talk !

Tinſ. This is a thundering dog.

Ab. What is he ?

Tinſ. A private gentleman.

Ab. Ay ! where does he live ?

Tinſ. In the horſe-guards———But he has one fault I muſt tell thee of. If thou canſt bear with that, he's a man for thy purpoſe.

Ab. Pray, Mr. *Tinſel,* what may that be ?

Tinſ. He's but five and twenty years old.

Ab. 'Tis no matter for his age, if he has been well educated.

Tinſ. No man better, child ; he'll tye a wig, toſs a dye, make a paſs, and ſwear with ſuch a grace, as wou'd make thy heart leap to hear him.

Ab.

Ab. Half these accomplishments will do, provided he has an Estate——Pray what has he?

Tinf. Not a farthing.

Ab. Pox on him, what do I give him the hearing for. [*Aside.*

Tinf. But as for that I wou'd make it up to him.

Ab. How?

Tinf. Why look ye, child, as soon as I have married thy lady, I design to discard this old prig of a steward, and to put this honest gentleman, I am speaking of, into his place.

Ab. This fellow's a fool—I'll have no more to say to him. [*Aside.*]—Hark! my Lady's a coming!

Tinf. Depend upon it, *Nab*, I'll remember my promise.

Ab. Ay, and so will I too—to your cost. [*Aside.*
[*Exit* Abigal.

Tinf. My dear is purely fitted up with a maid——but I shall rid the house of her.

Enter Lady.

Lady. Oh, Mr. *Tinsel*, I am glad to meet you here, I am going to give you an entertainment, that won't be disagreeable to a man of wit and pleasure of the town——There may be something diverting in a conversation between a Conjurer, and this conceited ass. [*Aside.*

Tinf. She loves me to distraction, I see that. [*Aside.*—Pr'ythee, widow, explain thyself.

Lady. You must know here is a strange sort of man come to town, who undertakes to free the house from this disturbance. The steward believes him a Conjurer.

Tinf. Ay; thy steward is a deep one!

Lady. He's to be here immediately. It is indeed an odd figure of a man.

Tinf. Oh! I warrant you he has study'd the black art! Ha, ha, ha! Is he not an *Oxford* Scholar?—— Widow, thy house is the most extraordinarily inhabited of any widow's this day in christendom—I think thy four chief domesticks are—— a wither'd *Abigal*—— a superannuated Steward—— a Ghost——and a Conjurer.

Lady. [*mimicking* Tinsel.] And you wou'd have it inhabited.

habited by a fifth, who is a more extraordinary Perſon than any of all theſe four.

Tinſ. It's a ſure ſign a woman loves you, when ſhe imitates your manner. [*aſide.*]—Thou'rt very ſmart, my dear. But ſee! ſmoak the doctor.

Enter Vellum, *and Sir* George *in his Conjurer's habit.*

Vel. I will introduce this profound perſon to your Ladyſhip, and then leave him with you—Sir, this is her Honour,

Sir Geo. I know it well. [*Exit* Vellum. [*Aſide, walking in a muſing Poſture.*] That dear Woman l the fight of her unmans me. I cou'd weep for tenderneſs, did not I, at the ſame time, feel an indignation riſe in me, to ſee that wretch with her : And yet I cannot but ſmile to ſee her in the company of her firſt and ſecond husband at the ſame time.

Lady. Mr. *Tinſel,* do you ſpeak to him; you are us'd to the company of men of learning.

Tinſ. Old Gentleman thou doſt not look like an inhabitant of this world; I ſuppoſe thou art lately come down from the ſtars. Pray what news is ſtirring in the *Zodiack?*

Sir Geo. News that ought to make the heart of a coward tremble. *Mars* is now entring into the firſt houſe, and will ſhortly appear in all his domal dignities————

Tinſ. Mars? Pr'ythee, father grey-beard, explain thy ſelf.

Sir Geo. The entrance of *Mars* into his houſe, portends the entrance of a maſter into this family—and that ſoon.

Tinſ. D'ye hear that, Widow? The ſtars have cut me out for thy husband. This houſe is to have a maſter, and that ſoon—Hark thee, old *Gadbury,* is not *Mars* very like a young fellow call'd *Tom Tinſel?*

Sir Geo. Not ſo much as *Venus* is like this Lady.

Tinſ. A word in your ear, Doctor; theſe two Planets will be in conjunction by and by; I can tell you that.

Sir Geo. [*aſide, walking diſturb'd*] Curſe on this impertinent fop! I ſhall ſcarce forbear diſcovering myſelf— Madam, I am told that your houſe is viſited with ſtrange noiſes.

Lady.

Lady. And I am told that you can quiet them I muſt confeſs I had a curioſity to ſee the perſon I had heard ſo much of; and, indeed, your aſpect ſhows that you have had much experience in the world. You muſt be a very aged Man.

Sir Geo. My aſpect deceives you; what do you think is my real age?

Tinſ. I ſhou'd gueſs thee within three years of *Methuſelah.* Pr'ythee tell me, waſt not thou born before the flood?

Lady. Truly I ſhou'd gueſs you to be in your ſecond or third century. I warrant you, you have great grandchildren with beards of a foot long.

Sir Geo. Ha, ha, ha! If there be truth in Man, I was but five and thirty laſt *Auguſt.* O! the ſtudy of the occult Sciences makes a Man's beard grow faſter than you wou'd imagine.

Lady. What an eſcape you have had, Mr *Tinſel,* that you were not bred a Scholar!

Tinſ. And ſo I fancy, Doctor, thou think'ſt me an illiterate fellow, becauſe I have a ſmooth chin?

Sir Geo. Hark ye, Sir, a word in your ear. You are a Coxcomb by all the rules of Phyſiognomy: but let that be a ſecret between you and me. [*Aſide to* Tinſel.

Lady. Pray, Mr. *Tinſel,* what is it the Doctor whiſpers.

Tinſ. Only a compliment child, upon two or three of my features. It does not become me to repeat it.

Lady. Pray Doctor, examine this Gentleman's face, and tell me his fortune.

Sir Geo. If I may believe the lines of his face, he likes it better than I do, or—than you do fair Lady.

Tinſ. Widow, I hope now thou'rt convinc'd he's a cheat.

Lady. For my part I believe he's a witch---go on Doctor.

Sir Geo. He will be croſs'd in love; and that ſoon.

Tinſ. Pr'ythee, Doctor, tell us the truth. Doſt not thou live in *Moor-Fields?*

Sir Geo. Take my word for it, thou ſhalt never live in my Lady *Trueman's* manſion-houſe.

Tinſ. Pray, old Gentleman, haſt thou never been pluck'd by the beard when thou wert ſaucy?

Lady. Nay, Mr. *Tinſel,* you are angry! do you think I wou'd marry a man that dares not have his fortune told?

Sir Geo. Let him be angry——I matter not——he is but fhort-liv'd. He will foon die of————

Tinf. Come, come, fpeak out old *Hocus*, he, he, he! this fellow makes me burft with laughing. [*Forces a laugh.*

Sir Geo. He will foon die of a fright——or of the——. let me fee your nofe————ay————'tis fo!

Tinf. You fon of a whore! I'll run ye through the body, I never yet made the fun fhine through a Conjurer—

Lady. Oh, fy, Mr. *Tinfel!* you will not kill an old man?

Tinf. An old man! the dog fays he's but five and thirty.

Lady. Oh, fy, Mr, *Tinfel,* I did not think you could have been fo paffionate; I hate a paffionate man. Put up your fword, or I muft never fee you again.

Tin. Ha, ha, ha! I was but in jeft my dear. I had a mind to have made an experiment upon the Doctor's body. I wou'd but have drill'd a little eyelet-hole in it, and have feen whether he had art enough to clofe it up again.

Sir Geo. Courage is but ill fhown before a Lady. But know, if ever I meet thee again, thou fhalt find this arm can wield other weapons befides this wand.

Tinf. Ha, ha, ha!

Lady. Well, learned Sir, you are to give a proof of your art, not of your courage. Or if you will fhow your courage, let it be at nine a-clock—for that is the time the noife is generally heard.

Tinf. And look you old gentleman, if thou doft not do thy bufinefs well, I can tell thee by the little fkill I have, that thou wilt be tofs'd in a blanket before ten. We'll do our endeavour to fend thee back to the ftars again.

Sir Geo. I'll go and prepare my felf for the ceremonies ————and Lady, as you expect they fhou'd fucceed to your wifhes, treat that fellow with the contempt he deferves. [*Exit* Sir G.

Tinf. The faucieft dog I ever talk'd with in my whole life!

Lady. Methinks he's a diverting fellow; one may fee he's no fool

Tinf. No fool! ay, but thou doft not take him for a Conjurer.

Lady. Truly I don't know what to take him for; I am refolv'd to employ him however. When a ficknefs is
desperate

defperate, we often try remedies that we have no great faith in.

Enter Abigal.

Ab. Madam, the Tea is ready in the parlour as you or-der'd.

Lady. Come, Mr. *Tinfel,* we may there talk of this fubject more at leifure.   [*Exeunt* Lady *and* Tinfel.

Ab. (*fola*) Sure never any Lady had fuch Servants as mine has! well, if I get this thoufand pound, I hope to have fome of my own.   Let me fee, I'll have a pretty tight Girl——juft fuch as I was ten years ago (I'm afraid I may fay twenty) fhe fhall drefs me and flatter me—— for I will be flatter'd, that's pos! my Lady's caft fuits will ferve her, after I have given them the wearing.   Befides, when I am worth a thoufand pound, I fhall certainly carry off the Steward—— Madam *Vellum!* —— how prettily that will found ! Here, bring out Madam *Vellum's* Chaife ————nay, I do not know but it may be a Chariot—— It will break the attorney's Wife's heart——for I fhall take place of every body in the Parifh but my Lady.   If I have a Son, he fhall be call'd *Fantome.*   But fee Mr. *Vellum,* as I could wifh.   I know his humour, and will do my utmoft to gain his heart.

Enter Vellum *with a Pint of Sack.*

Vel. Mrs. *Abigal,* don't I break in upon you unfeafon-ably ?

Ab. Oh, no, Mr. *Vellum,* your vifits are always fea-fonable.

Vel. I have brought with me a tafte of frefh canary, which I think is delicious.

Ab. Pray fet it down——I have a dram-glafs juft by——
[*Brings in a Rummer.*
I'll pledge you ; my Lady's good health.

Vel. And your own with it——fweet Mrs. *Abigal.*

Ab. Pray, good Mr. *Vellum,* buy me a little parcel of this Sack, and put it under the article of Tea——I would not have my name appear to it.

Vel. Mrs. *Abigal,* your name feldom appears in my Bills ——and yet——if you will allow me a merry expreffion ——you have been always in my books, Mrs. *Abigal.* Ha, ha, ha !
Ab.

Ab, Ha, ha, ha ! Mr. *Vellum,* you are such a dry jesting Man !

Vel. Why truly, Mrs. *Abigal,* I have been looking over my papers——and I find you have been a long time my Debtor.

Ab. Your Debtor ! for what, Mr. *Vellum?*

Vel. For my heart, Mrs. *Abigal*——and our accounts will not be balanc'd between us, till I have yours in exchange for it. Ha, ha, ha!

Ab. Ha, ha, ha ! you are the moſt gallant Dun, Mr. *Vellum.*

Vel. But I am not us'd to be paid by words only, Mrs. *Abigal;* when will you be out of my debt ?

Ab. Oh, Mr. *Vellum,* you make one bluſh———my humble ſervice to you.

Vel. I muſt anſwer you, Mrs. *Abigal,* in the country Phraſe———*Your Love is ſufficient.* Ha, ha, ha !

Ab. Ha, ha, ha ! Well, I muſt own I love a merry Man !

Vel. Let me ſee, how long is it, Mrs. *Abigal,* ſince I firſt broke my mind to you———It was, I think *Undecimo Gulielmi*—— we have convers'd together theſe fifteen Years——and yet, Mrs. *Abigal,* I muſt drink to our better acquaintance. He, he, he———Mrs. *Abigal,* you know I am naturally jocoſe.

Ab. Ah, you Men love to make ſport with us ſilly creatures.

Vel. Mrs. *Abigal,* I have a trifle about me, which I would willingly make you a preſent of. It is indeed but a little toy.

Ab. You are always exceedingly obliging.

Vel. It is but a little toy———ſcarce worth your acceptance.

Ab. Pray do not keep me in ſuſpence ; what is it, Mr. *Vellum ?*

Vel. A ſilver thimble.

Ab. I always ſaid Mr *Vellum* was a generous lover.

Vel. But I muſt put it on myſelf, Mrs. *Abigal*——you have the prettieſt tip of a finger———I muſt take the freedom to ſalute it.

Ab.

Ab. Oh fye ! you make me afham'd, Mr. *Vellum* ; how can you do fo ? I proteft I am in fuch a confufion——

[*A feign'd ftruggle.*

Vel. This finger is not the finger of idlenefs ; it bears the honourable fcars of the needle——but why are you fo cruel as not to pare your nails ?

Ab. Oh, I vow you prefs it fo hard ! pray give me my finger again.

Vel. This middle finger, Mrs. *Abigal,* has a pretty neighbour——a wedding ring would become it mightily ——He, he, he !

Ab. You're fo full of your Jokes. Ay, but where muft I find one for it ?

Vel. I defign this thimble only as the forerunner of it, they will fet off each other, and are——indeed a twofold emblem. The firft will put you in mind of being a good hufwife, and the other of being a good wife. Ha, ha, ha !

Ab. Yes, yes, I fee you laugh at me.

Vel. Indeed I am ferious.

Ab. I thought you had quite forfaken me——I am fure you cannot forget the many repeated vows and promifes you formerly made me.

Vel. I fhou'd as foon forget the multiplication table.

Ab. I have always taken your part before my Lady.

Vel. You have fo, and I have *Item'd* it in my memory.

Ab. For I have always look'd upon your intereft as my own.

Vel. It is nothing but your cruelty can hinder them from being fo.

Ab. I muft ftrike while the Iron's hot. [*afide.*] —— Well, Mr. *Vellum,* there is no refufing you, you have fuch a bewitching tongue !

Vel. How ? fpeak that again !

Ab. Why then in plain *English* I love yon.

Vel. I'm overjoy'd !

Ab. I muft own my paffion for you.

Vel. I'm tranfported ! [*Catches her in his arms.*

Ab. Dear charming man !

Vel.

Vel. Thou fum total of all my happinefs! I fhall grow extravagant! I can't forbear!——to drink thy virtuous inclinations in a bumper of Sack. Your Lady muft make hafte, my Duck, or we fhall provide a young fteward to the Eftate, before fhe has an air to it—Pr'ythee my dear, does fhe intend to marry Mr. *Tinfel?*

Ab. Marry him! my Love, no, no! we muft take care of that! there wou'd be no ftaying in the houfe for us if fhe did. That young Rake-hell wou'd fend all the old fervants a grazing. You and I fhou'd be difcarded before the honey-moon was at an end.

Vel. Pr'ythee, fweet one, does not this Drum put the thoughts of marriage out of her head?

Ab. This Drum, my Dear, if it be well manag'd, will be no lefs than a thoufand pound in our way.

Vel. Ay, fay'it thou fo, my Turtle?

Ab. Since we are now as good as Man and Wife——I mean, almoft as good as Man and Wiife——I ought to conceal nothing from you:

Vel. Certainly my Dove, not from thy yoke-fellow, thy help mate, thy own flefh and blood!

Ab. Hufh! I hear Mr. *Tinfel's* laugh, my Lady and he are a coming this way; if you will take a turn without, I'll tell you the whole contrivance.

Vel. Give me your hand, Chicken.

Ab. Here take it, you have my heart already.

Vel. We fhall have much iffue.   [*Exeunt.*

A C T IV. S C E N E I.

Enter Vellum *and* Butler.

V E L L U M.

*J*O H N, I have certain orders to give you——and therefore be attentive.

Butl.

Butl. Attentive! ay, let me alone for that.—I ſuppoſe he means being ſober. [*aſide*.

Vel. You know I have always recommended to you a method in your buſineſs ; I wou'd have your knives and forks, your ſpoons and napkins, your plate and glaſſes, laid in a method.

Butl. Ah, Maſter *Vellum,* you are ſuch a ſweet-ſpoken man, it does one's heart good to receive your orders.

Vel. Method, *John,* makes buſineſs eaſy, it baniſhes all perplexity and confuſion out of families.

Butl. How he talks ! I cou'd hear him all day.

Vel. And now *John,* let me know whether your table-linen, your ſide-board, your cellar, and every thing elſe within your province, are properly and methodically diſ-pos'd for an entertainment this evening.

Butl. Maſter *Vellum,* they ſhall be ready at a quarter of an hour's warning. But pray, Sir, is this entertain-ment to be made for the Conjurer ?

Vel. It is, *John,* for the Conjurer, and yet it is not for the Conjurer.

Butl. Why, look you Maſter *Vellum,* if it is for the Con-jurer, the cook-maid ſhou'd have orders to get him ſome diſhes to his palate. Perhaps he may like a little brimſtone in his ſauce.

Vel. This Conjurer, *John,* is a complicated creature, an amphibious animal, a perſon of a two-fold nature—— but he eats and drinks like other men.

Butl. Marry, Maſter *Vellum,* he ſhou'd eat and drink as much as two other men, by the account you give of him.

Vel. Thy conceit is not amiſs, he is indeed a double man, ha, ha, ha !

Butl. Ha! I underſtand you, he's one of your Herma-phrodites, as they call 'em.

Vel. He is married, and he is not married—— he hath a beard, and he hath no beard. He is old, and he is young.

Butl. How charmingly he talks ! I fancy, Maſter *Vel-lum,* you cou'd make a Riddle. The ſame man old and young ! how do you make that out, Maſter *Vellum ?*

Vel.

Vel. Thou haft heard of a fnake cafting his fkin, and recovering his youth.   Such is this fage perfon.

Butl. Nay, 'tis no wonder a Conjurer fhou'd be like a Serpent.

Vel. When he has thrown afide the old Conjurer's flough that hangs about him, he'll come out as fine a young Gentleman as ever was feen in this houfe.

Butl. Does he intend to fup in his flough?

Vel. That time will fhow.

Butl. Well I have not a head for thefe things. Indeed, Mr. *Vellum*, I have not underftood one word you have faid this half hour.

Vel. I did not intend thou fhou'dft—but to our bufinefs—let there be a table fpread in the great hall. Let your pots and glaffes be wafh'd, and in a readinefs. Bid the Cook provide a plentiful fupper, and fee that all the fervants be in their beft Liveries.

Butl. Ay! now I underftand every word you fay. But I wou'd rather hear you talk a little in that t'other way.

Vel. I fhall explain to thee what I have faid by and by ——bid *Sufan* lay two pillows upon your Lady's bed.

Butl. Two pillows! Madam won't fleep upon 'em both! fhe is not a double woman too?

Vel. She will fleep upon neither. But hark, Mrs. *Abigal*, I think I hear her chiding the Cook-maid.

Butl. Then I'll away, or it will be my turn next; fhe, I am fure, fpeaks plain *Englifh*, one may eafily underftand every word fhe fays.   [*Exit* Butler.

Vellum folus.

Vel. Servants are good for nothing, unlefs they have an Opinion of the Perfon's underftanding who has the direction of them——But fee Mrs. *Abigal!* fhe has a bewitching countenance, I wifh I may not be tempted to marry her in good earneft.

Enter Abigal.

Ab. Ha! Mr. *Vellum*.

Vel. What brings my fweet one hither?

Ab. I am coming to fpeak to my friend behind the wainfcot. It is fit, child, he fhould have an account of this Conjurer, that he may not be furpriz'd.

Vel.

Vel. That wou'd be as much as thy thouſand pound is worth.

Ab. I'll ſpeak low———walls have ears.

                         [Pointing to the Wainſcot.

Vel. But heark you Ducklin! be ſure you do not tell him that I am let into the ſecret.

Ab. That's a good one indeed! as if I ſhou'd ever tell what paſſes between you and me.

Vel. No, no, my child, that muſt not be; he, he, he! that muſt not be; he, he, he!

Ab. You will always be waggiſh.

Vel. Adieu, and let me hear the reſult of your conference.

Ab. How can you leave one ſo ſoon? I ſhall think it an age till I ſee you again.

Vel. Adieu my pretty one.

Ab. Adieu ſweet Mr. *Vellum.*

Vel. My pretty one———   *[As he is going off.*

Ab. Dear Mr. *Vellum.*

Vel. My pretty one!   *[Exit* Vellum.

               Abigal *ſola.*

Ab. I have him———if I can but get this thouſand pound.   *[*Fantome *gives three raps upon his Drum behind the wainſcot.*

Ab. Ha! three raps upon the Drum! the ſignal Mr. *Fantome* and I agreed upon, when he had a mind to ſpeak with me.   *[*Fantome *raps again.*

Ab. Very well, I hear you; come fox, come out of your hole.

      Scene *opens and* Fantome *comes out.*

Ab. You may leave your Drum in the ward-robe, till you have occaſion for it.

Fant. Well, Mrs. *Abigal,* I want to hear what is a doing in the World.

Ab. You are a very inquiſitive Spirit. But I muſt tell you, if you do not take care of your ſelf, you will be laid this evening.

Fant. I have overheard ſomething of that matter. But let me alone for the Doctor———I'll engage to give a good account of him. I am more in pain about *Tinſel.*

                                         When

When a Lady's in the caſe, I'm more afraid of one Fop than twenty Conjurers.

Ab. To tell you truly, he preſſes his attacks with ſo much impudence, that he has made more progreſs with my Lady in two days, than you did in two months.

Fant. I ſhall attack her in another manner, if thou canſt but procure me another interview. There's nothing makes a lover ſo keen, as being kept up in the dark.

Ab. Pray no more of your diſtant bows, your reſpectful compliments————Really, Mr. *Fantome*, you're only fit to make love a-croſs a tea-table.

Fant. My dear Girl, I can't forbear hugging thee for thy good advice.

Ab. Ay, now I have ſome hopes of you; but why don't you do ſo to my Lady?

Fant. Child, I always thought your Lady lov'd to be treated with reſpect.

Ab. Believe me, Mr. *Fantome*, there is not ſo great a difference between woman and woman, as you imagine. You ſee *Tinſel* has nothing but his ſaucineſs to recommend him.

Fant. *Tinſel* is too great a Coxcomb to be capable of love————And let me tell thee, *Abigal*, a man, who is ſincere in his paſſion, makes but a very awkward profeſſion of it————but I'll mend my manners.

Ab. Ay, or you'll never gain a widow————come, I muſt tutor you a little; ſuppoſe me to be my Lady, and let me ſee how you'll behave your ſelf.

Fant. I'm afraid, child, we han't time for ſuch a piece of mummery.

Ab. Oh, it will be quickly over, if you play your part well.

Fant. Why then, dear Mrs. *Ab*———— I mean my Lady *Truman.*

Ab. Ay! but you han't ſaluted me.

Fant. That's right; Faith! I forgot that circumſtance. [*Kiſſes her.*] Nectar and *Ambroſia!*

Ab. That's very well————

Fant. How long muſt I be condemn'd to languiſh! when ſhall my ſufferings have an end! my life! my happineſs, my all is wound up in you.————

Ab. Well! why don't you fqueeze my hand?

Fant What, thus?

Ab. Thus? Ay—now throw your arm about my middle; hug me; clofer—You are not afraid of hurting me! now pour forth a volley of rapture and nonfence, till you are out of breath.

Fant. Tranfport and ecftacy! where am I—my life, my blifs! I rage, I burn, I bleed, I die!

Ab. Go on, go on.

Fant. Flames and darts—bear me to the gloomy fhade, rocks and grottos—flowers, *Zephyrs,* and purling ftreams.

Ab. Oh! Mr. *Fantome,* you have a tongue wou'd undo a veftal! you were born for the ruin of our fex.

Fant. This will do then, *Abigal?*

Ab. Ay, this is talking like a lover. Tho' I only reprefent my Lady, I take a pleafure in hearing you. Well, o' my confcience when a man of fenfe has a little dafh of the coxcomb in him, no woman can refift him. Go on at this rate, and the thoufand pound is as good as in my pocket.

Fant. I fhall think it an age till I have an opportunity of putting this leffon in practice.

Ab. You may do it foon, if you make good ufe of your time; Mr. *Tinfel* will be here with my Lady at eight, and at nine the Conjurer is to take you in hand.

Fant. Let me alone with both of them.

Ab. Well! forewarn'd, fore-arm'd Get into your box, and I'll endeavour to difpofe every thing in your favour.

[*Fantome goes in. Exit* Abigal.

Enter Vellum.

Vel. Mrs. *Abigal* is withdrawn.——I was in hopes to have heard what pafs'd between her and her invifible correfpondent.

Enter Tinfel.

Tinf. Vellum! Vellum!

Vel. Vellum! We are methinks very familiar; I am not us'd to be call'd fo by any but their Ho-nours [*afide*] ——What wou'd you, Mr. *Tinfel?*

Tinf. Let me beg a favour of thee, old gentleman.

Vel. What is that, good Sir?

Tinf.

Tinſ. Pr'ythee run and fetch me the rent-roll of thy, Lady's eſtate.

Vel. The rent-roll ?

Tinſ. The rent-roll ? ay, the rent-roll! doſt not un-derſtand what that means ?

Vel. Why ? have you thoughts of purchaſing of it ?

Tinſ. Thou haſt hit it, old boy, that is my very intention.

Vel. The purchaſe will be conſiderable.

Tinſ. And for that reaſon I have bid thy Lady very high --ſhe is to have no leſs for it than this entire Perſon of mine.

Vel. Is your whole eſtate perſonal, Mr. *Tinſel* ?—he, he, he !

Tinſ. Why, you queer old dog, you don't pretend to jeſt, d'ye ? Look ye, *Vellum*, if you think of being continued my ſteward, you muſt learn to walk with your toes out.

Vel. An inſolent companion !   [*aſide.*

Tinſ. Thou'rt confounded rich·I ſee, by that dangling of thy arms.

Vel. An ungracious bird ! .   [*aſide.*

Tinſ. Thou ſhalt lend me a couple of thouſand pounds.

Vel. A very profligate !   [*aſide.*

Tinſ. Look ye, *Vellum*, I intend to be kind to you— I'll borrow ſome money of you.

Vel. I cannot but ſmile to conſider the diſappointment this young fellow will meet with ; I will make my ſelf merry with him [*aſide.*]—And ſo, Mr. *Tinſel*, you pro-miſe you will be a very kind maſter to me ? [*ſtifling a laugh.*

Tinſ. What will you give for a Life in the houſe you live in ;

Vel. What do you think of five hundred pounds ?—— ha, ha, ha !

Tinſ. That's too little.

Vel. And yet it is more than I ſhall give you——and I will offer you two reaſons for it.

Tinſ. Pr'ythee what are they ?

Vel. Firſt, becauſe the tenement is not in your diſpoſal ; and ſecondly, becauſe it never will be in your diſpoſal : and ſo fare you well, good Mr. *Tinſel.* Ha, ha, ha ! you will pardon me for being jocular.   -   [*Exit* Vellum.

           Tinſ.

Tinf. This rogue is as faucy as the Conjurer; I'll be hang'd if they are not a-kin.

Enter Lady.

Lady. Mr. *Tinfel!* what, all alone? You Free-thinkers are great admirers of folitude.

Tinf. No faith, I have been talking with thy fteward; a very grotefque figure of a fellow, the very picture of one of our Benchers. How can you bear his converfation?

Lady. I keep him for my fteward, and not my companion. He's a fober man.

Tinf. Yes, yes, he looks like a put——a queer old dog, as ever I faw in my life: We muft turn him off, widow. He cheats thee confoundedly, I fee that.

Lady. Indeed you're miftaken, he has always had the reputation of being a very honeft man.

Tinf. What I fuppofe he goes to church.

Lady. Goes to church! fo do you too, I hope.

Tinf. I wou'd for once, Widow, to make fure of you.

Lady. Ah, Mr. *Tinfel,* a hufband who would not continue to go thither, would quickly forget the promifes he made there.

Tinf. Faith very innocent and very ridiculous! Well then, I warrant thee widow, thou wou'dft not for the world marry a fabbath-breaker!

Lady. Truly they generally come to a bad end. I remember the Conjurer told you, you were fhort-liv'd.

Tinf. The Conjurer! Ha, ha, ha!

Lady. Indeed you're very witty!

Tinf. Indeed you're very handfome. [*Kiffes her hand.*

Lady. I wifh the Fool does not love me! [*Afide.*

Tinf. Thou art the idol I adore. Here muft I pay my devotion——Pr'ythee, Widow, haft thou any timber upon thy eftate?

Lady. The moft impudent fellow I ever met with.[*Afide.*

Tinf. I take notice thou haft a great deal of old plate here in the houfe, Widow.

Lady. Mr. *Tinfel,* you are a very obferving man.

Tinf. Thy large filver ciftern would make a very good coach; and half a dozen falvers that I faw on the fideboard might be turn'd into fix as pretty horfes as any that appear in the ring.

Lady.

Lady. You have a very good fancy, Mr. *Tinſel*——
what pretty transformations you could make in my houſe
——But I'll ſee where 'twill end. [*Aſide.*

Tinſ. Then I obſerve, child, you have two or three
ſervices of gilt plate ; we'd eat always in china, my dear.

Lady. I perceive you are an excellent manager— how
quickly you have taken an inventory of my goods !

Tinſ. Now hark ye, Widow, to ſhow you the love that
I have for you————

Lady. Very well, let me hear.

Tinſ. You have an old-faſhion'd gold caudle-cup, with
the figure of a Saint upon the lid on't.

Lady. I have : what then ?

Tinſ. Why look ye, I'd ſell the caudle-cup with the
eld Saint for as much money as they'd fetch, which I
wou'd convert into a diamond buckle, and make you a
preſent of it.

Lady. Oh you are generous to an extravagance. But
pray, Mr. *Tinſel*, don't diſpoſe of my goods before you
are ſure of my perſon. I find you have taken a great af-
feɛtion to my moveables.

Tinſ. My dear, I love every thing that belongs to you.

Lady. I ſee you do, Sir, you need not make any proteſtations upon that ſubjeɛt.

Tinſ. Pho, pho, my dear we are growing ſerious, and,
let me tell you, that's the very next ſtep to being dull.
Come, that pretty face was never made to look grave with.

Lady. Believe me, Sir, whatever you may think,
marriage is a ſerious ſubjeɛt.

Tinſ. For that very reaſon my dear, let us get over it
as faſt as we can.

Lady. I ſhou'd be very much in haſte for a huſband, if
I married within fourteen months after Sir*George*'s deceaſe.

Tinſ. Pray, my dear, let me aſk you a queſtion ; Do'ſt
not thou think that Sir *George* is as dead at preſent, to all
intents and purpoſes, as he will be a twelve-month hence?

Lady. Yes : but decency, Mr. *Tinſel*————

Tinſ. Or do'ſt thou think thou'lt be more a Widow
then, than thou art now ?

Lady.

Lady. The world would fay I never lov'd my firft husband.

Tinf. Ah, my dear, they would fay you lov'd your
fecond ; and they wou'd own I deferv'd it, for I fhall love
thee moft inordinately.

Lady. But what wou'd people think ?

Tinf. Think ! why they wou'd think thee the mirrour
of widowhood————That a woman fhou'd live fourteen
whole months after the deceafe of her Spoufe, without
having engaged herfelf. Why, about town, we know
many a woman of quality's fecond Hufband feveral years
before the death of the firft.

Lady. Ay, I know you Wits have your common place
jefts upon us poor widows.

Tinf. I'll tell you a ftory, Widow ; I know a certain
Lady, who confidering the crazinefs of her hufband, had,
in cafe of mortality, engaged her feif to two young fellows of my acquaintance. They grew fuch defperate rivals for her while her hufband was alive, that one of them
pink'd the t'other in a duel. But the good Lady was no
fooner a Widow, but what did my dowager do ? Why
faith, being a woman of honour, fhe married a third, to
whom, it feems fhe had given her firft promife.

Lady. And this is a true ftory upon your own knowledge ?

Tinf. Every tittle, as I hope to be marry'd, or never
believe *Tom Tinfel.*

Lady. Pray, Mr. *Tinfel,* do you call this talking like
a Wit, or like a Rake ?

Tinf. Innocent enough, he, he, he ! Why ! where's
the difference, my dear ?

Lady. Yes, Mr. *Tinfel,* the only man I ever lov'd in
my life, had a great deal of the one and nothing of the
other in him.

Tinf. Nay now you grow vapourifh ; thou'lt begin to
fancy thou hear'ft the Drum by and by.

Lady. If you had been here laft night about this time,
you would not have been fo merry.

Tinf. About this time, fay'ft thou ? Come faith, for
the humour's fake, we'll fit down and liften.

Lady. I will, if you'll promise to be serious.

Tinf. Serious! never fear me, child. Ha, ha, ha! do't not hear him?

Lady. You break your word already. Pray, Mr. *Tinsel,* do you laugh to show your wit or your teeth?

Tinf. Why, both! my dear——I'm glad however, that she has taken notice of my teeth [*Aside.*] But you look serious, Child; I fancy thou hear'st the Drum, do't not?

Lady. Don't talk so rashly.

Tinf. Why, my dear, you cou'd not look more frighted if you had *Lucifer*'s Drum-major in your house.

Lady. Mr. *Tinsel,* I must desire to see you no more in it, if you do not leave this idle way of talking.

Tinf. Child, I thought I had told you what is my opinion of Spirits, as we were drinking a dish of tea but just now.———There is no such thing, I give thee my word.

Lady. Oh, Mr. *Tinsel,* your authority must be of great weight to those that know you.

Tinf. For my part, Child, I have made myself easy in those points.

Lady. Sure nothing was ever like this fellow's vanity, but his ignorance.   [*Aside.*

Tinf. I'll tell thee what now, Widow——I wou'd engage by the help of a white sheet and a penny-worth of link in a dark night, to frighten you a whole country village out of their senses, and the vicar into the bargain. [*Drum beats.*] Hark! hark! what noise is that! Heaven defend us! this is more than fancy.

Lady. It beats more terrible than ever.

Tinf. 'Tis very dreadful—what a dog have I been to speak against my conscience, only to show my parts!

Lady. It comes nearer and nearer. I wish you have not anger'd it by your foolish discourse.

Tinf. Indeed, Madam, I did not speak from my heart; I hope it will do me no hurt, for a little harmless raillery.

Lady. Harmless, d'ye call it? it beats hard by us, as if it would break through the Wall.

Tinf.

Tinf. What a devil had I to do with a white ſheet ?

　　　　　　　[*Scene opens, and diſcovers* Fantome.

Tinſ. Mercy on us ! it appears.

. *Lady.* Oh ! 'tis he ! 'tis he himſelf, 'tis Sir *George !*
'tis my huſband !　　　　　　　　　　　[*She faints.*

Tinſ. Now wou'd I give ten thouſand pound that I were
in town.　　　　　[Fantome *advances to him drumming.*

I beg ten thouſand pardons. I'll never talk at this rate
any more.　　　　　　　[Fantome *ſtill advances drumming.*

By my ſoul, Sir *George,* I was not in earneſt [*falls on
his knees*] have compaſſion on my youth, and conſider I
am but a Coxcomb——[Fantome *points to the door.*] But
ſee he waves me off——ay with all my heart——What
a devil had I to do with a white ſheet ?　・

　　　　[*He ſteals off the ſtage, mending his pace as the
　　　　　　Drum beats.*

Fant. The ſcoundrel is gone, and has left his miſtreſs
behind him.　I'm miſtaken if he makes love in this houſe
any more.　I have now only the Conjurer to deal with.　I
don't queſtion but I ſhall make his reverence ſcamper as
faſt as the lover.　And then the day's my own.　But the
ſervants are coming,　I muſt get into my cup-board.　:

　　　　　　　　　　　　　　[*He goes in-*

Enter Abigal *and Servants.*

Ab. Oh my poor Lady ! this wicked Drum, has frighted Mr. *Tinſel* out of his wits, and my Lady into a ſwoon.
Let me bend her a little forward.　She revives.　Here,
carry her into the freſh air, and ſhe'll recover. [*They carry
her off.*]This is a little barbarous to my Lady, but 'tis all
for her good : and I know her ſo well, that ſhe wou'd not
be angry with me, if ſhe knew what I was to get by it.
And if any of her friends ſhou'd blame me for it hereafter,

*I'll clap my Hand upon my Purſe, and tell 'em,
'Twas for a thouſand Pound, and Mr. Vellum.*

A C T V. S C E N E I.

Enter Sir George, *in his Conjurer's Habit, the But-*
ler marching before him with two large candles,
and the two Servants coming after him, one bring-
ing a little table, and another a chair.

B U T L E R.

AN'T pleaſe your worſhip, Mr. Conjurer, the Steward
has given all of us orders to do whatſoever you ſhall
bid us, and to pay you the ſame reſpect, as if you were
our Maſter.

Sir Geo. Thou ſay'ſt well.

Gard. An't pleaſe your Conjurſhip's Worſhip, ſhall I ſet
the table down here ?

Sir Geo. Here, *Peter.*

Gard. *Peter !* ———— he knows my name by his
learning.   [*Aſide*

Coach. I have brought you, reverend Sir, the largeſt
elbow chair in the houſe ; 'tis that the Steward ſits in
when he holds a Court.

Sir Geo. Place it there.

Butl. Sir, will you pleaſe to want any thing elſe ?

Sir Geo. Paper, and a pen and ink.

Butl. Sir, I believe we have paper that is fit for your
purpoſe ! my Lady's mourning paper, that is black'd at
the edges———— wou'd you chuſe to write with a crow
quill ?

Sir Geo. There is none better.

Butl. Coachman, go fetch the paper and ſtandiſh out
of the little Parlour.

Coach.

Coach. [*to the Gard*] *Peter,* pr'ythee do thou go along with me——I'm afraid——you know I went with you laſt night into the garden, when the cook-maid wanted a handful of parſley.

Butl. Why, you don't think I'll ſtay with the Conjurer by my ſelf!

Gard. Come, we'll all three go and fetch the pen and ink together.

[*Exeunt Servants.*

Sir Geo. (*ſolus*) There's nothing, I ſee, makes ſuch ſtrong alliances as fear. Theſe fellows are all enter'd into a confederacy againſt the Ghoſt. There muſt be abundance of buſineſs done in the family at this rate. But here comes the triple alliance. Who cou'd have thought theſe three rogues cou'd have found each of 'em an employment in fetching a pen and ink ?

Enter Gardiner *with a Sheet of Paper,* Coachman *with a Standiſh, and* Butler *with a Pen.*

Gard. Sir, there is your paper.

Coach. Sir, there is your Standiſh.

Butl. Sir, there is your crow-quill pen——I'm glad I have got rid on't. [*Aſide.*

Gard. He forgets that he's to make a circle [*Aſide.*]— Doctor, ſhall I help you to a bit of chalk ?

Sir Geo. It is no matter.

Butl. Look ye, Sir, I ſhow'd you the ſpot where he's heard ofteneſt, if your worſhip can but ferret him out of that old wall in the next room————

Sir Geo. We ſhall try.

Gard. That's right, *John.* His worſhip muſt let fly all his learning at that old wall.

Butl. Sir, if I was worthy to adviſe you, I wou'd have a bottle of good *October* by me. Shall I ſet a cup of old ſtingo at your elbow ?

Sir Geo. I thank thee——we ſhall do without it.

Gard. John, he ſeems a very good-natur'd man for a Conjurer.

Butl. I'll take this opportunity of enquiring after a bit of plate I have loſt. I fancy, whilſt he is in my Lady's pay, one may hedge in a queſtion or two into the bargain. Sir, Sir, may I beg a word in your ear?

Sir Geo. What wouldſt thou?

Butl. Sir, I know I need not tell you, that I loſt one of my ſilver ſpoons laſt week.

Sir Geo. Mark'd with a Swan's neck————

Butl. My Lady's Creſt! He knows every thing. [*dſide.* How wou'd your Worſhip adviſe me to recover it again?

Sir Geo. Hum!

Butl. What muſt I do to come at it?

Sir Geo. Drink nothing but ſmall-beer for a fort-night————

Butl. Small beer! Rot-gut!

Sir Geo. If thou drink'ſt a ſingle drop of Ale before fifteen days are expir'd—it is as much—as thy ſpoon—is worth.

Butl. I ſhall never recover it that way; I'll e'en buy a new one. [*Aſide.*

Coach. D'ye mind how they whiſper?

Gard. I'll be hang'd if he be not aſking him ſomething about *Nell*————

Coach. I'll take this opportunity of putting a queſtion to him about poor *Dobbing*, I fancy he could give me better counſel than the farrier.

Butl. [*to the Gard.*] A prodigious Man! he knows every thing: Now is the time to find out thy pick-axe.

Gard. I have nothing to give him: Does not he expect to have his hand croſs'd with ſilver?

Coach. [*to Sir George.*] Sir, may a man venture to aſk you a queſtion?

Sir Geo. Aſk it.

Coach. I have a poor horſe in the Stable that's be-witch'd————

Sir Geo. A bay gelding.

Coach. How cou'd he know that———— [*Aſide.*

Sir Geo. Bought at *Banbury*.

Coach. Whew————— ſo it was o' my conſcience.
[*Whiſtles.*

Sir

Sir Geo. Six years old laſt *Lammas*.

Coach. To a day. [*aſide.*] Now, Sir, I wou'd know whether the poor beaſt is bewitch'd by Goody *Crouch* or Goody *Flye* ?

Sir Geo. Neither.

Coach. Then it muſt be Goody *Gurten* ! for ſhe is the next oldeſt woman in the pariſh.

Gard. Haſt thou done, *Robin* ?

Coach. [*to Gard.*] He can tell thee any thing.

Gard. [*to Sir George.*] Sir, I wou'd beg to take you a little further out of hearing——

Sir Geo. Speak.

Gard. The Butler and I, Mr. Doctor, were both of us in love at the ſame time with a certain perſon.

Sir Geo. A woman.

Gard. How cou'd he know that ?   [*Aſide.*

Sir Geo. Go on.

Gard. This woman has lately had two children at a birth.

Sir Geo. Twins.

Gard. Prodigious ! where could he hear that ?

                                                [*Aſide.*

Sir Geo. Proceed.

Gard. Now, becauſe I us'd to meet her ſometimes in the garden, ſhe had laid them both——

Sir Geo. To thee.

Gard. What a power of learning he muſt have ! he knows every thing.   [*Aſide.*

Sir Geo. Haſt thou done ?

Gard. I wou'd deſire to know whether I am really' father to them both ?

Sir Geo. Stand before me, let me ſurvey thee round.

        [*Lays his wand upon his head, and makes him
                turn about.*

Coach. Look yonder, *John*, the ſilly dog is turning about under the Conjurer's wand. If he has been ſaucy to him, we ſhall ſee him puff'd off in a whirlwind immediately.

Sir Geo. Twins, do'ſt thou ſay ?   [*Still turning him.*

Gard. Ay ; are they both mine, d'ye think ?

                                                        Sir

Sir Geo. Own but one of them.

Gard. Ah, but Mrs. *Abigal* will have me take care of them both——ſhe's always for the Butler——if my poor Maſter Sir *George* had been alive, he wou'd have made him go halves with me.

Sir Geo. What, was Sir *George* a kind maſter ?

Gard. Was he ! ay, my fellow-ſervants will bear me witneſs.

Sir Geo. Did ye love Sir *George ?*

Butl. Every body lov'd him————

Coach. There was not a dry eye in the Pariſh at the news of his death————

Gard. He was the beſt neighbour————

Butl. The kindeſt huſband——

Coach. The trueſt friend to the poor————

Butl. My good Lady took on mightily, we all thought it wou'd have been the death of her————

Sir Geo. I proteſt theſe fellows melt me ! I think the time long till I am their maſter again, that I may be kind to them.   [*Aſide.*

Enter Vellum.

Vel. Have you provided the Doctor ev'ry thing he has occaſion for ? if ſo—-you may depart. [*Exeunt Servants.*

Sir Geo. I can as yet ſee no hurt in my wife's behaviour ; but ſtill have ſome certain pangs and doubts, that are natural to the heart of a fond Man. I muſt take the advantage of my diſguiſe to be thoroughly ſatisfied. It wou'd neither be for her happineſs, nor mine, to make my ſelf known to her till I am ſo [*Aſide.*]—Dear *Vellum !* I am impatient to hear ſome news of my wife, how does ſhe after her fright ?

Vel. It is a ſaying ſomewhere in my Lord *Coke,* that a Widow————

Sir Geo. I ask of my Wife, and thou talk'ſt to me of my Lord *Coke*——pr'ythee tell me how ſhe does, for I am in pain for her.

Vel. She is pretty well recover'd, Mrs. *Abigal* has put her in good heart ; and I have given her great hopes from your ſkill.

Sir Geo. That I think cannot fail, since thou haft got this secret out of *Abigal.* But I could not have thought my friend *Fantome* would have ferved me thus——

Vel. You will ftill fancy you are a living Man——

Sir Geo. That he fhou'd endeavour to enfnare my Wife——

Vel. You have no right in her after your demife : Death extinguifhes all property,——*Quoad hanc*—it is a maxim in the law.

Sir Geo. A pox on your learning ! well, but what is become of *Tinfel?*

Vel. He rufh'd out of the houfe, call'd for his horfe, clap'd fpurs to his fides, and was out of fight in lefs time than I—can—tell—ten.

Sir Geo. This is whimfical enough ! my Wife will have a quick fucceffion of lovers in one day——*Fantome* has driven out *Tinfel,* and fhall I drive out *Fantome.*

Vel. Ev'n as one wedge driveth out another—he, he, he ! you muft pardon me for being jocular.

Sir Geo. Was there ever fuch a provoking blockhead ! but he means me well. [*Afide.*] Well ! I muft have fatis-faction of this traitor *Fantome* : and cannot take a more proper one, than by turning him out of my houfe, in a manner that fhall throw fhame upon him, and make him ridiculous as long as he lives —— You muft remember *Vellum,* you have abundance of bufinefs upon your hands, and I have but juft time to tell it you over ; all I require of you is difpatch, therefore hear me.

Vel. There is nothing more requifite in bufinefs than difpatch——

Sir Geo. Then hear me.

Vel. It is indeed the life of bufinefs——

Sir Geo. Hear me then, I fay.

Vel. And as one has rightly obferved, the benefit that attends it is four-fold. Firft——

Sir Geo. There is no bearing this ! thou art a going to defcribe difpatch, when thou fhould'ft be practifing it.

Vel. But your ho-nour will not give me the hearing——

Sir Geo. Thou wilt not give me the hearing—— [*Angrily.*

Vel. I am ftill.

Sir

Sir Geo. In the firſt place, you are to lay my wig, hat, and ſword ready for me in the cloſet, and one of my ſcarlet coats. You know how *Abigal* has deſcribed the Ghoſt to you.

Vel. It ſhall be done.

Sir Geo. Then you muſt remember, whilſt I am laying this Ghoſt, you are to prepare my wife for the reception of her real huſband; tell her the whole ſtory, and do it with all the art you are maſter of, that the ſurprize may not be too great for her.

Vel. It ſhall be done——but ſince her ho-nour has ſeen this apparition, ſhe deſires to ſee you once more, before you encounter it.

Sir Geo. I ſhall expect her impatiently. For now I can talk to her without being interrupted by that impertinent Rogue *Tinſel.* I hope thou haſt not told *Abigal* any thing of the ſecret.

Vel. Mrs. *Abigal* is a woman; there are many reaſons why ſhe ſhou'd not be acquainted with it: I ſhall only mention ſix———

Sir Geo. Huſh, here ſhe comes! oh my heart!

Enter Lady *and* Abigal.

Sir Geo. [*Aſide, while* Vellum *talks in dumb ſhow to* Lady. O that lov'd woman! how I long to take her in my arms! if I find I am ſtill dear to her memory, it will be a return to life indeed! But I muſt take care of indulging this tenderneſs, and put on a behaviour more ſuitable to my preſent character.

[*Walks at a diſtance in a penſive poſture, waving his wand.*

Lady [*to* Vellum] This is ſurprizing indeed! ſo all the ſervants tell me: they ſay he knows every thing that has happen'd in the family.

Ab. [*Aſide.*] A parcel of credulous fools! they firſt tell him their ſecrets, and then wonder how he comes to know them.

[*Exit* Vellum, *exchanging fond looks with* Abigal.

Lady. Learned Sir, may I have ſome converſation with you, before you begin your ceremonies?

Sir

Sir Geo. Speak! but hold——first let me feel your pulse.

Lady. What can you learn from that?

Sir Geo. I have already learn'd a fecret from it, that will aftonifh you.

Lady. Pray what is it?

Sir Geo. You will have a hufband within this half hour.

Ab. [*Afide.*] I'm glad to hear that——he muft mean Mr. *Fantome*; I begin to think there's a good deal of truth in his art.

Lady. Alas! I fear you mean I fhall fee Sir *George's* apparition a fecond time.

Sir Geo. Have courage, you fhall fee the aparition no more. The hufband I mention fhall be as much alive as I am.

Ab. Mr *Fantome* to be fure.   [*Afide.*

Lady. Impoffible! I lov'd my firft too well.

Sir Geo. You cou'd not love the firft better than you will love the fecond.

Ab. [*afide.*] I'll be hang'd if my dear Steward has not inftructed him; he means Mr. *Fantome* to be fure; the thoufand pound is our own!

Lady. Alas! you did not know Sir *George.*

Sir Geo. As well as I do my felf——I faw him with you in the red damask room, when he firft made love to you; your mother left you together, under pretence of receiving a vifit from Mrs. *Hawthorn,* on her return from *London.*

Lady. This is aftonifhing!

Sir Geo. You were a great admirer of a fingle life for the firft half hour; your refufals then grew ftill fainter and fainter. With what ecftafy did Sir *George* kifs your hand, when you told him you fhou'd always follow the advice of your *Mamma!*

Lady. Every circumftance to a title!

Sir Geo. Then Lady! the wedding night! I faw you in your white fattin night gown? you wou'd not come out of your dreffing-room, till Sir *George* took you out by force. He drew you gently by the hand——you ftrug-

gled

gled——but he was too ftrong for you——you blufh'd,
he——

Lady. Oh ! ftop there! go no farther! ——He knows
every thing.   [*afide.*

Ab. Truly Mr. Conjurer, I believe you have been a
wag in your youth.

. *Sir Geo.* Mrs. *Abigal*, you know what your good word
coft Sir *George*, a purfe of broad pieces, Mrs. *Abigal*—

Ab. The Devil's in him. [*afide.*] Pray, Sir, fince you
have told fo far, you fhould tell my Lady that I refus'd to
take them.

Sir Geo. 'Tis true, Child, he was forc'd to thruft them
into your bofom.

Ab. This rogue will mention the thoufand pound, if I
don't take care.[*afide*]Pray, Sir, though you are aConjurer,
methinks you need not be a Blab————

Lady. Sir, fince I have now no reafon to doubt of your
art, I muft befeech you to treat this Aparition gently——
it has the refemblance of my deceas'd hufband; if there
be any undifcover'd fecret, any thing that troubles his reft
learn it of him.

. *Sir Geo.* I muft to that end be fincerely informed by
you, whether your heart be engaged to another; have
not you receiv'd the Addreffes of many lovers fince his
death ?

Lady. I have been oblig'd to receive more vifits, than
have been agreeable.

Sir Geo. Was not *Tinfel* welcome?—I'm afraid to hear
an anfwer to my own queftion.   [*Afide.*

Lady. He was well recommended.

Sir Geo. Racks ¡   [*Afide.*

Lady. Of a good family.

Sir Geo. Tortures !   [*Afide.*

Lady. Heir to a confiderable Eftate !

Sir Geo. Death [*afide.*] And you ftill love him?—
I'm diftracted!   [*Afide.*

Lady. No, I defpife him. I found he had a defign upon
my fortune, was bafe, profligate, cowardly, and ev'ry
thing that cou'd be expected from a Man of the vileft principles—

                                          Sir

Sir Geo. I'm recover'd.   [*aside.*

Ab. Oh, Madam, had you feen how like a fcoundrel he look'd when he left your Ladyfhip in a fwoon. Where have you left my Lady? fays I. In an Elbow-chair, Child, fays he: And where are you going? fays I. ' To town, Child, fays he, For to tell thee truly, Child, fays he, I don't care for living under the fame roof with the Devil, fays he.

Sir Geo. Well, Lady, I fee nothing in all this that may hinder Sir *George's* Spirit from being at reft.

Lady. If he knows any thing of what paffes in my heart, he cannot but be fatisfy'd of that fondnefs which I bear to his memory. My forrow for him is always frefh when I think of him. He was the kindeft, trueft, tendereft—Tears will not let me go on—

Sir Geo. This quite o'erpowers me—I fhall difcover my felf before my time. [*aside.*] —Madam, you may now retire and leave me to my felf.

Lady. Succefs attend you!

Ab. I wifh Mr. *Fantome* gets well off from this old Don—I know he'll be with him immediately.

[*Exeunt* Lady *and* Abigal.

Sir George *folus.*

Sir Geo. My heart is now at eafe, fhe is the fame dear Woman I left her——now for my revenge upon *Fantome*——I fhall cut the ceremonies fhort——a few words will do his bufinefs——now let me feat my felf in form——a good eafy chair for a Conjurer this!——now for a few mathematical fcratches——a good lucky fcrawl, that——faith I think it looks very Aftrological——thefe two or three magical Pot-hooks about it, make it a compleat Conjurer's fcheme. [*Drum beats.*] Ha, ha, ha, Sir, are you there? Enter Drummer. Now muft I pore upon my Paper.

Enter Fantome, *beating his Drum.*
Sir Geo. Pr'ythee don't make a noife, I'm bufy.

[*Fantome beats.*

A pretty march! pr'ythee beat that over again.

[*He beats and advances.*

Sir

Sir Geo. [*Rifing.*] Ha! you're very perfect in the ftep of a Ghoft.   You ftalk it majeftically.

[*Fantome advances.*

How the Rogue ftares! he acts it to admiration! I'il be hang'd if he has not been practifing this half hour in Mrs. *Abigal's* Wardrobe.

[*Fantome ftarts, and gives a rap upon his Drum.*

Pry'thee don't play the fool!   [*Fantome beats.*

Nay, nay, enough of this good Mr. *Fantome.*

Fant. [*Afide.*] Death! I'm difcover'd. This Jade *Abigal* has betray'd me.

Sir Geo. Mr. *Fantome*, upon the word of an Aftrologer, your thoufand pound bribe will never gain my Lady *Truman.*

Fant. 'Tis plain, fhe has told him all.   [*afide.*

Sir Geo. Let me advife you to make off as faft as you can, or I plainly perceive by my art, Mr. *Ghoft* will have his bones broke.

Fant. [*to Sir George.*] Lookye, old Gentleman, I perceive you have learnt this fecret from Mrs. *Abigal.*

Sir Geo. I have learn'd it from my art.

Fant. Thy art! pr'ythee no more of that.   Look ye, I know you are a cheat as much as I am.   And if thou'lt keep my counfel, I'll give thee ten broad pieces.——

Sir Geo. I am not mercenary! young Man, I fcorn thy Gold.

Fant. I'll make them up twenty—

Sir Geo. Avaunt! and that quickly, or I'll raife fuch an Apparition, as fhall—

Fant. An Apparition, old Gentleman! you miftake your Man, I am not to be frighten'd with bugbears—

Sir Geo. Let me retire but for a few moments, and I will give thee fuch a proof of my art———

Fant. Why, if thou haft any *Hocus pocus* Tricks to play, why canft not do them here?

Sir Geo. The raifing of a Spirit, requires certain fecret myfteries to be performed, and words to be mutter'd in private—

Fant. Well, if I fee through your trick, will you promife to be my friend?

Sir

Sir Geo. I will—attend and tremble.   [*Exit.*

. Fantome *solus.*

Fant. A very folemn old Afs! but I fmoak him,—— he
has a mind to raife his price upon me.   I cou'd not think
this flut wou'd have us'd me thus—I begin to grow hor--
ribly tir'd of my Drum, I wifh I was well rid of it However I have got this by it, that it has driven off *Tinfel* for
good and all; I fhan't have the mortification to fee my
miftrefs carry'd off by fuch a Rival.   Well, whatever
happens, I muft ftop this old fellow's mouth, I muft not
be fparing in hufh-money.   But here he comes.

Enter Sir George *in his own habit,*

Fant. Ha! what's that! Sir *George Truman!* This can
be no counterfeit.   His drefs! his fhape! his face! the very
wound of which he dy'd! nay then 'tis time to decamp!

(*Runs off.*

Sir Geo. Ha, ha, ha! Fare you well, good Sir *George*
—the Enemy has left me mafter of the field: here are the
marks of my victory.   This Drum will I hang up in my
great hall as the trophy of the day.

Enter Abigal.

[*Sir* George *ftands with his hand before his face in a
mufing pofture.*

Ab. Yonder he is.   O'my confcience he has driven off
the Conjurer.   Mr. *Fantome,* Mr. *Fantome!* I give you
joy, I give you joy.   What do you think of your thoufand pounds now? Why does not the Man fpeak?

[*Pulls him by the fleeve.*

Sir Geo. Ha!   (*Taking his hand from his face.*

Ab. O! 'tis my Mafter!   (*Shrieks.*

(*Running away*) *he catches her.*

Sir Geo. Good Mrs. *Abigal* not fo faft.

Ab. Are you alive, Sir?—He has given my fhoulder
fuch a curfed tweak! they muft be real fingers.   I feel
'em I'm fure.

Sir Geo. What do'ft think?

Ab. Think, Sir? Troth I don't know what to think.
Pray, Sir, how.————

Sir Geo. No queftions, good *Abigal.* Thy curiofity
fhall be fatisfied in due time.   Where's your Lady?

Ab.

Ab. Oh, I'm ſo frighted————and ſo glad————

Sir Geo. Where's your Lady, I aſk you————

Ab. Marry I don't know where I am my ſelf————I can't forbear weeping for joy————

Sir Geo. Your Lady! I ſay your Lady! I muſt bring you to your ſelf with one pinch more————

Ab. Oh! ſhe has been talking a good while with the Steward.

Sir Geo. Then he has open'd the whole ſtory to her, I'm glad he has prepar'd her. Oh! here ſhe comes.

Enter Lady *follow'd by* Vellum.

Lady. Where is he? let me fly into his arms! My life! my ſoul! my huſband!

Sir Geo. Oh! let me catch thee to my heart, deareſt of women!

Lady. Are you then ſtill alive, and are you here! I can ſcarce believe my ſenſes! now am I happy indeed!

Sir Geo. My heart is too full to anſwer thee.

Lady. How could you be ſo cruel to defer giving me that joy which you knew I muſt receive from your pre-ſence? You have robb'd my life of ſome hours of hap-pineſs that ought to have been in it.

Sir Geo.—It was to make our happineſs the more ſincere and unmixt. There will be now no doubts to daſh it. What has been the affliction of our lives, has given a va-riety to them, and will hereafter ſupply us with a thouſand materials to talk of.

Lady. I'm now ſatisfy'd that it is not in the power of ab-ſence to leſſen your love towards me.

Sir Geo. And I am ſatisfy'd that it is not in the power of death to deſtroy that love which makes me the hap-pieſt of Men.

Lady. Was ever woman ſo bleſt! to find again the dar-ling of her Soul, when ſhe thought him loſt for ever! to enter into a kind of ſecond marriage with the only Man whom ſhe was ever capable of loving.

Sir Geo. May it be as happy as our firſt, I deſire no more! Believe me, my Dear, I want words to expreſs thoſe tranſports of joy and tenderneſs which are every mo-ment riſing in my heart whilſt I ſpeak to thee.

Enter

Enter Servants.

Butl. Juſt as the Steward told us, Lads! Look you there, if he ben't with my Lady already.

Gard. He! he! he! what a joyful night will this be for Madam!

Coach As I was coming in at the gate, a ſtrange gentleman whisk'd by me; but he took to his heels, and made away to the *George.* If I did not ſee maſter before me, I ſhou'd have ſworn it had been his Honour.

Gard. Ha'ſt given orders for the bells to be ſet a ringing?

Coach. Never trouble thy head about that, 'tis done.

Sir Geo. [*to* Lady.] My Dear, I long as much to tell you my whole ſtory, as you do to hear it. In the mean while, I am to look upon this as my wedding day. I'll have nothing but the voice of mirth and feaſting in my houſe. My poor neighbours and my ſervants ſhall rejoice with me. My hall ſhall be free to every one, and let my cellars be thrown open.

Butl. Ah! bleſs your Honour, may you never die again!

Coach. The ſame good man that ever he was!

Gard. Whurra!

Sir Geo. *Vellum,* thou haſt done me much ſervice to-day. I know thou lov'ſt *Abigal,* but ſhe's diſappointed in a fortune. I'll make it up to both of you. I'll give thee a thouſand pound with her. It is not fit there ſhould be one ſad heart in my houſe to-night.

Lady. What you do for *Abigal,* I know is meant as a compliment to me. This is a new inſtance of your love.

Ab. Mr. *Vellum,* you are a well-ſpoken man: Pray do you thank my Maſter and my Lady.

Sir Geo. *Vellum,* I hope you are not diſpleas'd with the Gift I make you.

Vel. *The gift is twofold. I receive from you*
   A virtuous partner, and a portion too;
   For which; in humble wiſe, I thank the Donors:
   And ſo we bid good night to both your Ho-nours.

THE

THE

EPILOGUE.

Spoken by Mrs. *Oldfield.*

TO-night the Poet's advocate I stand,
  And he deserves the favour at my hand,
Who in my equipage their cause debating
Has plac'd two Lovers, and a third in waiting;
If both the first should from their duty swerve,
There's one, behind the wainscote in reserve.
In his next Play, If I wou'd take this trouble,
He promis'd me to make the number double:
In troth 'twas spoke like an obliging creature,
For tho' 'tis simple, yet it shews good nature.

   My help thus ask'd, I cou'd not chuse but grant it,
And really I thought the Play wou'd want it,
Void as it is of all the usual arts
To warm your fancies, and to steal your hearts:
No Court-Intrigue, nor City-Cuckoldom,
No song, no dance, no musick ---- but a Drum ----
No smutty thought in doubtful phrase exprest;
And, Gentlemen, if so, pray where's the jest?
When we wou'd raise your mirth, you hardly know
Whether in strictness you should laugh or no,
But turn upon the Ladies in the pit,
And if they redden, you are sure 'tis wit.

Protect

EPILOGUE.

Protect him then, ye Fair-ones ; for the Fair
Of all conditions are his equal care.
He draws a Widow, who, of blameless carriage,
True to her jointure, hates a second marriage ;
And to improve a virtuous wife's delights,
Out of one man contrives two wedding-nights ;
Nay, to oblige the sex in every state,
A nymph of five and forty finds her mate.

Too long has Marriage, in this tasteless age,
With ill-bred raillery supply'd the stage ;
No little Scribbler is of wit so bare,
But has his fling at the poor wedded pair.
Our Author deals not in conceits so stale :
For shou'd th' examples of his Play prevail,
No man need blush, tho' true to marriage-vows,
Nor be a jest tho' he shou'd love his spouse.
Thus has he done you British consorts right,
Whose husbands, shou'd they pry like mine to night,
Wou'd never find you in your conduct slipping,
Tho' they turn'd Conjurers to take you tripping.

THE LATE

TRYAL

AND

CONVICTION

OF

Count *TARIFF*.

THE LATE
TRYAL *and* CONVICTION
OF
Count TARIFF.

TH E whole Nation is at prefent very inquifitive after the proceedings in the caufe of Goodman *Fact*, Plaintiff, and Count *Tariff*, Defendant ; as it was tried on the 18th of *June*, in the thirteenth year of her Majefty's reign, and in the year of the Lord 1713. I fhall therefore give my countrymen a fhort and faithful account of that whole matter. And in order to it, muft in the firft place premife fome particulars relating to the perfon and character of the faid Plaintiff Goodman *Fact*.

Goodman *Fact* is allowed by every body to be a plain fpoken perfon, and a man of very few words. Tropes and figures are his averfion. He affirms every thing roundly, without any art, rhetorick, or circumlocution. He is a declared enemy to all kinds of ceremony and complaifance. He flatters no body. Yet fo great is his natural eloquence, that he cuts down the fineft orator, and deftroys the beft contrived argument, as foon as ever he gets himfelf to be heard. He never applies to the paffions or prejudices of his audience : when they liften with attention and honeft minds, he never fails of carrying his point. He appeared in a fuit of *Englifh* broadcloth, very plain, but rich. Every thing he wore was fubftantial, honeft, home-fpun ware. His cane indeed came from the *Eaft-Indies*, and two or three little fuperfluities from *Turkey*, and other parts. It is faid that he encouraged himfelf with a bottle of neat *Port*, before he appeared at the tryal. He was huzzaed into the Court by feveral thoufands of *Weavers, Clothiers, Fullers, Dyers, Packers, Calenders, Setters, Silk-men, Spinners, Dreffers, Whitfters, Winders, Mercers, Throwfters, Sugar-bakers,*

Diftiller

Diftillers, Drapers, Hofiers, Planters, Merchant's and *Fi-fhermen*; who all unanimoufly declared that they could not live above two months longer, if their friend *Fact* did not gain his caufe.

Every body was over-joyed to hear that the good man was come to town. He no fooner made his appearance in Court, but feveral of his friends fell a weeping at the fight of him: for indeed he had not been feen there three years before.

The charge he exhibited againft Count *Tariff*, was drawn up in the following articles.

I. That the faid Count had given in falfe and fraudulent reports in the name of the Plaintiff.

II. That the faid Count had tampered with the faid Plaintiff, and made ufe of many indirect methods to bring him over to his party.

III. That the faid Count had wilfully and knowingly traduced the faid Plaintiff, having mifreprefented him in many cunningly-devifed fpeeches, as a perfon in the *French* intereft.

IV. That the faid Count had averred in the prefence of above five hundred perfons, that he had heard the Plaintiff fpeak in derogation of the *Portuguefe, Spaniards, Italians, Hollanders*, and others; who were the perfons whom the faid Plaintiff had always favoured in his difcourfe, and whom he fhould always continue to favour.

V. That the faid Count had given a very difadvantageous relation of three great farms, which had long flourifhed under the care and fuperintendency of the Plaintiff.

VI. That he would have obliged the owners of the faid farms to buy up many commodities which grew upon their own land. That he would have taken away the labour from the tenants, and put it into the hands of ftrangers, That he would have leffened and deftroyed the produce of the faid farms.

That by thefe and many other wicked devices he would have ftarved many honeft day-labourers; have impoverifhed the owner, and have filled his farms with beggars, &c.

VII.

VII. That the said Count had either funk or miflaid several books, papers, and receipts, by which the Plaintiff might fooner have found means to vindicate himfelf from fuch calumnies, afperfions, and mifreprefentations.

In all thefe particulars Goodman *Fact* was very fhort but pithy: for, as I faid before, he was a plain home-fpun man. His yea was yea, and his nay, nay. He had further fo much of the Quaker in him, that he never fwore, but his affirmation was as valid as another's oath.

It was obferved, that Count *Tariff* endeavoured to brow-beat the Plaintiff all the while he was fpeaking: but though he was not fo impudent as the Count, he was every whit as fturdy; and when it came to the Count's turn to fpeak, old *Fact* fo ftared him in the face, after his plain, down-right way, that the Count was very often ftruck dumb, and forc'd to hold his tongue in the middle of his difcourfe.

More witneffes appeared on this occafion to atteft Goodman *Fact*'s veracity than ever were feen in a court of juftice. His caufe was pleaded by the ableft men in the kingdom; among whom was a Gentleman of *Suffolk* who did him fignal fervice.

Count *Tariff* appeared juft the reverfe of Goodman *Fact*. He was dreffed in a fine brocade waftcoat, curi-rioufly embroidered with Flower-de-luces. He wore alfo a broad-brimmed hat, a fhoulder-knot, and a pair of filver-clock'd ftockins. His fpeeches were accompanied with much gefture and grimace. He abounded in empty phrafes, fuperficial flourifhes, violent affertions, and feeble proofs. To be brief, he had all the *French* affurance, cunning, and volubility of tongue; and would moft certainly have carried his caufe, had he dealt with any one antagonift in the world befides Goodman *Fact*.

The Count being called upon to anfwer to the charge which had been made againft him, did it after a manner peculiar to the family of the *Tariffs*, viz. by railing and calling names.

He in the firft place accufed his adverfary of *Scandalum magnatum*, and of fpeaking againft his fuperiors with faucinefs and contempt. As the plain good man was not of a make to have any friends at Court, he was a little startled at this accusation, till at length he made it appear, that it was impossible for any of his family to be either saucy or cringing ; for that their character was, above all others in the world, to do what was required of them by the Court, that is, To speak the Truth and nothing but the Truth.

The Count in the next place assured the Court, that his antagonist has taken upon him a wrong name, having curtailed it of two or three letters; for that in reality his name was not Fact but Faction. The Count was so pleased with this conceit, that for an hour together he repeated it in every sentence ; calling his antagonist's assertions, the reports of faction; his friends, the sons of faction : the testimonies of his witnesses, the dictates of faction : nay, with such a degree of impudence did he push this matter, that when he heard the cries of above a million of people begging for their bread, he termed the prayers and importunities of such a starving multitude, the Clamours of Faction.

As soon as the Count was driven out of this device, he affirmed roundly in the Court that Fact was not an Englishman by birth, but that he was of Dutch extraction and born in Holland. In consequence of this assertion, he began to rally the poor Plaintiff under the title of Mynheer van Fact; which took pretty well with the simpletons of his party, but the men of sense did not think the jest worth all their lands and tenements.

When the Count had finished his speech, he desired leave to call in his witnesses, which was granted : when immediately there came to the bar a man with a hat drawn over his eyes in such a manner that it was impossible to see his face. He spoke in the spirit, nay in the very language of the Count, repeated his arguments, and confirmed his assertions. Being asked his name; he said the world called him, Mercator : but as for his true name, his age, his lineage, his religion, his place of abode, they were particulars, which for certain reasons he was obliged to conceal. The Court found him such a false shuffling, prevaricating rascal, that they set him aside as a person unqualified to give his testimony in a Court of Justice ; advising vifing him at the same time, as he tendered his ears, to forbear uttering such notorious falfhoods as he had then publifhed. The witnefs however perfifted in his contumacy, telling them he was very forry to find, that notwithftanding what he had faid they were refolved to be as arrant fools as all their forefathers had been for a hundred years before them.

There came up another witnefs, who fpoke much to the reputation of Count *Tariff*. This was a tall, black, bluftering perfon, dreffed in a *Spanifh* habit, with a plume of feathers on his head, a *Golillio* about his neck, and a long *Toledo* fticking out by his fide; his garments were fo covered with tinfel and fpangles, that at a diftance he feemed to be made up of filver and gold. He called himfelf DON ASSIENTO, and mentioned feveral nations that had fought his friendfhip; but declared that he had been gained over by the Count; and that he was come into thefe parts to enrich every one that heard him. The Court was at firft very well pleafed with his figure, and the promifes he made them; but upon examination found him a true *Spaniard*: nothing but fhow and beggary. For it was fully proved, that notwithftanding the boafts and appearance which he made, he was not worth a groat: nay, that upon cafting up his annual expences, with the debts and incumbrances which lay upon his eftate, he was worfe than nothing.

There appeared another witnefs in favour of the Count, who fpoke with fo much violence and warmth, that the Court began to liften to him very attentively; 'till upon hearing his name they found he was a notorious Knight of the poft, being kept in pay, to give his teftimony on all occafions where it was wanted. This was the EXAMINER; a perfon who had abufed almoft every man in *England*, that deferved well of his country. He called Goodman *Fact* a lyar, a feditious perfon, a traytor, and a rebel; and fo much incenfed the honeft man, that he would certainly have knocked him down if he could have come at him. It was allowed by every body, that fo foul-mouthed a witnefs never appeared in any caufe. Seeing feveral perfons of great eminence, who had maintained

D 4 *tha*

the caufe of Goodman *Fact*, he called them ideots, block-heads, villains, knaves, infidels, atheifts, apoftates, fiends, and devils: never did man fhow fo much eloquence in ribaldry. The Court was at length fo juftly provoked with this fellow's behaviour, who fpared no age, nor fex, nor profeffion, which had fhown any friendfhip or inclination for the Plaintiff, that feveral began to whifper to one another, it was high time to bring him to punifhment. But the witnefs over-hearing the word *Pillory* repeated twice or thrice, flunk away privately, and hid himfelf among the people.

After a full hearing on both fides, Count *Tariff* was caft, and Goodman *Fact* got his caufe; but the Court fitting late, did not think it fit at that time to give him cofts, or indeed to enter into that matter. The honeft man immediately retired, after having affured his friends, that at any time when the Count fhould appear on the like occafion, he would undertake their defence, and come to their affiftance, if they would be at the pains to find him out.

It is incredible how general a joy Goodman *Fact*'s fuc-cefs created in the city of *London*; there was nothing to be feen or heard the next day, but fhaking of hands, congratulations, reflections on the danger they had efcaped; and gratitude to thofe who had delivered them from it

The night concluded with balls, bonfires, ringing of bells, and the like publick demonftrations of joy.

THE

THE

WHIG-EXAMINER;

AND

LOVER.

THE
WHIG-EXAMINER.

No. 1. *Thursday, September* 14, 1710.

Nescia mens hominum fati sortisque futuræ,
Et servare modum, rebus sublata secundis !
Turno tempus erit. magno cum optaverit emptum
Intactum Pallanta ; & cum spolia ista diemque
Oderit———— VIRG.

THE design of this work is to censure the writings of others, and to give all persons a rehearing, who have suffered under any unjust sentence of the *Examiner*. As that Author has hitherto proceeded, his paper would have been more properly entitled the *Executioner* : at least his examination is like that which is made by the rack and wheel. I have always admired a Critic that has discovered the beauties of an author, and never knew one who made it his business to lash the faults of other writers, that was not guilty of greater himself; as the hangman is generally a worse malefactor, than the Criminal that suffers by his hand. To prove what I say, there needs no more than to read the annotations which this Author has made upon Dr. *Garth*'s Poem, with the preface in the front, and a riddle at the end of them. To begin with the first : Did ever an advocate for a party open with such an unfortunate assertion ? *The collective body of the Whigs have already engrossed our*
riches :

riches : That is, in plain Englifh, the Whigs are poffeffed of all the riches in the nation.. Is not this giving up
all he has been contending for thefe fix Weeks? Is there
any thing more reafonable, than that thofe who have
all the riches of the nation in their poffeffion, or if he
likes his own phrafe better, as indeed I think it is ftronger, that thofe who have already *engroffed* our riches,
fhould have the management of our publick Treafure,
and the direction of our fleets and armies? But let us
proceed : *Their reprefentative the Kit Cat have pretended
to make a Monopoly of our fenfe.* Well, but what does all
this end in? If the author means any thing, it is this,
That to prevent fuch a Monopoly of fenfe, he is refolved to deal in it himfelf by retail, and fell a pennyworth
of it every week. In what follows, there is fuch a fhock-
ing familiarity both in his railleries, and civilities, that
one cannot long be in doubt who is the Author. The
remaining part of the preface has fo much of the pedant,
and fo little of the converfation of men in it, that 1 fhall
pafs it over, and haften to the riddles, which are as follows.

The R I D D L E.

S PHINX *was a monfter, that would eat
   Whatever ftranger fhe could get :
Unlefs his ready Wit difclos'd
The fubtle riddle fhe propos'd.
   Oedipus was refolv'd to go,
And try what ftrength of parts could do :
Says Sphinx, On this depends your fate ;
Tell me what animal is that,
Which has four feet at morning bright?
Has two at noon, and three at night ?
'Tis man, faid he, who weak by nature,
At firft creeps, like his fellow-creature,
Upon all four : As years accrue,
With fturdy fteps he walks on two :
In age, at length, grown weak and fick,
For his third leg adopts the ftick.*

Now in your turn, 'tis juſt, met hinks,
You ſhould reſolve me, Madam Sphinx,
What ſtranger creature yet is he,
Who has four-legs, then two, then three;
Then loſes one, then gets two more,
And runs away at laſt on four.

The firſt part of this little myſtical Poem is an old riddle, which we could have told the meaning of, had not
the Author given himſelf the trouble of explaining it;
but as for the expoſition of the ſecond, he leaves us altogether in the dark. The riddle runs thus: What creature is it that walks upon four legs in the morning, two
legs at noon, and three legs at night? This he ſolves, as
our forefathers have done for theſe two thouſand
years; and not according to *Rabelais*, who gives another
reaſon why a man is ſaid to be a creature, with three
legs at night. Then follows the ſecond riddle: What
creature, ſays he, is it that firſt uſes four legs, then two
legs, then three legs; then loſes one leg, then gets two
legs, and at laſt runs away upon four legs? Were I dif-
poſed to be ſplenetick, I ſhould ask if there was any
thing in the new garland of riddles *ſo wild, ſo childiſh,*
or ſo flat: But though I dare not go ſo far as that, I ſhall
take upon me to ſay, that the Author has ſtollen his hint
out of the garland, from a riddle which I was better acquainted with than the *Nile* when I was but twelve
years old. It runs thus, Riddle my riddle my ree, what
is this? Two legs ſate upon three legs, and held one leg
in her hand; in came four legs, and ſnatched away one
leg; up ſtarted two legs, and flung three legs at four
legs, and brought one leg back again. This Enigma,
joined with the foregoing two, rings all the changes
that can be made upon four legs. That I may deal more
ingenuouſly with my Reader than the above-mentioned
Enigmatiſt has done, I ſhall preſent him with a key to
my riddle; which upon application he will find exactly
fitted to all the words of it: one leg is a leg of mutton,
two legs is a ſervant maid, three legs is a joint ſtool,
which in the Sphinx's country was called a tripode; as

four

four legs is a dog, who in all nations and ages has been reckoned a quadruped. We have now the expofition of our firft and third riddles upon legs; let us here if you pleafe, endeavour to find out the meaning of our fecond, which is thus in the Author's words:

What ftranger creature yet is he,
That has four legs, then two, then three;
Then lofes one, then gets two more,
And runs away at laft on four?

This riddle, as the Poet tells us, was propofed by *Oedipus* to the Sphinx, after he had given his folution to that which the Sphinx had propofed to him. This *Oedipus*, you muft underftand, though the people did not believe it, was fon to a King of *Thebes*, and bore a particular grudge to the Tre————r of that Kingdom; which made him fo bitter upon *H. L.* in this Enigma.

What ftranger creature yet is he,
That has four legs, then two, then three?

By which he intimates, that this great man at *Thebes* being *weak by nature*, as he admirably exprefles it, could not walk as foon as he was born, but like other children fell upon all four when he attempted it; that he afterwards went upon two legs, like other men; and that in his more advanced age, he got a white ftaff in Queen *Jocafta*'s court, which the Author calls his third leg. Now it fo happened that the Treafurer fell, and by that means broke his third leg, which is intimated by the next word, *Then lofes one*—Thus far I think we have travelled through the riddle with good fuccefs.

What ftranger creature yet is he
That has four legs, then two, then three?
Then lofes one,————

But now comes the difficulty that has puzzled the whole town, and which I muft confefs has kept me awake for thefe three nights; ————*Then*

—————*Then gets two more,*
And runs away at laſt on four.

I at laſt thought the treaſurer of *Thebes* might have walked upon crutches, and ſo ran away on four legs, *viz.*
two natural and two artificial.   But this I have no autho·
rity for; and therefore upon mature conſideration do
find that theſe words *(Then gets two more)* are only Greek
expletives, introduced to make up the verſe, and to ſig-
nify nothing ; and that *runs,* in the next line, ſhould be
rides.   I ſhall therefore reſtore the true ancient reading
of this riddle, after which it will be able to explain it
ſelf.

  Oedipus ſpeaks:
Now in your turn, 'tis juſt methinks,
You ſhould reſolve me, Madam Sphinx,
What ſtranger creature yet is he,
Who has four legs, then two, then three;
Then loſes one, then gains two more,
And rides away at laſt on four ?

I muſt now inform the Reader, that *Thebes* was on the
continent, ſo that it was eaſy for a man to ride out of his
dominions on horſeback, an advantage that a *Britiſh*
Stateſman would be deprived of.   If he would run
away, he muſt do it *in an open boat* ; for to ſay of an *Eng-*
liſhman in this ſenſe, that he runs away on all four,
would be as abſurd as to ſay, he clapped Spurs to his
Horſe at St. *James*'s gate, and galloped away to the
Hague
 Before I take my farewel of this ſubject, I ſhall adviſe the Author for the future to ſpeak his meaning
more plainly.   I allow he has a happy talent at doggrel,
when he writes upon a known ſubject: where he tells
us in plain · intelligible language, how *Syriſca*'s ladle was
loſt in one hole, and *Hans Carvel*'s finger in another,
he is very jocular and diverting ; but when he wraps a
lampoon in a riddle, he muſt conſider that his jeſt is loſt
to every one, but the few merry wags that are in the ſecret.

cret. This is making darker satyrs than ever *Perſius* did.
After this curſory view of the *Examiner's* performance,
let us conſider his remarks upon the Doctor's. That general piece of raillery which he paſſes upon the Doctor's conſidering the Treaſurer in ſeveral different views,
is that which might fall upon any Poem in *Waller*, or
any other writer who has diverſity of thoughts and allu-
ſions : and tho' it may appear a pleaſant ridicule to an ignorant Reader, is wholly groundleſs and unjuſt. I do
likewiſe diſſent with the *Examiner*, upon the phraſes of
paſſions being poiſed, and of the *retrieving merit from de-
pendance*, which are very beautiful and poetical. It is the
ſame cavilling ſpirit that finds fault with that expreſſion of
the *pomp of peace among the woes of war*, as well as of
offering unaſked. As for the *Nile*, how *Icarus* and *Phaeton* came to be joined with it, I cannot conceive. I muſt
confeſs they have been formerly uſed to repreſent the fate
of raſh ambitious men ; and I cannot imagine why the
Author ſhould deprive us of thoſe particular Similes for
the future. The next Criticiſm upon the ſtars, ſeems introduced for no other reaſon but to mention Mr. *Bickerſtaffe*, whom the Author every where endeavours to i-
mitate and abuſe. But I ſhall refer the *Examiner* to the
frog's advice to her little one, that was blowing it ſelf
up to the ſize of an Ox :

————*Non ſi te ruperis, inquit,*
　Par eris————

The alluſion to the victim may be a Gallimatia in
French politicks, but is an apt and noble alluſion to a
true *Engliſh* ſpirit. And as for the *Examiner's* remarks
on the word *bleed* (though a man would laugh to ſee
impotent malice ſo little able to contain it ſelf) one can
not but obſerve in them the temper of the Banditti
whom he mentions in the ſame paper, who always
murder where they rob. The laſt obſervation is upon
the line, *Ingratitude's a weed of every clime.* Here he is
very much out of humour with the Doctor, for having
called that the weed, which *Dryden* only terms the
　　　　　　　　　　　　　　　　　　　　growth

growth of every Clime. But, for God-fake, why fo much tenderneſs for ingratitude?

But I ſhall ſay no more. We are now in an age wherein impudent aſſertions muſt paſs for arguments: and I do not queſtion but the ſame, who has endeavoured here to prove that he who wrote the *Diſpenſary* was no Poet, will very ſuddenly undertake to ſhew, that he who gained the battle of *Blenheim* is no General.

No. 2.   *Thurſday, September* 21.

———*Arcades ambo*
Et cantare pares———   VIRG.

I Never knew any Author who had not his admirers. *Bunyan* and *Quarels* have paſſed through ſeveral editions, and pleaſe as many Readers, as *Dryden* and *Tillotſon*: The *Examiner* had not written two half ſheets of paper, before he met with one that was aſtoniſhed at *the force he was maſter of,* and approaches him with awe, when he mentions State-Subjects, as *encroaching on the province that belong'd to him,* and treating of things *that deſerved to paſs under his Pen.* The ſame humble Author tells us, that the *Examiner* can furniſh mankind with an *Antidote to the Poiſon that is ſcattered through the nation.* This crying up of the *Examiner's* Antidote, puts me in mind of the firſt appearance that a celebrated *French* quack made in the ſtreets of *Paris.* A little boy walked before him, publiſhing with a ſhrill voice, *Mon pere guerit touies ſortes de maladies, My father cures all ſorts of diſtempers:* To which the Doctor, who walked behind him, added in a grave and compoſed manner, *L'enfant dit vrai, The child ſays true.*

That the Reader may ſee what party the Author of this Letter is of, I ſhall ſhew how he ſpeaks of the *French*
King

King and the Duke of *Anjou*, and how of our greateſt Allies, the Emperor of *Germany* and the States-General. *In the mean while the* French *King has withdrawn his troops from* Spain, *and has put it out of his power to reſtore that monarchy to us, was he reduced low enough really to deſire to do it.* The Duke of Anjou *has had leiſure to take off thoſe whom he ſuſpected, to confirm his friends, to regulate his revenues, to increaſe and form his troops, and above all, to rouze that ſpirit in the* Spaniſh *nation, which a ſucceſſion of lazy and indolent Princes had lulled aſleep. From hence it appears probable enough, that if the war continue much longer on the preſent foot, inſtead of regaining* Spain, *we ſhall find the Duke of* Anjou *in a condition to pay the debt of gratitude, and ſupport the grandfather in his declining years; by whoſe arms, in the days of his infancy, he was upheld.* What expreſſions of tenderneſs, duty, and ſubmiſſion! The Panegyrick on the Duke of *Anjou*, is by much the beſt written part of this whole Letter; the Apology for the *French* King is indeed the ſame which the *Poſt-boy* has often made, but worded with greater deference and reſpect to that great Prince. Theſe are many ſtrokes of the Author's good-will to our confederates, the *Dutch* and the Emperor, in ſeveral patrs of this notable Epiſtle; I ſhall only quote one of them, alluding to the concern which the Bank, the States-General, and the Emperor, expreſſed for the Miniſtry, by their humble applications to Her Majeſty, in theſe words.

Not daunted yet, they reſolve to try a new expedient and the intereſt of Europe *is to be repreſented as inſeparable from that of the Miniſters.*

Haud dubitant equidém implorare quod uſquam eſt;
Flectere ſi nequeunt Superos, Acheronta movebunt.

The members of the Bank, the Dutch, *and the Court of* Vienna, *are called in as confederates to the Miniſtry.* This, in the mildeſt *Engliſh* it will bear, runs thus. *They are reſolved to look for help where-ever they can find it; if they cannot have it from heaven, they will go to hell for it:*
That

That is, to the members of the Bank, the *Dutch* and the Court of *Vienna*. The *French* King, the Pope, and the Devil, have been often joined together by a well meaning *Englishman*; but I am very much furprifed to fee the Bank, the *Dutch* and the Court of *Vienna*, in fuch company. We may ftill fee this Gentleman's principles in the accounts which he gives of his own country: fpeaking of *the* G————l, *the quondam* T————r, *and the* J————*to*, which every one knows comprehends the *Whigs*, in their utmoft extent; he adds in oppofition to them, *For the Queen and the whole body of the* Britifh *nation,*——

Nos Numerus fumus.

In Englifh,

We are Cyphers.

How properly the Tories may be called the whole bo- dy of the *Britifh* nation, I leave to any one's judging: and wonder how an Author can be fo difrefpeftful to Her Majefty, as to feparate Her in fo faucy a manner from that part of her people, who according to the *Ex- aminer* himfelf *have engroffed the riches of the nation;* and all this to join her, with fo much impudence, under the common denomination *of We*; that is, W E *Queen and Tories* are cyphers. *Nos numerus fumus* is a fcrap of *Latin* more impudent than Cardinal *Woolfey*'s *Ego et Rex meus.* We find the fame particle W E, ufed with great emphafis and fignificancy in the eighth page of this Letter; *But nothing decifive, nothing which had the appearance of earneft has been fo much as attempted, ex- cept that wife expedition to* Toulon, *which* W E *fuffered to be defeated before it began.* Whoever did, God forgive them: there were indeed feveral ftories of difcoveries made, by letters and meffengers that were fent to *France.*

Having done with the Author's party and principles, we now fhall confider his performance, under the three
heads

heads of Wit, Language, and Argument. The firſt laſh of his Satyr falls upon the *Cenſor* of *Great Britain*, who, ſays he, reſembles the famous *Cenſor* of *Rome*, in no-thing but eſpouſing the *cauſe of the vanquiſhed.* Our Letter writer here alludes to that known verſe in *Lucan,*

Victrix cauſa Diis placuit, ſed victa Catoni.

The Gods eſpouſed the cauſe of the conquerors, but Cato *eſpouſed the cauſe of the vanquiſhed.* The misfortune is, that this verſe was not written of *Cato* the *Cenſor,* but of *Cato* of *Utica.* How Mr. *Bickerſtaffe,* who has written in favour of a party that is not vanquiſhed, reſembles the younger *Cato,* who was not a *Roman Cenſor,* I do not well conceive, unleſs it be in ſtruggling for the liber-ty of his country. To ſay therefore, that the *Cenſor* of *Great Britain* reſembles that famous *Cenſor* of *Rome in nothing but eſpouſing the cauſe of the vanquiſhed;* is juſt the ſame as if one ſhould ſay, in regard to the many ob-ſcure truths and ſecret hiſtories that are brought to light in this Letter, that the Author of theſe new Revelations, reſembles the ancient Author of the Revelations *in nothing but venturing his head.* Beſides that there would be no ground for ſuch a reſemblance, would not a man be laughed at by every common Reader, ſhould he thus miſtake one St. *John* for another; and apply that to St. *John* the Evangeliſt which relates to St. *John* the Bap-tiſt, who died many years before him ?.

Another ſmart touch of the Author we meet with in the fifth page, where without any preparation, he breaks out all on a ſudden into a vein of poetry ; and in-ſtead of writing a Letter to the *Examiner,* gives advice to a painter in theſe ſtrong lines : *Paint, Sir, with that force which you are maſter of, the preſent ſtate of the war abroad ; and expoſe to the publick view theſe principles upon which, of late, it has been carried on, ſo different from thoſe upon which it was originally entered into. Collect ſome of the indignities which have been this year offered to Her Majeſty, and of thoſe unnatural ſtruggles which have betrayed the weakneſs of a ſhattered conſtitution.* By the way, a man may be said to paint a battle, or if you please, a war; but I do not see how it is possible to paint the present state of a war. So a man may be said to describe or to collect accounts of indignities and unnatural struggles; but to collect the things themselves, is a figure which this Gentleman has introduced into our *English* prose. Well, but what will be the use of this picture of a state of the war? and this collection of indignities and struggles? It seems the chief design of them is to make a dead man blush, as we may see in those inimitable lines which immediately follow: *And when this is done,* D——n *shall blush in his grave among the dead,* W——le *among the living, and even* Vol——e *shall feel some remorse.* Was there ever any thing, I will nor say so stiff and so unnatural, but so brutal and so silly! This is downright hacking and hewing in Satyr. But we see a masterpiece of this kind of writing in the twelfth page; where, without any respect to a Dutchess of *Great Britain*, a Princess of the Empire, and one who was a bosom friend of her Royal Mistress, he calls a great Lady *an insolent woman, the worst of her sex, a fury, an executioner of divine vengeance, a plague*; and applies to her a line which *Virgil* writ originally upon ALECTO. One would think this foul-mouthed writer must have received some particular injuries, either from this great Lady or from her husband; and these the world shall be soon acquainted with, by a book which is now in the press, entitled, *An Essay towards proving that gratitude is no virtue.* This Author is so full of Satyr, and is so angry with every one that is pleased with the Duke of *Marlborough's* victories, that he goes out of his way to abuse one of the Queen's singing men, who it seems did his best to celebrate a thankfgiving day in an Anthem; as you may see in that passage: *Towns have been taken, and battles have been won; the mob has huzza'd round bonefires, the Senator of the chappel has strained his throat in the gallery, and the Senator of* S——m *has deafned his audience from the pulpit.* Thus you see how like a true son of the High-Church, he falls upon a learned and reverend Prelate, and for no other crime, but for preach-

ing

ing with an audible voice. If a man lifts up his voice like a trumpet to preach ſedition, he is received by ſome Men as a Confeſſor; but if he cries aloud, and ſpares not, to animate people with devotion and gratitude, for the greateſt publick Bleſſings that ever were beſtowed on a ſinful nation, he is reviled as a *Stentor.*

I promiſed in the next place to conſider the Language of this excellent Author, who I find takes himſelf for an Orator. In the firſt page he cenſures ſeveral for the poiſon which they *profuſely ſcatter* through the nation; that is in plain *Engliſh*, for *ſquandering away their poiſon.* In the ſecond he talks of *carrying probability through the thread of a fable*; and in the third, *of laying an odium at a man's door.* In the fourth he riſes in his expreſſions; where he ſpeaks of thoſe who would perſuade the people, that *the G———l, the quondam T———r, and the J————to, are the only objects of the confidence of the Allies, and of the fears of the enemies.* I would adviſe this Author to try the beauty of this expreſſion. Suppoſe a foreign Miniſter ſhould addreſs Her Majeſty in the following manner, (for certainly it is Her Majeſty only to whom the ſenſe of the compliment ought to be paid) Madam, you are *the object of the confidence of the Allies*; or, Madam, your Majeſty is *the only object of the fears of the enemies.* Would a man think that he had learned *Engliſh?* I would have the Author try, by the ſame rule, ſome of his other phraſes, as *Page* 7. where he tells us, *that the ballance of power in* Europe *would be ſtill precarious.* What would a tradeſman think, if one ſhould tell him in a paſſion, that his *ſcales were precarious*; and mean by it, that they were not fixed? In the thirteenth page he ſpeaks of certain *profligate wretches, who have uſurped the Royal Seat, reſolved to venture the overturning the chariot of government, rather than to loſe their place in it.* A plain ſpoken-man would have left the *Chariot* out of this ſentence, and ſo have made it good *Engliſh.* As it is there, it is not only an impropriety of ſpeech, but of metaphor; it being impoſſible for a man to have a place in the Chariot which he drives. I would therefore adviſe this Gentleman, in the next edition of his Letter, to change

change the Chariot of Government into the Chaife of Government, which will found as well, and ferve his turn much better. I could be longer on the *errata* of this very fmall work, but will conclude this head with taking notice of a certain figure which was unknown to the ancients, and in which this Letter-writer very much excels. This is called by fome an *Anti-climax*, an inftance of which we have in the tenth page; where he tells us, that *Britain* may expect to have this only glory left her, *that fhe has proved a farm to the Bank, a province to* Holland, *and a jeft to the whole world.* I never met with fo fudden a downfal in fo promifing a fentence; *a jeft to the whole world* gives fuch an unexpected turn to this happy period, that I was heartily troubled and furprifed to meet with it. I do not remember in all my reading, to have obferved more than two couplets of verfes that have been written in this figure; the firft are thus quoted by Mr. *Dryden.*

Not only London *ecchoes with thy fame,*
But alfo Iflington *has heard the* fame.

The other are in *French.*

Allez vous, luy dit il, fans bruit chez vos parens,
Ou vous avez laiffè votre honneur & vos gans.

But we need not go further than the Letter before us for examples of this nature, as we may find in page the eleventh. *Mankind remains convinced, that a Queen poffeffed of all the virtues requifite to blefs a nation, or make a private family happy, fits one the throne.* Is this Panegyrick or Burlefque? To fee fo glorious a Queen celebrated in fuch a manner, gives every good fubject a fecret indignation; and looks like *Scarron*'s character of the great Queen *Semiramis,* who, fays that Author, " was the " Founder of *Babylon,* Conqueror of the *Eaft,* and an " excellent Houfewife.

The third fubject being the argumentative part of this Letter, I fhall leave till another occafion.

Thurfday,

❀❀❀❀❀❀❀❀❀❀❀❀❀❀❀❀❀❀❀❀❀❀

No. 3. *Thurſday, September 28, 1710.*

―――*Non defenſoribus iſtis*
Tempus eget―――   VIRG.

I Was once talking with an old humdrum fellow, and
before I had heard his ſtory out, was called away by
buſineſs. About three years after I met him again; when
he immediately reaſſumed the thread of his ſtory, and
began his ſalutation with, *but, Sir, as I was telling you.*
The ſame method has been made uſe of by very polite
writers; as, in particular, the Author of *Don Quixote,*
who inſerts ſeveral novels in his works, and after a paren-
theſis of about a dozen leaves, returns again to his ſtory.
Hudibras has broke off the *Adventure of the Bear and
Fiddle.* The *Tatler* has frequently interrupted the courſe
of a Lucubration, and taken it up again after a fortnight's
reſpite; as the *Examiner* who is capable of imitating him
in this particular, has likewiſe done.

This may ſerve as an apology for my poſtponing the
examination of the argumentative part of *the Letter to
the Examiner* to a furtherday, though I muſt confeſs, this
was occaſioned by a 'Letter, which I received laſt poſt.
Upon opening it I found it to contain a very curious piece
of antiquity: which without preface or application, was
introduced as follows.

" *Alcibiades* was a man of wit and pleaſure, bred up
" in the ſchool of *Socrates*; and one of the beſt Orators
" of his age, notwithſtanding he lived at a time when
" learning was at its higheſt pitch: he was likewiſe ve-
" ry famous for his military exploits, having gained
" great conqueſts over the *Lacedæmonians,* who had
" formerly been the confederates of his country-men
" againſt the great King of *Perſia,* but were at that time
" in alliance with the *Perſians.* He had been once ſo
                                                  " far

" far mifreprefented and traduced by the malice of his
" enemies, that the Priefts curfed him.   But after the
" great fervices which he had done for his country, they
" publickly repealed their curfes, and changed them into
" applaufes and benedictions.

" *Plutarch* tells us, in *the life of* Alcibiades, that one
" *Taureas*, an obfcure man, contended with him for a
" certain prize, which was to be conferred by vote; at
" which time each of the competitors recommended him-
" felf to the *Athenians* by an oration.   The Speech which
" *Alcibiades* made on that occafion, has been lately dif-
" covered among the Manufcripts of *King's-college* in
" *Cambridge*; and communicated to me by my learned
" friend Dr. B———*ley*; who tells me, that by a mar-
" ginal note it appears, that this *Taureas*, or, as the
" Doctor rather chufes to call him, *Toryas*, was an *Athe-*
" *nian* Brewer.   This fpeech I have tranflated literally,
" changing very little in it, except where it was abfo-
" lutely neceffary to make it underftood by an *Englifh*
" Reader.   It is as follows.

" **I**S it then poffible, O ye *Athenians*, that I who hi-
"   " therto have had none but Generals to oppofe
" me, muft now have an artifan for my antagonift?
" That I who have overthrown the Princes of *Lacedæ-*
" *mon*, muft now fee my felf in danger of being defeat-
" ed by a Brewer? What will the world fay of the
" Goddefs that prefides over you, fhould they fuppofe
" you follow her dictates? would they think fhe acted
" like herfelf, like the great *Minerva?* would they now
" fay, fhe infpires her fons with wifdom? or would
" they not rather fay, fhe has a fecond time chofen
" owls for her favourites? But O ye men of *Athens*,
" what has this man done to deferve your voices? You
" fay he is honeft; I believe it, and therefore he fhall
" brew for me.   You fay he is affiduous in his calling:
" and is he not grown rich by it? let him have your
" cuftom, but not your votes: you are now to caft your
" eyes on thofe who can detect the artifices of the com-
" mon enemy, that can difappoint your fecret foes in

Vol. II.   E   " Council,

" Council, and your open ones in the field. Let it not
" avail my Competitor, that he has been tapping his li-
" quors, while I have been spilling my blood ; that he
" has been gathering hops for you, while I have been
" reaping lawrels. Have I not born the dust and heat
" of the day, while he has been sweating at the furnace ?
" behold these scars, behold this wound which still
" bleeds in your service ; what can *Taureas* shew you of
" this nature ? What are his marks of honour ? Has he
" any other wound about him, except the accidental
" scaldings of his wort, or bruises from the tub or bar-
" rel ? Let it not, O *Athenians,* let it not be said, that
" your Generals have conquered themselves into your
" displeasure, and lost your favour by gaining you vic-
" tories. Shall those atchievements that have redeemed
" the present age from slavery, be undervalued by those
" who feel the benefits of them ? Shall those names that
" have made your city the glory of the whole earth, be
" mentioned in it with obloquy and detraction ? Will
" not your posterity blush at their forefathers, when
" they shall read in the annals of their country, that *Al-*
" *cibiades* in the 90*th* Olympiad, after having conquer-
" the *Lacedæmenians,* and recovered *Byzantium,* con-
" tended for a prize against *Taureas* the Brewer ? The
" competition is dishonourable, the defeat would be
" shameful. I shall not however slacken my endea-
" vours for the security of my country. If she is un-
" grateful, she is still *Athens.* On the contrary, as she
" will stand more in need of defence, when she has so
" degenerate a people, I will pursue my victories, 'till
" such time as it shall be out of your power to hurt
" yourselves, and that you may be in safety even un-
" der your present leaders. But oh ! thou genius of *A-*
" *thens* whither art thou fled ? Where is now the race
" of those glorious spirits that perished at the battle of
" *Thermopylæ,* and fought upon the plains of *Mara-*
" *thon?* Are you weary of conquering, or have you for-
" gotten the oath which you took at *Agraulos, That*
" *you would look upon the bounds of* Attica *to be those soils*
" *only which are incapable of bearing wheat and barley*

" *vines and olives?* Confider your enemies the *Lacedæ-*
" *monians* ; did you ever hear that they preferred a
" Coffee-man to *Agefilaus?* No, though their Gene-
" rals have been unfortunate, though they have loft
" feveral battels, though they have not been able to
" cope with the troops of *Athens*, which I have con-
" ducted ; they are comforted and condoled, nay cele-
" brated and extolled, by their fellow-citizens... Their
" Generals have been received with honour after their
" defeat, yours with ignominy after conqueft. Are
" there not men of *Taureas*'s temper and character,
" who tremble in their hearts at the name of the great
" King of *Perfia?* who have been *againft* entering into
" a war with him, or *for* making a peace upon bafe
" conditions ? that have grudged thofe contributions
" which have fet our country at the head of all the go-
" vernments of *Greece ?* that would difhonour thofe
" who have raifed her to fuch a pitch of glory ? that
" would betray thofe liberties which your fathers in
" all ages have purchafed or recovered with their
" blood ? and would profecute your fellow-citizens
" with as much rigour and fury, as of late years we
" have attacked the common enemy ? I fhall trouble
" you no more, O ye men of *Athens* ; you know my
" actions, let my antagonift relate what he has done for
" you. Let him produce his vatts and tubs, in op-
" pofition to the heaps of arms and ftandards which
" were employed againft you, and which I have wrefted
" out of the hands of your enemies. And when this is
" done, let him be brought into the field of election upon
" his dray-cart ; and if I can finifh my conqueft fooner,
" I will not fail to meet him there in a triumphant cha-
" riot. But, O ye Gods ! let not the King of *Perfia*
" laugh at the fall of *Alcibiades !* Let him not fay, *the*
" Athenians *have avenged me upon their own Generals* ;
" or let me be rather ftruck dead by the hand of a *Lace-*
" *dæmonian,* than difgraced by the voices of my fellow-
" citizens.

No. 4.   *Thurſday, October* 5.

Satis eloquentiæ, ſapientiæ parum.   . . SAL.

HUdibras has defined nonſenſe (as *Cowley* does wit) by negatives. Nonſenſe (ſays he) is that which is neither true nor falſe. Theſe two great properties of nonſenſe which are always eſſential to i, give it ſuch a peculiar advantage over all other writings, that it is incapable of being either anſwered or contradicted. It ſtands upon its own baſis like a rock of adamant, ſecured by its natural ſituation againſt all conqueſts or attacks. There is no one place about it weaker than another, to favour an enemy in his approaches. The major and the minor are of equal ſtrength. Its queſtions admit of no reply, and its aſſertions are not to be invalidated. A man may as well hope to diſtinguiſh colours in the midſt of darkneſs, as to find out what to approve and diſapprove in nonſenſe: you may as well aſſault an army that is buried in intrenchments. If it affirms any thing, you cannot lay hold of it; or if it denies, you cannot confute it. In a word, there are greater depths and obſcurities, greater intricacies and perplexities, in an elaborate and well written piece of nonſenſe, than in the moſt abſtruſe and profound tract of ſchool-divinity.

After this ſhort panegyrick upon nonſenſe, which may appear as extravagant to an ordinary Reader, as *Eraſmus's Encomium of folly*; I muſt here ſolemnly proteſt, that I have not done it to curry favour with my antagoniſt, or to reflect any praiſe in an oblique manner upon the *Letter to the Examiner:* I have no private conſiderations to warp me in this controverſy, ſince my fiſt entering upon it. But before I proceed any further, becauſe it may be of great uſe to me in this diſpute, to ſtate the whole nature of nonſenſe; and becauſe 'tis a ſubject

subject entirely new, I must take notice that there are two kinds of it, *viz.* high nonsense and low nonsense.

Low nonsense is the talent of a cold phlegmatick temper, that in a poor dispirited style creeps along servilely through darkness and confusion. A writer of this complexion gropes his way softly among self-contradictions, and grovels in absurdities.

Videri vult pauper, & est pauper.

He has neither wit nor sense, and pretends to none.

On the contrary, your high nonsense blusters and makes a noise, it stalks upon hard words, and rattles through polysyllables. It is loud and sonorous, smooth and periodical. It has something in it like manliness and force, and makes one think of the name of Sir *Hercules Nonsense* in the play called *the nest of fools*. In a word, your high nonsense has a majestick appearance, and wears a most tremendous garb, like *Æsop*'s ass cloathed in a lion's skin.

When *Aristotle* lay upon his death-bed, and was asked whom he would appoint for his successor in the school, two of his scholars being Candidates for it; he called for two different sorts of wine, and by the character which he gave of them, denoted the different qualities and perfections that shewed themselves in the style and writings of each of the Competitors. As rational writings have been represented by *wine*, I shall represent those kinds of writings we are now speaking of, by *small-beer*.

Low nonsense is like that in the barrel, which is altogether flat, tasteless, and insipid. High nonsense is like that in the bottle, which has in reality no more strength and spirit than the other, but frets and flies, and bounces, and by the help of a little wind that is got into it, imitates the passions of a much nobler liquor.

We meet with a low groveling nonsense in every *Grub-street* production; but I think there are none of our present writers who have hit the sublime in nonsense, besides Dr. S——l in divinity, and the Author of this letter in politicks; between whose characters in their respective professions, there seems to be a very nice resemblance. There

E 3

There is ftill another qualification in nonfenfe which I muft not pafs over, being that which gives it the laft finifhing and perfection; and eminently difcovers it felf in the letter to the Examiner.————This is when an Author without any meaning, feems to have it; and fo impofes upon us by the found and ranging of his words, that one is apt to fancy they fignify fomething. Any one who reads this letter, as he goes through it, will lie under the fame delufion; but after having read it, let him confider what he has learnt from it, and he will immediately difcover the deceit. I did not indeed at firft imagine there was in it fuch a jargon of Ideas, fuch an inconfiftency of notions, fuch a confufion of particles, that rather puzzle than connect the fenfe, which in fome places he feems to have aimed at, as I found upon my nearer perufal of it: Neverthelefs, as no body writes a book without meaning fomething, though he may not have the faculty of writing confe-quential'y, and expreffing his meaning; I think, I have with a great deal of attention and difficulty found out what this Gentleman would fay, had he the gift of ut-terance. The Syftem of his politicks, when difembroi-led and cleared of all thofe incoherences and indepen-dent matters that are woven into this motley piece, will be as follows. The conduct of the late Miniftry is con-fidered firft of all in refpect to foreign affairs; and fe-condly to domeftick: As to the firft, he tells us, that *the motives which engaged* Britain *in the prefent war, were both wife and generous;* fo that the Miniftry is cleared as to that particular. Thefe motives he tells us, *were to reftore the* Spanifh *monarchy to the houfe of* Auftria, *and to regain a barrier for* Holland. *The laft of thefe two motives,* he fays, *was effectually anfwered by the reduc-tion of the* Netherlands *in the year* 1706, *or might have been fo by the conceffions which it is notorious that the enemy offered.* So that the Miniftry are here blamed for not contenting themfelves with the barrier they had gained in the year 1706, nor with the conceffions which the enemy then offered. The other motive of our entering into the war, *viz. The reftoring the* Spanifh *monarchy* to the houfe of Auftria, he tells us, *remained ftill in its full force; and we were told,* fays he, *that though the barrier of* Holland *was fecured, the trade of* Britain *and the ballance of power in* Europe *would be ftill precarious:* Spain *therefore muft be conquered.* He then lofes himfelf in matter foreign to his purpofe: But what he endeavours in the fequel of his difcourfe, is to fhew, that we have not taken the proper method to recover the *Spanifh* monarchy; *that the whole ftrefs of the war has been wantonly laid where* France *is beft able to keep us at bay; that the* French King *has made it impoffible for himfelf to give up* Spain, and that the Duke of *Anjou* has made it as impoffible for us to conquer it: Nay, *that inftead of regaining* Spain, *we fhall find the Duke of* Anjou *in a condition to pay the debt of gratitude, and fupport the Grandfather in his declining years, by whofe arms in the days of his infancy he was upheld.* He then intimates to us, that the *Dutch* and the Emperor will be fo very well fatisfied with what they have already conquered, that they may probably leave the houfe of *Bourbon* in the quiet poffeffion of the *Spanifh* Monarchy.

This ftrange huddle of politicks has been fo fully anfwered by General *Stanhope*, that if the Author had delayed the publifhing of his letter but a fortnight, the world would have been deprived of that elaborate production. Notwithftanding all that the *French*-King or the Duke of *Anjou* have been able to do, notwithftanding the feeble efforts we have made in *Spain*, notwithftanding *the little care the Emperor takes to fupport King* Charles, notwithftanding the *Dutch* might have been contented *with a larger and better country than their own already conquered for them,* that victorious General at the head of *Englifh* and *Dutch* forces, in conjunction with thofe of the Emperor, has wrefted *Spain* out of the hands of the houfe of *Bourbon;* and added the conqueft of *Navarre, Arragon,* and *Caftile,* to thofe of *Catalonia, Bavaria, Flanders, Mantua, Milan, Naples, Sicily, Majorca, Minorca,* and *Sardinia.* Such a wonderful feries of victories, and thofe aftonifhing returns of ingratitude which they have met with, appear both of

them

them rather like Dreams than realities: They puzzle and confound the prefent age, and it is to be hoped they will not be believed by pofterity. Will the trifling Author of this letter fay, that the Miniftry did not apply themfelves to the reduction of *Spain*, when the whole Kingdom was twice conquered in their adminiftration? The Letter-writer fays; *that the* Dutch *had gain'd a good barrier after the battle of* Ramillies *in the year* 1706. But I would fain afk him, whether he thinks *Antwerp* and *Bruffels*, *Ghent* and *Burges*, could be thought a ftrong barrier, or that thofe important conquefts did not want feveral towns and forts to cover them? But it feems our great General on that fide has done more for us than we expected of him, and made the barrier too impregnable. *But,* fays the Letter-writer, *the ftrefs of the war was laid in the wrong place:* But if the laying the ftrefs of the war in the *Low-Countries* drew thither the whole ftrength of *France*; if it weakened *Spain*, and left it expofed to an equal force, if *France*, without being preffed on this fide, could have affifted the Duke of *Anjou* with a numerous army; and if by the advantage of the fituation, it could have fent and maintained in *Spain* ten regiments with as little trouble and expence, as *England* could two regiments; every impartial Judge would think that the ftrefs of the war has been laid in the right place.

The Author in this confufed differtation on foreign affairs, would fain make us believe, that *England* has gained nothing by thefe conquefts, and put us out of humour with our chief Allies, the Emperor and the *Dutch*. He tells us, *they hoped* England *would have been taken care of, after having fecured a barrier for* Holland: As if *England* were not taken care of by this very fecuring a barrier for *Holland*; which has always been looked upon as our Bulwark, or as Mr. *Waller* expreffes it, our *out-guard on the continent*; and which if it had fallen into the hands of the *French*, would have made *France* more ftrong by fea than all *Europe* befides. Has not *England* been taken care of by gaining a new mart in *Flanders*, by opening our trade into the *Levant*, by fecuring

curing ports for us in *Gibraltar*, *Minorca*, and *Naples*, and by that happy profpect we have of renewing that great branch of our commerce into *Spain*, which will be of more advantage to *England* than any conqueft we can make of towns and provinces ? Not to mention the demolifhing of *Dunkirk*, which we were in a fair way of obtaining during the laft Parliament, and which we never fo much as propofed to our felves at our firft engaging in this war.

As for this Author's afperfions of the *Dutch* and *Germans*, I have fometimes wonder'd that he has not been complained of for it to the Secretary of ftate. Had not he been looked upon as an infignificant fcribler, he muft have occafioned remonftrances and memorials: Such national injuries are not to be put up, but when the offender is below refentment. This puts me in mind of an honeft *Scotchman*, who as he was walking along the ftreets of *London*, heard one calling out after him *Scot*, *Scot*, and cafting forth in a clamorous manner a great deal of opprobrious language againft that antient nation: *Sawny* turned about in a great paffion, and found, to his furprize, that the perfon who abufed him was a fawcy parrot that hung up not far from him in a cage ; upon which he clapped his hand to his fword, and told him, were he a man as he was a green-goofe, he would have run him through the wemb.

The next head our Politician goes upon, relates to our domeftick affairs; where I am extremely at a lofs to know what he wou'd be at: All that I can gather from him, is, that *the Queen had grieved her fubjects* in making choice of fuch men for her Minifters, as raifed the nation to a greater pitch of glory than ever it was in the days of our forefathers, or than any other nation in thefe our days.

No. 5. *Thurſday, October* 12.

Parere jam non ſcelus eſt. Mart.

WE live in a nation where at preſent there is ſcarce
a ſingle head that does not teem with politicks.
The whole Iſland is peopled with Stateſmen, and not un-
like *Trinculo's* Kingdom of Vice-roys. Every man has
contrived a ſcheme of government for the benefit of his
fellow-ſubjects, which they may follow and be ſafe.

After this ſhort preface, by which as an Engliſhman,
I lay my claim to be a Politician; I ſhall enter on my
diſcourſe.

The chief point that has puzzled the freeholders of
Great Britain, as well as all thoſe that pay ſcot and lot,
for about theſe ſix months laſt paſt, is this, Whether
they would rather be governed by a Prince that is obliged by laws to be good and gracious, juſt and upright,
a friend, father, and a defender of his people; or by
one who, if he pleaſes, may drive away or plunder, im-
priſon or kill, without oppoſition or reſiſtance. This is
the true ſtate of the controverſy relating to *paſſive-obedience* and *non-reſiſtance*. For I muſt obſerve, that the Ad-
vocates for this doctrine have ſtated the caſe in the ſoft-
eſt and moſt palatable terms that it will bear: And we
very well know, that there is great art in moulding a
queſtion; and that many a motion will paſs with a *nemine
contradicente* in ſome words, that would have been as una-
nimouſly rejected in others. *Paſſive obedience* and *non-reſiſtance* are of a mild, gentle, and meek-ſpirited ſound:
They have reſpect but to one ſide of the relation between
the ſovereign and the ſubject, and are apt to fill the mind
with no other ideas but thoſe of peace, tranquillity, and
reſignation. To ſhew this doctrine in thoſe black and
odious colours that are natural to it, we ſhould conſider

it

it with regard to the Prince as well as to the people: The queſtion will then take another turn, and it will not be debated whether reſiſtance may be lawful, or whether we may take up Arms againſt our Prince; but whether the Engliſh form of government be a tyranny or a limited monarchy? Whether our Prince be obliged by our conſtitution to act according to law, or whether he be arbitrary and deſpotical.

It is impoſſible to ſtate the meaſures of *Obedience*, without ſettling the extent of *Power*; or to deſcribe the *Subject*, without defining the *King*. An arbitrary Prince is in juſtice and equity the maſter of a non-reſiſting people; for where the power is uncircumſcribed, the obedience ought to be unlimited. *Paſſive-obedience* and *non-reſiſtance* are the duties of *Turks* and *Indians*, who have no laws above the Will of a *Grand Signior* or a *Mogul*. The ſame power which thoſe Princes enjoy in their reſpective governments, belongs to the legiſlative body in our conſtitution; and that for the ſame reaſon; becauſe no body of men is ſubject to laws, or can be controuled by them, who have the authority of making, altering, or repealing whatever laws they ſhall think fit. Were our legiſlature veſted in the perſon of our Prince, he might doubtleſs wind and turn our conſtitution at his pleaſure; he might ſhape our government to his fancy. In a word, he might oppreſs, perſecute, or deſtroy, and no man ſay to him, what doſt thou?

If therefore we would rightly conſider our form of government, we ſhould diſcover the proper meaſures of our duty and obedience; which can never riſe too high to our Sovereign, whilſt he maintains us in thoſe rights and liberties we were born to. But to ſay that we have rights which we ought not to vindicate and aſſert; that Liberty and Property are the birth-right of the *Engliſh* nation, but that if a Prince invades them by violent and illegal methods, we muſt upon no pretence reſiſt, but remain altogether paſſive; nay, that in ſuch a caſe we muſt all loſe our lives unjuſtly rather than defend them: this, I ſay, is to confound governments, and to

join

join things together that are wholly repugnant in their
natures; since it is plain, that such a passive subjection,
such an unconditional obedience, can be only due to an
arbitrary Prince or to a legislative body.

Were these smooth ensnaring terms rightly explained to the people, and the controversy of Non-resistance
set in this just light, we should have wanted many thousands of hands to some late Addresses. I would fain
know what Free-holder in *England* would have sub-
scribed the following Address, had it been offered to
him; or whether Her Majesty, who values the rights
of her subjects as much as her own prerogative, would
not have been very much offended at it? and yet I will
appeal to the Reader, if this has not been the sense of
many Addresses, when taken out of several artificial
qualifying expressions, and exposed in their true and genuine light.

Madam,

"IT is with unspeakable grief of heart, that we hear
"a set of men daily preaching up among us,
"that pernicious and damnable doctrine of self-preser-
"vation; and boldly affirming, as well in their publick
"writings, as in their private discourses, that it is law-
"ful to resist a tyrant, and take up arms in defence of
"their lives and liberties. We have the utmost horror
"and detestation of these diabolical principles, that
"may induce your people to rise up in vindication of
"their rights and freedoms, whenever a wicked
"Prince shall make use of his Royal authority to sub-
"vert them. We are astonished at the bold and impious
"attempts of those men, who under the reign of the
"best of Sovereigns, would avow such dangerous te-
"nets as may secure them under the worst. We are re-
"solved to beat down and discountenance these sediti-
"ous notions, as being altogether republican, jesuiti-
"cal, and conformable to the practice of our rebelli-
"ous fore-fathers; who in all ages, at an infinite ex-
"pence of blood and treasure, asserted their rights and
"properties, and consulted the good of their posterity
"by

" by refiftance, arms, and pitched battles, to the great
" trouble and difquiet of their lawful Prince. We do
" therefore in the moft humble and dutiful manner fo-
" lemnly proteft and declare, that we will never refift
" a Sovereign that fhall think fit to deftroy our *Magna*
" *Charta,* or invade thofe rights and liberties which
" thofe traytors procured for us; but will venture our
" lives and fortunes againft fuch of our fellow-fubjefts
" who think they may ftand up in defence of them.

It happens very unluckily that there is fomething fo
fupple and infinuating in this abfurd unnatural doctrine, as makes it extremely agreeable to a Prince's ear:
for which reafon the publifhers of it have always been
the favourites of weak Kings. Even thofe who have *no
inclination* to do hurt to others, fays the famous Saty-
rift, would have *the power* of doing it if they pleafed.
Honeft men who tell their Sovereigns what they expeft
from them, and what obedience they fhall be always
ready to pay them, are not upon an equal foot with
fuch bafe and abjeft flatterers; and are therefore always
in danger of being the laft in the Royal favour. Nor indeed would that be unreafonable, if the profeffors of
Non-refiftance and Paffive-obedience would ftand to
their principle: but inftead of that, we fee they never
fail to exert themfelves againft an arbitrary power, and
to caft off the oppreffion when they feel the weight
of it. Did they not in the late Revolution rife up unanimoufly with thofe who always declared their fubjeftion
to be conditional, and their obedience limited? and very lately, when their Queen had offended them in nothing but by the promotion of a few great men to pofts
of truft and honour, who had diftinguifhed themfelves
by their moderation and humanity to all their fellow-
fubjefts, what was the behaviour of thefe men of meek
and refigned principles? Did not the *Church-memorial,*
which they all applauded and cried up as the language
and fentiments of their party, tell H. M. that it would
not be fafe for Her to rely upon their doftrines of Paffive-obedience and Non-refiftance, for that *nature*
might

might rebel againft principles? Is not this, in plain terms,
that they will only practife Non-refiftance to a Prince
that pleafes them, and Paffive-obedience when they fuffer nothing? I remember one of the rabble in *Oedipus*,
when he is upbraided with his rebellion, and asked by
the Prophet if he had not taken an oath to be loyal, falls
a fcratching his head, and tells him, Why yes, truly, he
had taken fuch an oath, *but it was an hard thing that an
oath fhould be a man's mafter.* This is in effect the language of the Church in the above-mentioned Memorial.
Men of thefe foft peaceable difpofitions in times of pro-
fperity, put me in mind of *Kirke's Lambs*; for that was
the name he ufed to give his dragoons that had fignali-
zed themfelves above the reft of the army by many military atchievements among their own country-men.

There are two or three fatal confequences of this
doctrine, which I cannot forbear pointing out. The
firft of which is, That it has a natural tendency to make
a good King a very bad one. When a man is told he
may do what he pleafes with impunity, he will be lefs
careful and cautious of doing what he fhould do, than a
man who is influenced by fear as well as by other motives to virtue. It was a faying of *Thales* the wife *Mi-
lefian*, that *of all wild beafts a tyrant is the worft, and
of all tame beafts a flatterer.* They do indeed naturally
beget one another, and always exift together. Perfuade a
Prince that he is irrefiftible, and he will take care not to
let fo glorious an attribute lie dead and ufelefs by him.
An arbitrary power has fomething fo great in it, that he
muft be more than man who is endowed with it, but
never exerts it.

This confequence of the doctrine I have been fpeaking of, is very often a fatal one to the people; there is
another which is no lefs deftructive to the Prince. A
late unfortunate King very vifibly owed his ruin to it.
He relied upon the affurances of his people, that they
would never refift him upon any pretence whatfoever,
and accordingly began to act like a King who was not
under the reftraint of laws, by difpenfing with them,
and taking on him that power which was vefted in

the

the whole legiflative body. And what was the dreadful end of fuch a proceeding? It is too frefh in every body's memory. Thus is a Prince corrupted by the profeffors of this doctrine, and afterwards betrayed by them. The fame perfons are the Actors, both in the temptation and the punifhment. They affure him they will never refift, but retain their obedience under the utmoft fufferings, he tries them in a few inftances, and is depofed by them for his credulity.

I remember at the beginning of King *James's* reign the Quakers prefented an Addrefs, which gave great offence to the High Church-men of thofe times. But notwithftanding the uncourtlinefs of their phrafes, the fenfe was very honeft. The Addrefs was as follows, to the beft of my memory, for I then took great notice of it; and may ferve as a counter-part to the foregoing one.

"THefe are to teftify to thee our forrow for our friend *Charles,* whom we hope thou wilt follow in every thing that is good.

"We hear that thou art not of the religion of the land any more than we, and therefore may reafonably expect that thou wilt give us the fame liberty that thou takeft thy felf.

"We hope that in this and all things elfe thou wilt promote the good of thy people, which will oblige us to pray that thy reign over us may be long and profperous.

Had all King *James's* fubjects addreffed him with the fame integrity; he had, in all probability, fat upon his throne till death had removed him from it.

THE

LOVER.

No. 10. *Thursday, March* 18, 1714.

——*Magis illa placent quæ pluris emuntur.*

I Have lately been very much teized with the thought of Mrs. *Anne Page,* and the memory of thofe many cruelties which I fuffered from that obdurate fair one. Mrs. *Anne* was in a particular manner very fond of *China* ware, againft which I had unfortunately declared my averfion. I do not know but this was the firft occafion of her coldnefs towards me, which makes me fick at the very fight of a *China* difh ever fince. This is the beft introduction I can make for my prefent difcourfe, which may ferve to fill up a gap till I am more at leizure to refume the thread of my amours.

There are no inclinations in women which more furprife me than their paffions for chalk and *China.* The firft of thefe maladies wears out in a little time; but when a woman is vifited with the fecond it generally takes poffeffion of her for life. *China* veffels are playthings for women of all ages. An old Lady of fourfcore fhall be as bufie in cleaning an *Indian* Mandarin, as her great-grand-daughter is in dreffing her baby.

The

The common way of purchasing such trifles, if I may
believe my female informers, is by exchanging old suits
of cloths for this brittle ware. The potters of *China*
have, it seems, their factors at this distance, who retail
out their several manufactures for cast cloths and superannuated garments. I have known an old petticoat me-
tamorphosed into a punch-bowl, and a pair of breeches
into a tea-pot. For this reason my friend *Tradswell* in
the city calls his great room, that is nobly furnished out
with *China*, his wife's wardrobe. In yonder corner,
says he are above twenty suits of cloths, and on that
scrutore above a hundred yards of furbelowed silk. You
cannot imagine how many night-gowns, stays and man-
toes, went to the raising of that pyramid. The worst
of it is, says he, a suit of cloths is not suffered to last
half its time, that it may be the more vendible ; so that
in reality this is but a more dextrous way of picking the
husband's pocket, who is often purchasing a great vase
of *China*, when he fancies that he is buying a fine head,
or a silk gown for his wife. There is likewise another
inconvenience in this female passion for *China*, namely,
that it administers to them great matter of wrath and
sorrow. How much anger and affliction are produced
daily in the hearts of my dear country women, by the
breach of this frail furniture. Some of them pay half
their servants wages in *China* fragments, which their
carelesness has produced. *If thou hast a piece of earthen
ware, consider, says* Epictetus, *that it is a piece of earthen
ware, and very easy and obnoxious to be broken : be not
therefore so void of reason as to be angry or grieved when
this comes to pass.* In order, therefore, to exempt my
fair Readers from such additional and supernumerary
calamities of life, I would advise them to forbear deal-
ing in these perishable commodities, till such time as
they are philosophers enough to keep their temper at
the fall of a tea-pot or a *China* cup. I shall further recommend to their serious consideration these three particulars : First, That all *China* ware is of a weak and
transitory nature. Secondly, that the fashion of it is
changeable : and Thirdly, that it is of no use. And first of
the

the firſt: the fragility of *China* is ſuch as a reaſonable Being ought by no means to ſet its heart upon, though at
the ſame time I am afraid I may complain with *Seneca*
on the like occaſion, that this very conſideration recommends them to our choice ; our luxury being grown ſo
wanton, that this kind of treaſure becomes the more valuable, the more eaſily we may be deprived of it, and
that it receives a price from its brittleneſs. There is a
kind of oſtentation in wealth, which ſets the poſſeſſors
of it upon diſtinguiſhing themſelves in thoſe things
where it is hard for the poor to follow them. For this
reaſon I have often wondered that our Ladies have not
taken pleaſure in egg-ſhells, eſpecially in thoſe which
are curiouſly ſtained and ſtreaked, and which are ſo very
tender, that they require the niceſt hand to hold without breaking them. But as if the brittleneſs of this
ware were not ſufficient to make it coſtly, the very fa-
ſhion of it is changeable, which brings me to the ſecond
particular.

It may chance that a piece of *China* may ſurvive all
thoſe accidents to which it is by nature liable, and laſt
for ſome years, if rightly ſituated and taken care of. To
remedy, therefore, this inconvenience, it is ſo ordered that the ſhape of it ſhall grow unfaſhionable, which
makes new ſupplies always neceſſary, and furniſhes employment for life to women of great and generous
Souls, who cannot live out of the mode. I myſelf remember when there were few *China* veſſels to be ſeen
that held more than a diſh of Coffee ; but their ſize is ſo
gradually enlarged, that there are many at preſent,
which are capable of holding half a hogſhead. The fa-
ſhion of the tea-cup is alſo greatly altered, and has run
through a wonderful variety of colour, ſhape and ſize.

But, in the laſt place, *China* ware is of no uſe. Who
would not laugh to ſee a ſmith's ſhop furniſhed with an-
vils and hammers of *China* ? The furniture of a Lady's favourite room is altogether as abſurd : you ſee Jars of a
prodigious capacity that are to hold nothing. I have
ſeen horſes and herds of cattel in this fine ſort of Porſe-
lain, not to mention the ſeveral *Chineſe* Ladies who,

per-

perhaps, are naturally enough reprefented in thefe frail materials.

Did our women take delight in heaping up piles of earthen platters, brown juggs, and the like ufeful pro-ducts of our *Britifh* potteries, there would be fome fenfe in it. They might be ranged in as fine figures, and dif-pofed of in as beautiful pieces of Architecture; but there is an objection to thefe which cannot be overcome, namely, that they would be of fome ufe, and might be taken down on all occafions to be employed in fervices of the family, befides that they are intolerably cheap, and moft fhamefully durable and lafting.

No. 39. *Tuefday, May* 25.

Nec verbum verbo curabis reddere fidus.
Interpres――― HOR.

SINCE I have given publick notice of my abode, I have had many vifits from unfortunate fellow-fuffer-ers who have been croffed in love as well as my felf.

Will. Wormwood, who is related to me by my mother's fide, is one of thofe who often repair to me for my ad-vice. *Will.* is a fellow of good fenfe, but puts it to little other ufe than to torment himfelf. He is a man of fo re-fined an underftanding, that he can fet a conftruction upon every thing to his own difadvantage, and turn even a civility into an affront. He groans under imaginary in-juries, finds himfelf abufed by his friends, and fancies the whole world in a kind of combination againft him. In fhort, poor *Wormwood* is devoured with the fpleen: you may be fure a man of this humour makes a very whimfi-cal lover. Be that as it will, he is now over head and ears in that paffion, and by a very curious interpretation of his Miftrefs's behaviour, has in lefs than three months
reduced

reduced himfelf to a perfect fkeleton. As her fortune is
inferior to his, fhe gives him all the encouragement another man could wifh, but has the mortification to find
that her lover ftill fowers upon her hands. *Will.* is dif-
fatisfied with her, whether fhe fmiles or frowns upon
him ; and always thinks her too referved, or too coming.
A kind word, that would make another lover's heart
dance for joy, pangs poor *Will.* and makes him lie awake
all night——— As I was going on with *Will Wormwood's*
amour, I received a prefent from my Bookfeller, which
I found to be *The Characters of* Theophraftus, tranflated
from the *Greek* into *Englifh* by Mr. *Budgell.*

It was with me, as I believe it will be with all who
look into this tranflation ; when I had begun to perufe
it, I could not lay it by, until I had gone through the
whole book ; and was agreeably furprifed to meet with
a chapter in it, intitled, *A difcontented temper,* which
gives a livelier picture of my coufin *Wormwood,* than that
which I was drawing for him myfelf. It is as follows,

C H A P. XVII. *A Difcontented Temper.*

" A difcontented temper, is *a frame of mind which*
" *fets a man upon complaining without reafon.* When one
" of his neighbours who makes an entertainment, fends
" a fervant to him with a plate of any thing that is nice,
" *What,* fays he, *your Mafter did not think me good enough*
" *to dine with him ?* He complains of his Miftrifs at the
" very time fhe is careffing him ; and when fhe redou
" bles her kiffes and endearments, *I wifh,* fays he, *all*
" *this came from your heart.* In a dry feafon he grum-
" bles for want of rain, and when a fhower falls, mut-
" ters to himfelf, *Why could not this have come fooner ?*
" If he happens to find a purfe of money, *Had it been a*
" *pot of gold,* fays he, *it would have been worth ftooping*
" *for.* He takes a great deal of pains to beat down the
" price of a flave ; and after he has paid his money for
" him, *I am fure,* fays he, *Thou art good for nothing, or*
" *I fhould not have had thee fo cheap.* When a meffenger
" comes with great joy to acquaint him that his wife is
                                                    " brought

" brought to bed of a son, he anfwers, *That is as much*
" *as to fay, Friend, I am poorer by half to day than I was*
" *yefterday.* Tho' he has gained a caufe with full
" cofts and damages, he complains that his Council did
" not infift upon the moft material points. If after any
" misfortune has befallen him, his friends raife a volun-
" tary contribution for him, and defire him to be mer-
" ry, *How is that poffible,* fays he, *when I am to pay*
" *every one of you his money again, and be obliged to you*
" *into the bargain.*

The inftances of a difcontented temper which *Theophraftus* has here made ufe of, like thofe which he fingles
out to illuftrate the reft of his characters, are chofen
with the greateft nicety, and full of humour. His ftrokes
are always fine and exquifite, and though they are not
fometimes violent enough to affect the imagination of a
coarfe Reader, cannot but give the higheft pleafure to e-
very man of a refined tafte, who has a thorough infight
into human nature.

As for the tranflation, I have never feen any of a profe
Author which has pleafed me more. The Gentleman
who has obliged the publick with it, has followed the
rule which *Horace* has laid down for tranflators, by pre-
ferving every where the life and fpirit of his Author,
without fervilely copying after him word for word. This
is what the *French*, who have moft diftinguifhed themfelves by performances of this nature, fo often inculcate
when they advife a tranflator to find out fuch particular
elegancies in his own tongue as bear fome analogy to
thofe he fees in the original, and to exprefs himfelf to
fuch phrafes as his Author would probably have made
ufe of, had he written in the language into which he is
tranflated. By this means, as well as by throwing in a
lucky word, or a fhort circumftance, the meaning of
Theophraftus is all along explained, and the humour very
often carried to a greater height. A tranflator, who does
not thus confider the different genius of the two languages in which he is concerned, with fuch parallel
turns of thoughts and expreffion as correfpond with one
ano-

another in both of them, may value himself upon being a *faithful interpreter*; but in works of wit and humour will never do juſtice to his author, or credit to himſelf.

· As this is every where a judicious and a reaſonable liberty, I ſee no chapter in *Theophraſtus* where it has been ſo much indulged, and in which it was ſo abſolutely neceſſary as in the character of the *Sloven*. I find the tranſlator himſelf, though he has taken pains to qualify it, is ſtill apprehenſive that there may be ſomething too groſs in the deſcription. The Reader will ſee with how much *Delicacy* he has touched upon every particular, and caſt into ſhades every thing that was ſhocking in ſo nauſeous a figure.

CHAP. XIX. *A SLOVEN.*

" Slovenlineſs is *ſuch a neglect of a man's perſon, as*
" *makes him offenſive to other people.* The ſloven comes
" into company with a dirty pair of hands, and a ſet of
" long nails at the end of them, and tells you for an exc-
" cuſe, that his father and grandfather uſed to do ſo be-
" fore him. However, that he may out-go his fore-fa-
" thers, his fingers are covered with warts of his own
" raiſing. He is as hairy as a goat, and takes care to let
" you ſee it. His teeth and breath are perfectly well
" ſuited to one another. He lays about him at table
" after a very extraordinary manner, and takes in a meal
" at a mouthful; which he ſeldom diſpoſes of without
" offending the company. In drinking he generally
" makes more haſte than good ſpeed. When he goes
" into the bath, you may eaſily find him out by the
" ſcent of his oyl, and diſtinguiſh him when he is dreſ-
" ſed by the ſpots in his coat. He does not ſtand upon
" decency in converſation, but will talk ſmut, though a
" prieſt and his mother be in the room. He commits a
" blunder in the moſt ſolemn offices of devotion; and
" afterwards falls a laughing at it. At a conſort of mu-
" ſick he breaks in upon the performance, hums over
" the tune to himſelf, or if he thinks it long, aſks the
" Muſicians *Whether they will never have done?* He al-
" ways

" ways fpits at random, and if he is at an entertainment,
" it is ten to one but it is upon the fervant who ftands
" behind him.

The foregoing tranflation brings to my remembrance
that excellent obfervation of my Lord *Rofcommon*'s.

None yet have been with Admiration *read,*
But who (befides their Learning) *were* well-bred.
Lord Rofcommon's *Effay on tranflated verfe.*

If after this the Reader can endure the filthy reprefentation of the fame figure expofed in its worft light, he
may fee how it looks in the former *Englifh* verfion, which
was publifhed fome years fince, and is done from the
French of *Bruyere*.

Naftinefs or Slovenlinefs.

" Slovenlinefs is a lazy and beaftly negligence of a
" man's own perfon, whereby he becomes fo fordid, as
" to be offenfive to thofe about him. You will fee him
" come into company when he is covered all over with
" a leprofy and fcurf, and with very long nails, and fays,
" thofe diftempers were hereditary, that his father and
" grandfather had them before him. He has ulcers in
" his thighs, and boils upon his hands, which he takes
" no care to have cured, but lets them run on till they
" are gone beyond remedy. His arm-pits are all hairy
" and moft part of his body like a wild beaft. His teeth
" are black and rotten, which makes his breath ftink fo
" that you cannot endure him to come nigh you ; he
" will alfo fnuff up his nofe and fpit it out as he eats, and
" ufes to fpeak with his mouth crammed full, and lets
" his victuals come out at both corners. He belches in
" the cup as he is drinking, and ufes nafty ftinking oyl
" in the bath. He will intrude into the beft company in
" fordid ragged cloths. If he goes with his mother to
" the foothfayers, he cannot then refrain from wicked
" and prophane expreffions. When he is making his ob-
" lations

" lations at the temple, he will let the diſh drop out of
" his hand, and fall a laughing, as if he had done ſome
" brave exploit. At the fineſt conſort of muſick he can-
" not forbear clapping his hands, and making a rude
" noiſe ; will pretend to ſing along with them, and fall
" a railing at them to leave off. Sitting at table, he ſpits
" full upon the ſervants who waited there.

I cannot cloſe this paper without obſerving, That if
Gentlemen of leiſure and genius would take the ſame
pains upon ſome other *Greek* or *Roman* Author, that has
been beſtowed upon this, we ſhould no longer be abuſed
by our Bookſellers, who ſet their hackney-writers at
work for ſo much a ſheet. The world would ſoon be convinced, that there is a great deal of difference between
putting an Author into *Engliſh*, and *Tranſlating* him.

DIALOGUES

DIALOGUES

UPON THE

USEFULNESS

OF

ANTIENT MEDALS.

Especially in relation to the

LATIN *and* GREEK *Poets.*

—————quoniam *hæc Ratio plerumque videtur*
Triſtor eſſe, quibus non eſt tractata, retroque
Volgus abhorret ad hac: volui tibi ſuaviloquenti
Carmine Pierio rationem exponere noſtram,
Et quaſi muſæo dulci contingere melle,
Si tibi forte animum tali ratione tenerem. Lucretius.

Printed in the Year, 1735.

VERSES

OCCASIONED BY

Mr. ADDISON's *Treatise*

OF

MEDALS.

SEE *the wild waste of all devouring years !*
    How Rome *her own sad sepulchre appears :*
With nodding arches, broken temples spread !
The very tombs now vanish'd like their dead !
Some felt the silent stroke of mould'ring age ;
Some, hostile fury ; some, religious rage.
Barbarian blindness, Christian *zeal conspire ;*
And Papal piety, and Gothick *fire.*
Perhaps by its own ruins sav'd from flame,
Some bury'd marble half preserves a Name ;
That Name, the learn'd with fierce disputes pursue,
And give to Titus *old* Vespasian's *due.*

F 2   Ambition

Ambition *figh'd.   She found it vain to truſt*
The faithleſs Column; and the crumbling Buſt ;
Huge Moles whoſe ſhadow ſtretch'd from ſhore to ſhore,
Their ruines periſh'd, and their place no more !
Convinc'd, ſhe now contraƈts her vaſt deſign ;
And all her triumphs ſhrink into a Coin.
A narrow orb each crowded conqueſt keeps ;
Beneath her Palm here ſad Judæa *weeps ;*
Now ſcantier limits the proud Arch confine,
And ſcarce are ſeen the proſtrate Nile *and* Rhine *:*
A ſmall Euphrates *thro' the piece is roll'd ;*
And little Eagles wave their wings in Gold.

The Medal, faithful to its charge of fame,
Thro' climes and ages bears each form and name :
In one ſhort view, ſubjeƈted to our eye,
Gods, Emp'rors, *Heroes,* Sages, *Beauties lye.*
With ſharpen'd ſight pale Antiquaries pore,
Th' Inſcription value, but the Ruſt adore :
This, the Blue varniſh, that, the Green endears,
The ſacred Ruſt of twice-ten hundred years.
To gain Peſcennius *one employs his ſchemes :*
One graſps a Cecrops *in ecſtatic dreams :*
Poor Vadius, *long with learned ſpleen devour'd,*
Can taſte no pleaſure ſince his Shield was ſcour'd ;
And Curio, *reſtleſs by the fair one's ſide,*
Sighs for an Otho, *and negleƈts his Bride.*

Theirs is the Vanity, the Learning thine.
Touch'd by thy hand, again Rome's *glories ſhine :*
Her Gods, and godlike Heroes riſe to view,
And all her faded garlands bloom anew.
Nor bluſh, theſe ſtudies thy regard engage ;
Theſe pleas'd the Fathers of poetic rage ;

The Verse and Sculpture bore an equal part,
And Art reflected images to Art.

Oh when shall Britain, conscious of her claim,
Stand emulous of Greek and Roman fame?
In living Medals see her wars enroll'd,
And vanquish'd realms supply recording Gold?
Here, rising bold, the Patriot's honest face;
There Warriors frowning in historic brass.
Then future ages with delight shall see,
How Plato's, Bacon's, Newton's looks agree:
Or in fair series laurel'd Bards be shown,
A Virgil there, and here an Addison.
Then shall Thy Craggs (and let me call him Mine)
On the cast Ore, another Pollio, shine;
With aspect open shall erect his head,
And round the Orb in lasting notes be read.
" Statesman, yet friend to Truth! in soul sincere,
" In action faithful, and in honour clear;
" Who broke no promise, serv'd no private end,
" Who gain'd no title, and who lost no friend;
" Ennobled by Himself, by all approv'd,
" And prais'd, unenvy'd by the Muse he lov'd.

A. POPE.

DIA-

DIALOGUES

Upon the Usefulness of ANCIENT
MEDALS.

DIALOGUE I.

Y NTH IO, Eugenius and *Philander* had retired together from the town to a country village, that lies upon the *Thames.* Their defign was to pafs away the heats of the Summer among the frefh breezes, that rife from the river, and the agreeable mixture of fhades and fountains, in which the whole country naturally abounds. They were all three very well verfed in the politer parts of learning, and had travelled into the moft refined nations of *Europe:* fo that they were capable of entertaining themfelves on a thoufand different fubjects without running into the common topics of defaming publick parties, or particular perfons. As they were intimate friends they took the freedom to diffent from one another in difcourfe, or upon occafion to fpeak

F 4.

a.

a *Latin* sentence without fearing the imputation of pedantry or ill breeding.

They were one evening taking a walk together in the fields when their discourse accidentally fell upon several unprofitable parts of learning. It was *Cynthio's* humour to run down every thing that was rather for ostentation than use. He was still preferring good sense to arts and sciences, and often took a pleasure to appear ignorant, that he might the better turn to ridicule those that valued themselves on their books and studies, though at the same time one might very well see that he could not have attacked many parts of learning so successfully, had he not borrowed his assistances from them. After having rally'd a set or two of *Virtuoso's,* he fell upon the Medalists.

These gentlemen, says he, value themselves upon being critics in Rust, and will undertake to tell you the different ages of it, by its colour. They are possessed with a kind of learned avarice, and are for getting together hoards of such money only as was current among the *Greeks* and *Latins*. There are several of them that are better acquainted with the faces of the *Antonines*, than of the *Stuarts*, and would rather chuse to count out a sum in Sesterces, than in pounds sterling. I have heard of one in *Italy* that used to swear *by the head of Otho*. Nothing can be pleasanter than to see a circle of these *Virtuoso's* about a cabinet of Medals, descanting upon the value, rarity and authenticalness of the several pieces that lie before them. One takes up a coin of gold, and after having well weighed the figures and inscription, tells you very gravely, if it were Brass, it would be invaluable. Another falls a ringing a *Pescennius Niger,* and judiciously distinguishes the sound of it to be modern. A third desires you to observe well the *Toga* on such a reverse, and asks you whether you can in conscience believe the sleeve of it to be of the true *Roman* cut.

I must confess, says *Philander*, the knowledge of Medals has most of those disadvantages that can render

der

der a fcience ridiculóus, to fuch as are not well verfed in it. Nothing is more eafy than to reprefent as
impertinencies any parts of learning that have no immediate relation to the happinefs or convenience of
mankind. When a man fpends his whole life among
the Stars and Planets, or lays out a twelve-month on
the fpots in the Sun, however noble his fpeculations
may be, they are very apt to fall into burlefque. But
it is ftill more natural to laugh at fuch ftudies as are
employed on low and vulgar objects. What curious
obfervations have been made on Spiders, Lobfters and
Cockle-fhells? yet the very naming of them is almoft
fufficient to turn them into raillery. It is no wonder
therefore that the fcience of Medals, which is charged
with fo many unconcerning parts of knowledge, and
built on fuch mean materials, fhould appear ridiculous to
thofe that have not taken the pains to examine it.

Eugenius was very attentive to what *Philander* faid
on the fubject of Medals. He was one that endeavoured rather to be agreeable than fhining in converfation, for which reafon he was more beloved, though
not fo much admired as *Cynthio.* I muft confefs, fays
he, I find my felf very much inclined to fpeak againft
a fort of ftudy that I know nothing of. I have, however one ftrong Prejudice in favour of it, that *Philander* has thought it worth his while to employ fome
time upon it. I am glad then, fays *Cynthio,* that I
have thrown him on a fcience of which I have long
wifhed to hear the Ufefulnefs. There, fays *Philander,*
you muft excufe me. At prefent you do not know
but it may have its ufefulnefs. But fhould I endeavour to convince you of it, I might fail in my attempt,
and fo render my fcience ftill more contemptible. On
the contrary, fays *Cynthio,* we are already fo perfuaded of the unprofitablenefs of your fcience, that you
can but leave us where you find us, but if you fucceed,
you increafe the number of your party. Well, fays
Philander, in hopes of making two fuch confiderable
profelytes, I am very well content to talk away an e-

F 5 vening

vening .with you on , the fubject; but on this condition, that you will communicate your thoughts to me freely when you diffent from me or have any difficulties that you think me capable of removing. To make ufe of the liberty you give us, fays *Eugenius*, I muft tell you what I believe furprizes all beginners as well as my felf. We are apt to think your Medalifts a little fantaftical in the different prices they fet upon their coins, without any regard to the ancient value or the metal of which they are compofed. A filver Medal, for example, fhall be more efteemed than a golden one, and a piece of brafs than either. To anfwer you, fays *Philander*, in the language of a Medallift, you are not to look upon a cabinet of Medals as a treafure of money, but of knowledge, nor muft you fancy any charms in gold, but in the figures and infcriptions that adorn it. The intrinfic value of an old coin does not confift in its metal but its erudition. It is the Device that has raifed the fpecies, fo that at prefent an *As* or an *Obolus* may carry a higher price than a *Denarius* or a *Drachma*; and a piece of money that was not worth a penny fifteen hundred years ago, may be now rated at fifty crowns, or perhaps a hundred guineas. I find, fays *Cynthio*, that to have a relifh for ancient coins it is neceffary to have a contempt of the modern. But I am afraid you will never be able with all your Medallic eloquence, to perfuade *Eugenius* and my felf that it is better to have a pocket full of *Otho*'s and *Gordians* than of *Jacobus*'s or *Louis d'ors*. This however we fhall be judges of, when you have let us know the feveral ufes of old coins.

The firft and moft obvious one, fays *Philander*, is the fhewing us the Faces of all the great perfons of antiquity. A cabinet of Medals is a collection of pictures in miniature: *Juvenal* calls them very humoroufly, *Concifum argentum in titulos, faciefque minutas*. Sat. 5. You here fee the *Alexanders, Cæfars, Pompeys, Trajans*, and the whole catalogue of Heroes; who have many of them fo diftinguifhed themfelves from the reft of

mankind

mankind that we almoſt look upon them as another ſpecies. It is an agreeable amuſement to compare in our own thoughts the face of a great Man with the character that authors have given us of him, and to try if we can find out in his looks and features either the haughty, cruel, or merciful temper that diſcovers it ſelf in the hiſtory of his actions. We find too on Medals the repreſentations of Ladies that have given occaſion to whole volumes on the account only of a face. We have here the pleaſure to examine their looks and dreſſes, and to ſurvey at leiſure thoſe beauties that have ſometimes been the happineſs or miſery of whole kingdoms. Nor do you only meet the faces of ſuch as are famous in hiſtory, but of ſeveral whoſe Names are not to be found any where except on Medals. Some of the Emperors, for example, have had Wives, and ſome of them Children, that no authors have mentioned. We are therefore obliged to the ſtudy of coins for having made new diſcoveries to the learned, and given them information of ſuch perſons as are to be met with on no other kind of records; You muſt give me leave, ſays *Cynthio*, to reject this laſt uſe of Medals. I do not think it worth while to trouble my ſelf with a perſon's name or face that receives all his reputation from the mint, and would never have been known in the world had there not been ſuch things as Medals. A man's memory finds ſufficient employment on ſuch as have really ſignalized themſelves by their great actions, without charging it ſelf with the names of an inſignificant people whoſe whole hiſtory is written on the edges of an old coin.

If you are only for ſuch perſons as have made a noiſe in the world, ſays *Philander*, you have on Medals a long liſt of heathen Deities, diſtinguiſhed from each other by their proper titles and ornaments. You ſee the copies of ſeveral ſtatues that have had the politeſt nations of the world fall down before them. You have here too ſeveral perſons of a more thin and ſhadowy nature, as Hope, Conſtancy, Fidelity, Abundance, Honour, Virtue, Eternity, Juſtice, Moderation, Happineſs pines, and in short a whole creation of the like imaginary substances. To these you may add the Genius of nations, provinces, cities, high-ways, and the like Allegorical Beings. In devices of this nature one sees a pretty poetical invention, and may often find as much thought on the reverse of a Medal as in a Canto of *Spenser.* Not to interrupt you, says *Eugenius,* I fancy it is this use of Medals that has recommended them to several history-painters, who perhaps without this assistance would have found it very difficult to have invented such an airy species of beings, when they are obliged to put a moral virtue into colours, or to find out a proper dress for a passion. It is doubtless for this reason, says *Philander,* that Painters have not a little contributed to bring the study of Medals in vogue. For not to mention several others, *Caraccio* is said to have assisted *Aretine* by designs that he took from the *Spintræ* of *Tiberius.* *Raphel* had thoroughly studied the figures on old Coins. *Patin* tells us that *Le Brun* had done the same. And it is well known that *Rubens* had a noble collection of Medals in his own possession. But I must not quit this head before I tell you, that you see on Medals not only the names and persons of Emperors, Kings, Consuls, Pro-consuls, Prætors, and the like characters of importance, but of some of the Poets, and of several who had won the prizes at the olympick games. It was a noble time, says *Cynthio,* when Trips and *Cornish* hugs could make a man immortal. How many Heroes would *Moor-fields* have furnished out in the days of old ? A fellow that can now only win a hat or a belt, had he lived among the *Greeks,* might have had his face stampt upon their Coins. But these were the wise Ancients, who had more esteem for a *Milo* than a *Homer,* and heapt up greater Honours on *Pindar's* Jockies, than on the Poet himself. But by this time I suppose you have drawn up all your medallic people, and indeed they make a much more formidable body than I could have imagined. You have shewn us all conditions,

tions, sexes and ages, emperors and empresses, men and children, gods and wrestlers. Nay you have conjured up persons that exist no where else but on old Coins, and have made our Passions and Virtues and Vices visible. I could never have thought that a cabinet of Medals had been so well peopled. But in the next place, says *Philander*, as we see on coins the different faces of persons, we see on them too their different Habits and Dresses, according to the mode that prevailed in the several ages when the Medals were stampt. This is another use, says *Cynthio*, that in my opinion contributes rather to make a man learned than wise, and is neither capable of pleasing the understanding or imagination. I know there are several supercilious Critics that will treat an author with the greatest contempt imaginable, if he fancies the old *Romans* wore a girdle, and are amazed at a man's ignorance, who believes the *Toga* had any Sleeves to it 'till the declension of the *Roman* Empire. Now I would fain know the great importance of this kind of learning, and why it should not be as noble a task to write upon a Bib and hanging-sleeves, as on the *Bulla* and *Prætexta*. The reason is, that we are familiar with the names of the one, and meet with the other no where but in learned authors. An Antiquary will scorn to mention a pinner or a night-rail, a petticoat or a manteau; but will talk as gravely as a father of the church on the *Vitta* and *Peplus*, the *Stola* and *Instita*. How would an old *Roman* laugh, were it possible for him to see the solemn dissertations that have been made on these weighty subjects. To set them in their natural light, let us fancy, if you please, that about a thousand years hence, some profound author shall write a learned treatise on the Habits of the present age, distinguished into the following Titles and Chapters.

Of the old British Trowser.

Of the Ruff and Collar band.

The opinion of several learned men concerning the use of the Shoulder-knot.

Such a one mistaken in his account of the Surtout, &c.

I

I must confess, says *Eugenius* interrupting him, the knowledge of these affairs is in itself very little improving, but as it is impossible without it to understand several parts of your ancient authors, it certainly hath its use. It is pity indeed there is not a nearer way of coming at it. I have sometimes fancied it would not be an impertinent design to make a kind of an old *Roman* wardrobe, where you should see *Toga*'s and *Tunica*'s, the *Chlamys* and *Trabea*, and in short all the different vests and ornaments that are so often mentioned in the *Greek* and *Roman* authors. By this means a man would comprehend better and remember much longer the shape of an ancient garment, than he possibly can from the help of tedious quotations and descriptions. The design, says *Philander*, might be very useful, but after what models would you work? *Sigonius*, for example, will tell you that the *Vestis Trabeata* was of such a particular fashion, *Scaliger* is for another, and *Dacier* thinks them both in the wrong. These are, says *Cynthio*, I suppose the names of three *Roman* taylors: for is it possible men of learning can have any disputes of this nature? May not we as well believe that hereafter the whole learned world will be divided upon the make of a modern pair of breeches? And yet, says *Eugenius*, the Critics have fallen as foul upon each other for matters of the same moment. But as to this point, where the make of the garment is controverted, let them, if they can find cloth enough, work after all the most probable fashions. To enlarge the design, I would have another room for the old *Roman* instruments of war, where you might see the *Pilum* and the shield, the eagles, ensigns, helmets, battering-rams and trophies, in a word, all the ancient military furniture in the same manner as it might have been in an Arsenal of old *Rome*. A third apartment should be a kind of Sacristie for altars, idols, sacrificing instruments, and other religious utensils. Not to be tedious, one might make a magazine for all sorts of antiquities, that would show a man in an afternoon more than he could learn out of books in a twelvemonth.

month. This would cut fhort the whole ftudy of antiquities, and perhaps be much more ufeful to Uni-
verfities than thofe .collections of Whale-bone and Cro-
codile-fkins in which they commonly abound. You
will find it very difficult, fays *Cynthio*, to perfuade
thofe focieties of learned men to fall in with your project. They will tell you that things of this importance muft not be taken on truft; you ought to learn
them among the Claffic Authors and at the fountain-
head. Pray confider what a figure a man would make
in the republick of letters, fhould he appeal to your
Univerfity-wardrobe, when they expect a fentence out
of the *Re Veftiaria?* or how do you think a man that
has read *Vegetius* will relifh your *Roman* Arfenal? In
the mean time, fays *Philander*, you find on Medals e-
very thing that you could meet with in your magazine
of antiquities, and when you have built your arfenals,
wardrobes, and facrifties, it is from Medals that you
muft fetch their furniture. It is here too that you fee
the figures of feveral inftruments of mufick, mathema-
tics and mechanics. One might make an entire gal-
ley out of the plans that are to be met with on the reverfes of feveral old Coins. Nor are they only charged with Things but with many ancient cuftoms as
facrifices, triumphs, congiaries, allocutions, decurfions,
lectifterniums, and a thoufand other antiquated names
and ceremonies that we fhould not have had fo juft a
notion of, were they not ftill preferved on Coins. I
might add under this head of antiquities that we find
on Medals the manner of fpelling in the old *Roman* infcriptions. That is, fays *Cynthio*, we find that *Felix*
is never written with an *æ* dipthongue, and that in *Auguftus*'s days *Civis* ftood for *Cives*, with other fecrets in
Orthography of the fame importance.

To come then to a more weighty ufe, fays *Philander*, it is certain that Medals give a very great light to
hiftory, in confirming fuch paffages as are true in old
Authors, in fettling fuch as are told after different
manners, and in recording fuch as have been omitted.
In this cafe a cabinet of Medals is a body of hiftory.

It

It was indeed the beft way in the world to perpetuate the memory of great actions, thus to coin out the life of an Emperor, and to put every great exploit into the mint. It was a kind of *Printing*, before the *Art* was invented. It is by this means that Monfieur *Vaillant* has difembroiled a hiftory that was loft to the world before his time, and out of a fhort collection of Medals has given us a chronicle of the Kings of *Syria*. For this too is an advantage Medals have over books, that they tell their ftory much quicker, and fum up a whole volume in twenty or thirty reverfes. They are indeed the beft epitomes in the world, and let you fee with one caft of an eye the fubftance of above a hundred pages. Another ufe of Medals is, that they not only fhew you the actions of an Emperor, but at the fame time mark out the year in which they were performed. Every exploit has its date fet to it. A feries of an Emperor's Coins is his life digefted into annals. Hiftorians feldom break their relation with a mixture of chronology, nor diftribute the particulars of an Emperor's ftory in the feveral years of his reign: or where they do it they often differ in their feveral periods. Here therefore it is much fafer to quote a Medal than an Author, for in this cafe you do not appeal to a *Suetonius* or a *Lampridius*, but to the Emperor himfelf, or to the whole body of a *Roman* Senate. Befides that a Coin is in no danger of having its characters altered by copiers and tranfcribers. This I muft confefs, fays *Cynthio*, may in fome cafes be of great moment, but confidering the fubjects on which your chronologers are generally employed, I fee but little ufe that rifes from it. For example, what fignifies it to the world whether fuch an Elephant appeared in the Amphi-theatre in the fecond or the third year of *Domitian?* Or what am I the wifer for knowing that *Trajan* was in the fifth year of his Tribunefhip when he entertained the people with fuch a Horfe-race, or Bull-beating? Yet it is the fixing of thefe great periods that gives a man the firft rank in the republic of letters,

and

and recommends him to the world for a perfon of various reading and profound erudition.

You muft always give your men of great reading
leave to fhow their talents on the meaneft fubjects,
fays *Eugenius*; it is a kind of fhooting at rovers:
where a man lets fly his arrow without taking any
aim, to fhew his ftrength. But there is one advantage, fays he, turning to *Philander*, that feems to me
very confiderable, although you Medallifts feldom
throw it into the account, which is the great help to
memory one finds in Medals: for my own part I am
very much embarraffed in the names and ranks of
the feveral *Roman* Emperors, and find it difficult to
recollect upon occafion the different parts of their
hiftory: but your Medallifts upon the firft naming of
an Emperor will immediately tell you his age, family and life. To remember where he enters in the
fucceffion, they only confider in what part of the cabinet he lies; and by running over in their thoughts
fuch a particular drawer, will give you an account of
all the remarkable parts of his reign.

I thank you, fays *Philander*, for helping me to an
ufe that perhaps I fhould not have thought on. But
there is another of which I am fure you could not
but be fenfible when you were at *Rome*. I muft own to
you it furprized me to fee my *Ciceroni* fo well acquainted with the bufts and ftatues of all the great people
of antiquity. There was not an Emperor or Emprefs
but he knew by fight, and as he was feldom without
Medals in his pocket, he would often fhew us the
fame face on an old Coin that we faw in the Statue.
He would difcover a *Commodus* through the difguife
of the club and lion's fkin, and find out fuch a one to
be *Livia* that was dreffed up like a *Ceres*. Let a buft
be never fo disfigured, they have a thoufand marks by
which to decipher it. They will know a *Zenobia* by
the fitting of her Diadem, and will diftinguifh the
Fauftina's by their different way of tying up their hair.
Oh! Sir, fays *Cynthio*, they will go a great deal farther, they will give you the name and titles of a Sta-
tue

tue that has lost his nose and ears; or if there is but half
a beard remaining, will tell you at first sight who was
the owner of it. Now I must confess to you, I used
to fancy they imposed upon me an Emperor or Emprefs at pleasure, rather than appear ignorant.

All this however is easily learnt from Medals, says
Philander, where you may see likewise the plans of
many the most confiderable buildings of Old *Rome.*
There is an ingenious Gentleman of our own nation
extremely well versed in this study, who has a design
of publishing the whole history of Architecture, with
its several improvements and decays as it is to be met
with on ancient Coins. He has assured me that he has
observed all the nicety of proportion in the figures of
the different orders that compose the buildings on the
best preserved Medals. You here see the copies of
such Ports and triumphal Arches as there are not the
least traces of in the places where they once stood.
You have here the models of several ancient Temples,
though the Temples themselves, and the Gods that
were worshipped in them, are perished many hundred
years ago. Or if there are still any foundations or
ruines of former edifices, you may learn from Coins
what was their Architecture when they stood whole and
entire. These are buildings which the *Goths* and *Vandals*
could not demolish, that are infinitely more durable
than stone or marble, and will perhaps last as long
as the earth it self. They are in short so many real
monuments of Brass.

> *Quod non imber edax non aquilo impotens*
> *Possit diruere, aut innumerabilis*
> *Annorum series, & fuga temporum.*

Which eating show'rs, nor northwind's feeble blast,
Nor whirle of time, nor flight of years can waste.

Mr. Creech.

This is a noble Panegyric on an old copper Coin,
says *Cynthio.* But I am afraid a little malicious rust
would demolish one of your brazen edifices as effectually as a *Goth* or *Vandal.* You would laugh at me,

says

fays *Philander*, fhould I make you a learned differtation on the nature of Rufts. I fhall only tell you
there are two or three forts of them which are extremely beautiful in the eye of an Antiquary, and
preferve a Coin better than the beft artificial varnifh.
As for other kinds, a fkilful Medallift knows very
well how to deal with them. He will recover you
a Temple or a triumphal Arch out of its rubbifh, if I may fo call it, and with a few repa-
rations of the gràving tool reftore it to its firft fplen-
dour and magnificence. I have known an Emperor
quite hid under a cruft of drofs, who after two or
three days cleanfing has appeared with all his Titles
about him as frefh and beautiful as at his firft coming
out of the Mint. I am forry, fays *Eugenius*, I did
not know this laft ufe of Medals when I was at *Rome*.
It might perhaps have given me a greater tafte of its
Antiquities, and have fixed in my memory feveral of
the ruines that I have now forgotten. For my part,
fays *Cynthio*, I think there are at *Rome* enow modern
works of Architecture to employ any reafonable man.
I never could have a tafte for old bricks and rubbifh,
nor would trouble my felf about the ruines of *Auguftus*'s Palace fo long as I could fee the *Vatican*, the
Borghefe, and the *Farnefe* as they now ftand ; I muft
own to you at the fame time this is talking like an ignorant man. Were I in other company I would perhaps change my ftyle, and tell them that I would rather fee the fragments of *Apollo*'s Temple than St.
Peter's. I remember when our Antiquary at *Rome* had
led us a whole day together from one ruine to another, he at laft brought us to the *Rotunda* ; And this,
fays he, is the moft valuable Antiquity in *Italy*, notwithftanding it is fo entire.

The fame kind of fancy, fays *Philander*, has formerly gained upon feveral of your Medallifts, who
were for hoarding up fuch pieces of money only as
had been half confumed by time or ruft. There were
no Coins pleafed them more than thofe which had
paffed through the hands of an old *Roman* Clipper.
I have

I have read an Author of this taste that compares a
ragged Coin to a tattered Colours. But to come a-
gain to our subject. As we find on Medals the plans
of several buildings that are now demolished, we see
on them too the Models of many ancient Statues that
are now lost. There are several Reverses which
are owned to be the representations of antique figures,
and I question not but there are many others that
were formed on the like Models, though at present
they lie under no suspicion of it. The *Hercules Far-
nese*, the *Venus* of *Medicis*, the *Apollo* in the *Belvideria*,
and the famous *Marcus Aurelius* on horse-back, which
are perhaps the four most beautiful Statues extant,
make their appearance all of them on ancient Medals,
though the figures that represent them were never
thought to be the copies of statues till the statues themselves were discovered. There is no question, I think,
but the same reflexion may extend itself to antique
Pictures : for I doubt not but in the designs of several *Greek* Medals in particular, one might often see
the hand of an *Apelles* or *Protogenes*, were we as well
acquainted with their works as we are with *Titian*'s
or *Vandike*'s. I might here make a much greater show
of the usefulness of Medals, if I would take the method of others, and prove to you that all arts and
sciences receive a considerable illustration from this
study. I must however tell you, that Medals and the
Civil Law, as we are assured by those who are well
read in both, give a considerable light to each other,
and that several old Coins are like so many maps for
explaining of the antient Geography. But besides the
more solid parts of learning, there are several little
intimations to be met with on Medals that are very
pleasant to such as are conversant in this kind of study.
Should I tell you gravely, that without the help of
Coins we should never have known which was the
first of the Emperors that wore a beard, or rode in
stirrups, I might turn my science into ridicule. Yet
it is certain there are a thousand little impertinencies of this nature that are very gratifying to curiosi-
ty.

ty, tho' perhaps not very improving to the underſtanding. To ſee the dreſs that ſuch an Empreſs delighted to be drawn in, the titles that were moſt agreeable to ſuch an Emperor, the flatteries that he lay moſt open to, the honours that he paid to his children, wives, predeceſſors, friends, or collegues, with the like particularities only to be met with on Medals, are certainly not a little pleaſing to that inquiſitive temper which is ſo natural to the mind of man.

I declare to you, ſays *Cynthio,* you have aſtoniſhed me with the ſeveral parts of knowledge, that you have diſcovered on Medals. I could never fancy before this evening, that a Coin could have any nobler uſe in it than to pay a reckoning.

You have not heard all yet, ſays *Philander*, there is ſtill an advantage to be drawn from Medals, which I am ſure will heighten your eſteem for them. It is indeed an uſe that no body has hitherto dwelt upon. If any of the Antiquaries have touched upon it, they have immediately quitted it, without conſidering it in its full latitude, light and extent. Not to keep you in ſuſpence, I think there is a great affinity between Coins and Poetry, and that your Medalliſt and Critic are much nearer related than the world generally imagines. A reverſe often clears up the paſſage of an old poet, as the poet often ſerves to unriddle a reverſe. I could be longer on this head, but I fear I have already tired you. Nay, ſays *Eugenius*, ſince you have gone ſo far with us, we muſt beg you to finiſh your lecture, eſpecially ſince you are on a ſubject, that I dare promiſe you will be very agreeable to *Cynthio,* who is ſo profeſſed an admirer of the ancient poets. I muſt only warn you, that you do not charge your Coins with more uſes than they can bear. It is generally the method of ſuch as are in love with any particular ſcience to diſcover all others in it. Who would imagine, for example, that architecture ſhould comprehend the knowledge of hiſtory, ethics, muſic, aſtronomy, natural philoſophy, phyſic and the civil law ? Yet *Vitruvius* will give you his reaſons, ſuch as they

are,

are, why a good architect is master of these several
arts and sciences. Sure, says *Cynthio, Martial* had
never read *Vitruvius* when he threw the Cryer and
the Architect into the same class.

> *Duri si puer ingeni videtur*
> *Præconem facias vel architectum.*
> If of dull parts the stripling you suspect,
> A herald make him, or an architect.

But to give you an instance out of a very celebrated
discourse on poetry, because we are on that subject,
of an author's finding out imaginary beauties in his
own art. *I have observed,* says he,
Vossius de viri- (speaking of the natural propension
bus Rythmi. that all men have to numbers and harmony) *that my barber has often combed
my head in Dactyls and Spondees, that is, with two
short strokes and a long one, or with two long ones suc-
cessively. Nay,* says he, *I have known him sometimes
run even into Pyrrhichius's and Anapæstus's.* This you
will think perhaps a very extravagant fancy, but I
must own I should as soon expect to find the *Prosodia*
in a Comb as Poetry in a Medal. Before I endeavour to convince you of it, says *Philander,* I must
confess to you that this science has its visionaries as
well as all others. There are several, for example,
that will find a mystery in every tooth of *Neptune's*
trident, and are amazed at the wisdom of the ancients that represented a thunder-bolt with three forks,
since, they will tell you, nothing could have better
explained its triple quality of piercing, burning and
melting. I have seen a long discourse on the figure
and nature of horn, to shew it was impossible to have
found out a fitter emblem for plenty than the *Cornu-
Copiæ.* These are a sort of authors who scorn to take
up with appearances, and fancy an interpretation vulgar when it is natural. What could have been more
proper to shew the beauty and friendship of the Three
Graces, than to represent them naked and knit together in a kind of dance? It is thus they always appear in ancient sculpture, whether on Medals or in

Marble,

Marble, as I doubt not but *Horace* alludes to defigns
of this nature, when he defcribes them after the fame
manner.

——————*Gratia*
Junctis nuda fororibus :
——————*Segnefque nodum folvere Gratiæ.*

The Sifter-*Graces* hand in hand
Conjoin'd by love's eternal band.

Several of your Medallifts will be here again aftonifhed at the wifdom of the ancients, that knew how to
couch fuch excellent precepts of morality under vifible objects. The nature of Gratitude, they will tell
you, is better illuftrated by this fingle device, than by
Seneca's whole book *de Beneficiis*. The three Graces
teach us three things. I. To remark the doing of a
courtefie. II. The return of it from the receiver.
III. The obligation of the receiver to acknowledge it.
The three Graces are always hand in hand to fhow
us that thefe three duties fhould be never feparated.
They are naked, to admonifh us that Gratitude fhould
be returned with a free and open heart ; and dancing,
to fhew us that no vertue is more active than Gratitude. May not we here fay with *Lucretius ?*

Quæ bene & eximie quanquam difpofta ferantur,
Sunt longè tamen à verâ ratione repulfa.

It is an eafy thing, fays *Eugenius*, to find out defigns
that never entered into the thoughts of the fculptor
or the coiner. I dare fay, the fame Gentlemen who
have fixed this piece of morality on the three naked
Sifters dancing hand in hand, would have found out
as good a one for them, had there been four of them
fitting at a diftance from each other, and covered
from head to foot. It is here therefore, fays *Philander*, that the old poets ftep in to the affiftance of
the Medallift, when they give us the fame thought in
words as the mafters of the *Roman* mint have done in
figures. A man may fee a metaphor or an allegory
in picture, as well as read them in a defcription.
When therefore I confront a Medal with a Verfe, I
only fhew you the fame defign executed by different
hands,

hands, and appeal from one mafter to another of the fame age and tafte. -- This is certainly a much furer way than to build on the interpretations of an author who does not confider how the ancients ufed to think, but will be ftill inventing myfteries and applications out of his own fancy. To make my felf more intelligible, I find a fhield on the reverfe of an Emperor's Coin, defigned as a complement to him from the fenate of *Rome*. I meet with the fame metaphor in ancient poets to exprefs protection or defence. I conclude therefore that this Medal compliments the Emperor in the fame fenfe as the old *Romans* did their Dictator *Fabius*, when they called him the Buckler of *Rome*. Put this reverfe now if you pleafe into the hands of a myftical antiquary; He fhall tell you that the ufe of the fhield being to defend the body from the weapons of an enemy, it very aptly fhadows out to us the refolution or continence of the Emperor, which made him proof to all the attacks of fortune or of pleafure. In the next place, the figure of the fhield being round, it is an emblem of perfection, for *Ariftotle* has faid the round figure is the moft perfect. It may likewife fignify the immortal reputation that the Emperor has acquired by his great actions, rotundity being an emblem of eternity that has neither beginning nor end. After this I dare not anfwer for the fhield's convexity that it does not cover a myftery, nay there fhall not be the leaft wrinkle or flourifh upon it which will not turn to fome account. In this cafe therefore * Poetry being in fome refpects an Art of defigning as well as Painting or Sculpture; they may ferve as Comments on each other. I am very well fatisfied, fays *Eugenius*, by what you have faid on this fubject, that the Poets may contribute to the explication of fuch reverfes as are purely emblematical, or when the perfons are of that fhadowy allegorical nature you have before mentioned, but I fuppofe there are many other reverfes that reprefent things and perfons of a

more

---

* *Poema eft pictura loquax.*

more real existence. In this case too, says *Philander*, a Poet lets you into the knowledge of a device better than a Profe-Writer, as his descriptions are often more diffuse, his story more naturally circumstanced, and his language enriched with a greater variety of epithets: So that you often meet with little hints and suggestions in a Poet that give a great illustration to the customs, actions, ornaments, and all kinds of Antiquities that are to be met with on ancient Coins. I fancy, says *Cynthio*, there is nothing more ridiculous than an Antiquary's reading the *Greek* or *Latin* Poets. He never thinks of the beauty of the thought or language, but is for searching into what he calls the Erudition of the Author. He will turn you over all *Virgil* to find out the figure of an old *Rostrum*, and has the greatest esteem imaginable for *Homer*, because he has given us the fashion of a *Greek* scepter. It is indeed odd enough to consider how all kinds of Readers find their account in the old Poets. Not only your Men of the more refined or solid parts of Learning, but even your Alchymist and Fortune-teller will discover the secrets of their art in *Homer* and *Virgil*. This, says *Eugenius*, is a prejudice of a very ancient standing. Read but *Plutarch*'s discourse on *Homer*, and you will see that the Iliad contains the whole circle of arts, and that *Thales* and *Pythagoras* stole all their philosophy out of this Poet's works. One would be amazed to see what pains he takes to prove that *Homer* understood all the figures in Rhétoric, before they were invented. I do not question, says *Philander*, were it possible for *Homer* to read his praises in this Author, but he would be as much surprized as ever Monsieur *Jordain* was when he had found he had talked Profe all his life-time without ever knowing what it was. But to finish the task you have set me, we may observe that not only the Virtues, and the like imaginary persons, but all the heathen Divinities appear generally in the same dress among the Poets that they were in Medals. I must confess, I believe both the one and the other took the Mode from the

ancient

ancient *Greek* Statuaries. It will not perhaps be an improper transition to pass from the heathen gods to the several monsters of antiquity, as *Chimæra's, Gorgon's, Sphinxes,* and many other that make the same figure in verse as on coins. It often happens too, that the Poet and the Senate of *Rome* have both chosen the same Topic to flatter their Emperor upon, and have sometimes fallen upon the same thought. It is certain, they both of them lay upon the catch for a great action: It is no wonder therefore, that they were often engaged on one subject, the Medal and the Poem being nothing else but occasional compliments to the Emperor. Nay, I question not but you may sometimes find certain passages among the Poets that relate to the particular device of a Medal.

I wonder, says *Eugenius,* that your Medallists have not been as diligent in searching the Poets as the Historians, since I find they are so capable of enlightning their art. I would have some body put the Muses under a kind of contribution to furnish out whatever they have in them that bears any relation to Coins. Though they taught us but the same things that might be learnt in other writings, they would at least teach us more agreeably, and draw several over to the study of Medals that would rather be instructed in verse than in prose. I am glad, says *Philander,* to hear you of this opinion, for to tell you truly, when I was at *Rome,* I took occasion to buy up many Imperial Medals that have any affinity with passages of the ancient Poets. So that I have by me a sort of poetical Cash, which I fancy I could count over to you in *Latin* and *Greek* verse. If you will drink a dish of Tea with me to-morrow morning, I will lay my whole collection before you. I cannot tell, says *Cynthio,* how the Poets will succeed in the explication of coins, to which they are generally very great strangers. We are however obliged to you for preventing us with the offer of a kindness that you might well imagine we should have asked you.

Our

Our three friends had been ſo intent to their diſcourſe, that they had rambled very far into the fields without taking notice of it. *Philander* firſt put them in mind, that unleſs they turned back quickly they would endanger being benighted. Their converſation ran inſenſibly into other ſubjects, but as I deſign only to report ſuch parts of it as have any relation to Medals, I ſhall leave them to return home as faſt as they pleaſe, without troubling my ſelf with their talk on the way thither, or with their ceremonies at parting.

DIALOGUE II.

SOME of the fineſt treatiſes of the moſt polite *Latin* and *Greek* writers are in Dialogue, as many very valued pieces of *French*, *Italian*, and *Engliſh* appear in the ſame dreſs. I have ſometimes however been very much diſtaſted at this way of writing, by reaſon of the long prefaces and exordiums into which it often betrays an Author. There is ſo much time taken up in ceremony, that before they enter on their ſubject the Dialogue is half ended. To avoid the fault I have found in others, I ſhall not trouble my ſelf nor my Reader with the firſt ſalutes of our three friends, nor with any part of their diſcourſe over the Tea table. We will ſuppoſe the *China* diſhes taken off, and a Drawer of Medals ſupplying their room. *Philander*, who is to be the Hero in my Dialogue, takes it in his hand, and addreſſing himſelf to *Cynthio* and *Eugenius*, I will firſt of all, ſays he, ſhow you an aſſembly of the moſt virtuous Ladies that you have ever perhaps convers'd with. I do not know, ſays *Cynthio*, regarding them, what their virtue may be, but methinks they are a little fantaſtical in their dreſs. You will find, ſays *Philander*,

there

there is good sense in it. They have not a single ornament that they cannot give a reason for. I was going to ask you, says *Eugenius*, in what country you find these Ladies. But I see they are some of those imaginary persons you told us of last night that inhabit old Coins, and appear no where else but on the reverse of a Medal. Their proper country, says *Philander*, is the breast of a good man: for I think they are most of them the figures of Virtues. It is a great compliment methinks to the -sex, says *Cynthio*, that your Virtues are generally shown in petticoats. I can give no other reason for it, says *Philander*, but because they chanced to be of the feminine gender in the *First Series.* learned languages. You find however something bold and masculine in the air and posture of the first figure, which is that of *Virtue* her self, and agrees very well with the description we find of her in *Silius Italicus*,

Fig. 1.

> *Virtutis dispar habitus, frons hirta, nec unquam*
> *Composita mutata coma, stans vultus, et ore*
> *Incessuque viro propior, lætique pudoris,*
> *Celsa humeris, niveæ fulgebat stamine pallæ.* Sil.It.l.15.

> A different form did *Virtue* wear,
> Rude from her forehead fell th' unplaited hair,
> With dauntless mien aloft she rear'd her head,
> And next to manly was the virgin's tread,
> Her height, her sprightly blush, the Goddess show,
> And robes unsully'd as the falling snow.

Virtue and *Honour* had their Temples bordering on each other, and are sometimes both on the same coin, as in the following one of *Galba*. *Silius Italicus* makes them companions in the glorious equipage that he gives his *Virtue*.

Fig. 2.

> *Mecum Honor, et Laudes, et læto Gloria vultu,*
> [Virtus loquitur.
> *Et Decus, et niveis Victoria concolor alis.* Ibid.

> With me the foremost place let *Honour* gain,
> [*Virtue speaks.*
> *Fame*, and the *Praises* mingling in her train;
> Gay *Glory* next, and *Victory* on high,
> White like my self, on snowy wings shall fly, *Tu*

Tu cujus placido posuere in pectore sedem
Blandus Honos, hilarisque (tamen cum pondere) Virtus.
Stat. Sil. l. 2.

The head of *Honour* is crowned with a Laurel, as *Martial* has adorned his *Glory* after the fame manner, which indeed is but another name for the fame perſon.

Mitte coronatas Gloria mœsta comas.

I find, ſays *Cynthio*, the *Latins* mean Courage by the figure of Virtue, as well as by the word it ſelf. Courage was eſteemed the greateſt perfeêtion among them, and therefore went under the name of Virtue in general, as the modern *Italians* give the fame name on the fame account to the Knowledge of Curioſities. Should a *Roman* Painter at preſent diaw the piêture of Virtue, inſtead of the Spear and Paratonium that ſhe bears on old coins, he would give her a Buſt in one hand and a Fiddle in the other.

Fig. 3. The next, ſays *Philander*, is a Lady of a more peaceful charaêter, and had her Temple at *Rome.*

———*Salutato crepitat Concordia nido.*

She is often placed on the reverſe of an Imperial coin to ſhow the good underſtanding between the Emperor and the Empreſs. She has always a *Cornu-copiæ* in her hand, to denote that Plenty is the fruit of Concord. After this ſhort account of the Goddeſs, I deſire you will give me your opinion of the Deity that is deſcribed in the following verſes of *Seneca,* who would have her propitious to the marriage of *Jaſon* and *Creuſa.* He mentions her by her qualities, and not by her name.

———————————————*Aſperi*
Martis ſanguineas quæ cohibet manus,
Quæ dat belligeris fœdera gentibus,
Et cornu retinet divite copiam.   Sen. Med. Aêt. 1.

Who ſooths great *Mars* the warrior God,
And checks his arm diſtain'd with blood,
Who joins in leagues the jarring lands,
The horn of plenty fills her hands.

The deſcription, ſays *Eugenius*, is a copy of the figure we have before us: and for the future, inſtead of any

G 3.   further

further note on this paſſagē, I would have the reverſe
you have ſhown us ſtamped on the ſide of it.   The
interpreters of *Seneca*, ſays *Philander*, will underſtand
the preceding verſes as a deſcription of *Venus*, though
in my opinion there is only the firſt of them that can
aptly relate to her, which at the ſame time agrees as
well with *Concord*: and that this was a Goddeſs who
uſed to intereſt her ſelf in marriages, we may ſee in
the following deſcription,

—————————————*Jamdudum poſte reclinis,*
Quærit Hymen thalamis intactum dicere carmen,
Quo vatem mulcere queat; dat Juno verenda
Vincula, et inſigni geminat Concordia tœdâ.

           Statii Epithalamion. Silv. li. 1.

Already leaning at the door too long
Sweet *Hymen* waits to raiſe the nuptial ſong,
Her ſacred bards majeſtick *Juno* lends,
And *Concord* with her flaming torch attends.

Fig. 4. *Peace* differs as little in her Dreſs as in her
Character from *Concord*. You may obſerve in both
theſe figures that the Veſt is gathered up before them,
like an Apron, which you muſt ſuppoſe filled with fruits
as well as the *Cornu-copiæ*. It is to this part of the
Dreſs that *Tibullus* aludes.

At nobis, Pax alma, veni, ſpicamque teneto,
   Perfluat et pomis candidus antè ſinus.

           Kind *Peace* appear,
And in thy right hand hold the wheaten ear,
From thy white lap th'o'erflowing fruits ſhall fall.
Prudentius has given us the ſame circumſtance in his de-
ſcription of Avarice.

—————*Avaritia gremio præcincta capaci.* Prud. Pſych.
How proper the emblems of Plenty are to Peace, may
be ſeen in the ſame Poet.

Interea Pax arva colat, Pax candida primùm
   Duxit araturos ſub juga curva boves;
Pax aluit vites, et ſuccos condidit uvæ,
   Funderet ut nato teſta paterna merum:
Pace bidens vomerque vigent.--- Tibul. El. 10. Lib. 1.

                             She

She firſt, White *Peace,* the earth with plough-ſhares
    broke,
And bent the oxen to the crooked yoke,
Firſt rear'd the vine, and hoarded firſt with care
The father's vintage for his drunken heir.

The Olive-branch in her hand is frequently touched upon in the old Poets as a token of Peace.

Pace orare manu———————— Virg. Æn. 10.
*Ingreditur, ramumque tenens popularis Olivæ.*Ov.M.l 7
In his right hand an Olive branch he holds.

————————————*furorem*
Indomitum duramque viri deflectere mentem
Pacifico ſermone parant, hoſtemque propinquum
Orant Cecropiæ prælatâ fronde Minervæ. Luc lib. 3.
————To move his haughty ſoul they try
Intreaties, and perſuaſion ſoft apply ;
Their brows *Minerva's* peaceful branches wear,
And thus in gentleſt terms they greet his ear.
                        Mr. *Rowe.*

Which by the way one would think had been ſpoken
rather of an *Attila,* or a *Maximin,* than *Julius Cæſar.*

Fig. 5. You ſee *Abundance* or *Plenty* makes the ſame
figure in Medals as in *Horace.*

————————————*tibi Copia*
Manabit ad plenum benigno
Ruris honorum opulenta cornu. Hor. Lib. 1. Od. 17.
————Here to thee ſhall Plenty flow
And all her riches ſhow,
To raiſe the honour of the quiet plain.   Mr. *Creech.*
The Compliment on this reverſe to *Gordianus Pius* is
expreſſed in the ſame manner as that of *Horace* to *Au-
guſtus.*

————————————*Aurea fruges*
Italiam pleno diffudit Copia cornu. Hor. Ep. 12: lib. 1.
————Golden *Plenty* with a bounteous hand
Rich harveſts freely ſcatters o'er our land. Mr. *Creech.*

Fig. 6. But to return again to our Virtues. You
have here the picture of *Fidelity,* who was worſhipped
as a Goddeſs among the *Romans.*

                       G. 4.   *Situ*

Si tu oblitus es at Dii meminerunt, meminit Fides.

Catul. ad Alphen.

I should fancy from the following verses of *Virgil* and *Silius Italicus*, that she was represented under the figure of an old woman.

Cana Fides, et Vesta, Remo cum fratre Quirinus
Jura dabunt——— . . . Virg. Æn. Lib. 1.

Then banish'd *Faith* shall once again return,
And vestal fires in hallow'd temples burn,
And *Remus* with *Quirinus* shall sustain
The righteous laws, and fraud and force restrain.

Mr. *Dryden.*

————————ad limina sanctæ
Tendebat Fidei, secretaque pectora tentat.
Arcanis dea læta, polo tum forte remoto.
Cælicolum magnas volvebat conscia curas.
Ante Jovem generata, decus divumque hominumque,
Quâ sine non tellus pacem, non æquora norunt,
Justitiæ consors——— Sil. It. Lib. 2.

He to the shrines of *Faith* his steps addrest;
She pleas'd with secrets rowling in her breast,
Far from the world remote, revolv'd on high
The cares of gods, and counsels of the sky.
E'er *Jove* was born she grac'd the bright-abodes,
Consort of *Justice*, boast of men and gods;
Without whose heavenly aid no peace below
The stedfast earth, and rowling ocean know.

Fig. 7. There is a medal of *Heliogabalus* inscrib'd FIDES EXERCITUS, that receives a great light from the preceding verses. She is posted between two military Ensigns, for the good quality that the Poet ascribes to her of preserving the public peace, by keeping the Army true to its Allegiance.

I fancy, says *Eugenius*, as you have discovered the Age of this imaginary Lady, from the description that the Poets have made of her, you may find too the colour of the Drapery that she wore in the old *Roman* paintings from that Verse in *Horace*,

Te Spes et albo rara Fides colit
Velata panno——— Hor. Od. 35. Lib. 1.

Sure

Sure *Hope* and *Friendſhip* cloath'd in White,
Attend on thee——— Mr. *Creech.*

One would think, ſays *Philander*, by this verſe, that *Hope* and *Fidelity* have both the ſame kind of Dreſs. It is certain *Hope* might have a fair pretence to White, in alluſion to thoſe that were Candidates for an employ.

———*quem ducit hiantem*
Cretata ambitio——— Perſ. Sat. 5.

And how properly the Epithet of *Rara* agrees with her, you may ſee in the tranſparency of the
next figure. She is here dreſſed in ſuch *Fig.* 8.
a kind of Veſt as the *Latins* call a *Mul-*
ticium from the fineneſs of its Tiſſue. Your *Roman* Beaus had their ſummer *toga* of ſuch a light airy make.

Quem tenues decuere togæ nitidique capilli.
Hor. Ep. 14. Lib. 1.

I that lov'd———
Curl'd powder'd locks, a fine and gawdy gown.
Mr. *Creech.*

I remember, ſays *Cynthio*, *Juvenal* rallys *Creticus*, that was otherwiſe a brave rough fellow, very handſomely, on this kind of garment.

———————————————*ſed quid*
Non facient alii cum tu multitia ſumas,
Cretice? et hanc veſtem populo mirante perores
In Proculas et Pollineas.—— Juv. Sat. 2.
Acer et indomitus Libertatiſque magiſter,
Cretice, pelluces——— ——— Ibid.

———Nor, vain *Metellus*, ſhall
From *Rome*'s Tribunal thy harangues prevail
'Gainſt harlotry, while thou art clad ſo thin,
That through thy Cobweb-robe we ſee thy ſkin,
As thou declaim'ſt——— Mr. *Tate.*
Canſt thou reſtore old manners or retrench
Rome's pride, who com'ſt tranſparent to the Bench ?
Idem.

But pray what is the meaning that this tranſparent Lady holds up her train in her left hand ? for I find your women on Medals do nothing without a mean-ing. Beſides, I ſuppoſe there is a moral precept at

leaſt

least couch'd under the figure she holds in her other hand. She draws back her garment, says *Philander*, that it may not incumber her in her march. For she is always drawn in a posture of walking, it being as natural for *Hope* to press forward to her proper objects, as for *Fear* to fly from them.

> *Ut canis in vacuo leporem cum Gallicus arvo*
> *Vidit, et hic prædam pedibus petit, ille salutem :*
> *Alter in-hæsuro similis, jam jamque tenere*
> *Sperat, et extento stringit vestigia rostro ;*
> *Alter in ambiguo est an sit comprensus, et ipsis*
> *Morsibus eripitur, tangentiaque ora relinquit :*
> *Sic deus et virgo est : hic spe celer, illa timore.*

De Apol. et Daph. Ov. Met. Lib. 1.

As when th' impatient Greyhound slipt from far,
Bounds o'er the glebe to catch the fearful Hare,
She in her speed does all her safety lay :
And he with double speed pursues the prey ;
O'er-runs her at the fitting turn, and licks
His chaps in vain, and blows upon the flix :
She 'scapes, and for the neighb'ring covert strives,
And gaining shelter doubts if yet she lives :—
Such was the god, and such the flying fair,
She, urg'd by Fear, her feet did swiftly move,
But he more swiftly, who was urg'd by Love.

Mr. *Dryden.*

This beautiful similitude is, I think, the prettiest emblem in the world of *Hope* and *Fear* in extremity. A flower or blossom that you see in the right hand is a proper ornament for *Hope*, since they are these that we term in poetical language the Hopes of the year.

> *Vere novo, tunc herba nitens, et roboris expers*
> *Turget et insolida est, et Spe delectat agrestes,*
> *Omnia tum florent florumque coloribus almus*
> *Ridet ager*———— Ov. Met. Lib. 15.

The green stem grows in stature and in size,
But only feeds with Hope the farmer's eyes;
Then laughs the childish year with flowrets crown'd,
And lavishly perfumes the fields around. Mr. *Dryden.*

The

The fame Poet in his *De faftis,* fpeaking of the Vine in flower, expreffes it.

In fpe vitis erat——— . Ov. de Faft. Lib. 9.·

Fig. 9. The next on the Lift is a Lady of·a contrary character, and therefore in a quite different pofture. As *Security* is free from all. purfuits, fhe is reprefented leaning carelefly on a pillar. *Horace* has drawn a pretty metaphor from this pofture.·

Nullum me à labore reclinat otium.

No eafe doth lay me down from pain. . Mr. *Creech.* She refts her felf on a pillar, for the fame reafon as the poets do often compare an obftinate refolution or a great firmnefs of mind, to rock that is not to be moved by all the affaults of winds or waves..

Non civium ardor prava jubentium,
Non vultus inftantis tyranni,
Mente quatit folidâ, neque Aufter
Dux inquietæ turbidus Adriæ, &c.   Hor.

The man refolv'd, and fteady to his truft,
Inflexible to ill, and obftinately juft,
May the rude Rabble's·infolence defpife,
Their fenfelefs clamours and tumultuous cries;
    The tyrant's fiercenefs he beguiles,
·And the ftern·brow and the harfh voice defies,
    And with fuperior greatnefs fmiles.
Not the rough whirlwind that deforms·
Adrea's black gulph———*&c.*   Mr. *Creech.*

I am apt to think it was on.devices of this nature that *Horace* had. his eye in his Ode to *Fortune.* It is certain he alludes to a·pillar that figured out *Security,* or fomething very like it; and.'till any body finds out another that will ftand better in its place, I think: we may content our felves with this before us.

Te Dacus afper, te profugi Scythæ
Urbéfque gentefque et. Latium ferox;
    Regumque matres barbarorum, et.
    · *Purpurei metuunt tyranni:*
Injuriofo nè pede proruas
Stantem columnam; neu populus frequens
    · *Ad arma ceffantes, ad arma.*

                                        Concitet;.

Concitet, imperiumque frangat.

Ad Fortunam. Hor. Lib. 1. Od. 35.

,To thee their vows rough *Germans* pay,
To thee the wandring *Scythians* bend,
Thee mighty, *Rome* proclaims a friend:
  And for their Tyrant fons
  The barb'rous Mothers pray.
To thee, the greateſt guardian of their Thrones.
  They bend, they vow, and ſtill they fear,
  Left you ſhould kick their Column down,
  And cloud the glory of their Crown;
    They fear that you would raiſe
    The lazy crowd to war,
And break their Empire, or confine their praiſe.

Mr. Creech.

I muſt however be ſo fair as to let you know that *Peace* and *Felicity* have their pillars in ſeveral Medals as well as *Security*, ſo that if you do not like one of them, you may take the other.

Fig. 10. The next Figure is that of *Chaſtity*, who was worſhipped as a Goddeſs, and had her Temple.

——*deinde ad ſuperos Aſtræa receſſit*
Hâc comite, atque duæ pariter fugere ſorores.

De pudicitia. Juv. Sat. 6.

At length uneaſy *Juſtice* upwards flew,
And both the Siſters to the Stars withdrew.Mr. *Dryden.*
Templa pudicitiæ quid opus ſtatuiſſe puellis,
  Si cuivis nuptæ quidlibet eſſe licet?   Tib. Lib. 2.
Since wives whate'er they pleaſe unblam'd can be,
Why rear we uſeleſs Fanes to *Chaſtity?*

How her poſture and dreſs become her, you may ſee in he following verſes.

Ergo ſedens velat vultus, obnubit ocellos,
  Iſta verecundi ſigna Pudoris erant.   Alciat.
She ſits, her viſage veil'd, her eyes conceal'd,
By marks like theſe was *Chaſtity* reveal'd.
Ite procul vittæ tenues, inſigne pudoris,
Quæque tegit medios inſtita longa pedes. Ov. de Ar. Am.
——*frontem limbo velata pudicam.*

. . . . . . Claud. de Theod. Conf.
Hence !

Hence ! ye fmooth fillets on the forehead bound,
Whofe bands the brows of *Chaftity* furround,
And her coy Robe that lengthens to the ground.

She is reprefented in the habit of a *Roman* Matron.

Matronæ præter faciem nil cernere poſſis,
Cæterà; ni Catia eſt, demiſſâ veſte tegentis.

Hor. Sat 2. Lib. 1.

Befides, a Matron's face is feen alone;
But *Cate*'s that female bully of the town,
For all the reft is cover'd with a gown.

Mr. *Creech.*

That *ni Catia eſt*, fays *Cynthio*, is a beauty unknown to moft of our *Engliſh* Satyrifts. *Horace* knew how to ftab with addrefs, and to give a thruft where he was leaft expected. *Boilcau* has nicely imitated him in this, as well as his other beauties. But our *Engliſh* Libellers are for hewing a man down-right, and for letting him fee at a diftance that he is to look for no mercy. I own to you, fays *Eugenius*, I have often admired this piece of art in the two Satyrifts you mention, and have been furprized to meet with a man in a Satire that I never in the leaft expected to find there. They have a particular way of hiding their ill nature, and introduce a criminal rather to illuftrate a precept or paffage, than out of any feeming defign to abufe him. Our *Engliſh* Poets on the contrary fhow a kind of malice prepenfe in their Satires, and inftead of bringing in the perfon to give light to any part of the Poem, let you fee they writ the whole Poem on purpofe to abufe the perfon. But we muft not leave the Ladies thus. Pray what kind of head-drefs is that of *Piety*?

Fig. 11. As *Chaſtity*, fays *Philander*, appears in the habit of a *Roman* matron, in whom that Virtue was fuppofed to reign in its perfection, *Piety* wears the drefs of the Veftal Virgins, who were the greateft and moft fhining examples of it. *Vittata Sacerdos* is you know an expreffion among the *Latin* Poets. I do not queftion but you have feen in the Duke of *Flo-*

rence's

rence's gallery a beautiful antique figure of a woman standing before an Altar, which some of the Antiquaries call a *Piety*, and others a Vestal Virgin. The woman, altar, and fire burning on it, are seen in marble exactly as in this coin, and bring to my mind a part of a speech that *Religion* makes in *Phædrus*'s fables.

Sed ne ignis noster facinori præluceat,
Per quem verendos excolit Pietas deos. Fab. 10. Li. 4.

It is to this Goddess that *Statius* addresses himself in the following lines.

Summa deum pietas! cujus gratissima cœlo
Rara profanatas inspectant numina terras,
Huc vittata comam, niveoque insignis amictu,
Qualis adhuc præsens, nullaque expulsa nocentum
Fraude rudes populos atque aurea regna colebas,
Mitibus exequiis ades, et lugentis Hetrusci
Cerne pios fletus, laudataque lumina terge.

Statius Silv. Li. 3.

Chief of the Skies, celestial Piety!
Whose god-head, priz'd by those of heavenly birth,
Revisits rare these tainted realms of Earth,
Mild in thy milk-white vest, to sooth my friend,
With holy fillets on thy brows descend;
Such as of old (e'er chac'd by Guilt and Rage)
A race unpolisht, and a golden age,
Beheld thee frequent. Once more come below,
Mix in the soft solemnities of woe,
See, see, thy own *Hetruscus* wastes the day,
In pious grief; and wipe his tears away.

The little trunk she holds in her left hand is the *Acerra* that you so often find among the Poets, in which the frankincense was preserv'd that Piety is here supposed to strow on the fire.

Dantque sacerdoti custodem thuris acerram.

Ov. Met. Li. 13.

Hæc tibi pro nato plena dat lætus acerra,
Phœbe———   Mart. Li. 4. Epig. 45.

Fig. 12. The figure of *Equity* differs but little from that our painters make of her at present. The scales she

she carries in her hand are so natural an emblem of justice, that *Perfius* has turned them into an allegory to express the decisions of right or wrong.

———— *Quirites*
Hoc puto non justum est, illud male, rectius istud;
Scis etenim, justum geminâ suspendere lance
Ancipitis Libræ———   Socrat. ad Alcibiad. Sat. 4.

———— *Romans*, know,
Against right reason all your counsels go;
This is not fair; nor profitable that:
Nor t'other question proper for debate.
But thou, no doubt, can'st set the business right,
And give each argument its proper weight:
Know'st with an equal hand to hold the scale, &c.

Mr. Dryden.

Fig. 13. The next figure I present you with is *Eternity*. She holds in her hand a globe with a Phœnix on it. How proper a type of *Eternity* is each of these you may see in the following quotations. I am sure you will pardon the length of the latter as it is not improper to the occasion, and shows at the same time the great fruitfulness of the Poet's fancy that could turn the same thought to so many different ways.

Hæc Æterna manet, divisque simillima forma est;
Cui neque principium est usquam, nec finis: in ipso
Sed similis toto remanet, perque omnia par est.

De Rotunditate Corporum. Manil. Li. 1.

This form's eternal, and may justly claim
A god-like nature, all its parts the same;
Alike, and equal to its self 'tis found,
No end's and no beginning in a round:
Nought can molest its Being, nought controul,
And this ennobles, and confines the whole.

Mr. Creech.

Par volucer superis: Stellas qui vividas æquat
Durando, membrisque terit redeuntibus ævum.———
Nam pater est prolesque sui, nulloque creante
Emeritos artus fœcunda morte reformat,
Et petit alternam totidem per funera vitam———
O senium posture rogo, falsique sepulchris

Nata-

Natales habiture vices, quæ sæpe renasci
Exitio, proprioque soles pubescere letho——
O felix, hæresque tui! quo solvimur omnes,
Hoc tibi suppeditat vires, præbetur origo
Per cinerem, moritur te non pereunte senectus.
Vidisti quodcunque fuit. Te secula teste
Cuncta revolvuntur: nosti quo tempore pontus
Fuderit elatas scopulis stagnantibus undas:
Quis Phaetonteis erroribus arserit annus.
Et clades Te nulla rapit, solusque superstes
Edomitâ tellure manes, non flamina Parcæ
In Te dura legunt, non jus habuere nocendi.

De Phœnice. Claud.

A God-like bird ! whose endless round of years
Outlasts the stars, and tires the circling spheres;——
Begot by none himself, begetting none,
Sire of himself he is, and of himself the son;
His life in fruitful death renews its date,
And kind destruction but prolongs his fate.——
O thou, says he, whom harmless fires shall burn,
Thy age the flame to second youth shall turn,
An infant's cradle is thy fun'ral urn.——
Thrice happy *Phœnix* ! Heav'n's peculiar care
Has made thy self thy self's surviving heir.
By Death thy deathless vigour is supply'd,
Which sinks to ruine all the world beside.
Thy age, not thee, assisting *Phœbus* burns,
And vital flames light up thy fun'ral Urns.
Whate'er events have been thy eyes survey,
And thou art fix'd while ages roll away.
Thou saw'st when raging ocean burst his bed,
O'ertop'd the mountains, and the earth o'erspread;
When the rash youth inflam'd the high abodes,
Scorch'd up the skies, and scar'd the deathless Gods.
When nature ceases, thou shalt still remain,
Nor second Chaos bound thy endless reign ;
Fate's tyrant laws thy happier lot shall brave,
Baffle destruction, and elude the grave,

The

The circle of rays that you see round the head of the
Phœnix diftinguifh him to be the bird and offspring of
the Sun.

Solis avi fpecimen————
Una eft quæ reparet feque ipfa refeminet ales;
Affyrii Phœnica vocant : non fruge neque herbis,
Sed Thuris lacrymis, et fucco vivit amomi.
Hæc ubi quinque fuæ complevit fecula vitæ,
Ilicis in ramis, tremulæve cacumine palmæ,
Unguibus et duro fibi nidum confruit ore :
Quo fimul ac cafias, ac nardi lenis arifas
Quaffaque cum fulwâ fubfravit cinnama myrrhâ,
Se fuper imponit, finitque in odoribus ævum.
Inde ferunt totidem qui vivere debeat annos
Corpore de patrio parvum phœnica renafci.
Cum dedit huic ætas vires, onerique ferendo eft,
Ponderibus nidi ramos levat arboris altæ,
Fertque pius cunafque fuas, patriumque Sepulchrum,
Perque leves auras Hyperionis urbe potitus
Ante fores facras Hyperionis ede reponit.

Ov. Met. Lib. 15.

————————Titanius ales.

Claud. de Phœnice.

————From himfelf the *Phœnix* only fprings :
Self-born, begotten by the parent Flame.
In which he burn'd, another and the fame.
Who not by corn or herbs his life fuftains,
But the fweet effence of *Amomum* drains :
And watches the rich gums *Arabia* bears,
While yet in tender dew they drop their tears.
He (his five centuries of life fulfill'd)
His neft on oaken boughs begins to build,
Or trembling tops of palm, and firft he draws
The plan with his broad bill and crooked claws,
Nature's artificers ; on this the pile
Is form'd, and rifes round ; then with the fpoil
Of *Caffia, Cynnamon,* and ftems of *Nard,*
(For foftnefs ftrew'd beneath) his fun'ral bed is rear'd.
Fun'ral and bridal both ; and all around
The borders with corruptlefs Myrrh are crown'd,

On

On this incumbent; 'till ætherial flame
First catches, then confumes the coftly frame;
Confumes him too, as on the pile he lies;
He liv'd on odours, and in odours dies.

 An Infant-*Phœnix* from the former springs,
His father's heir, and from his tender wings
Shakes off his parent duft, his method he purfues,
And the fame leafe of life on the fame teims renews.
When grown to manhood he begins his reign,
And with ftiff pinions can his flight fuftain,
He lightens of its load, the tree that bore
His father's royal fepulchre before,
And his own cradle : This (with pious care,
Plac'd on his back) he cuts the buxom air,
Seeks the Sun's city, and his facred church,
And decently lays down his burden in the porch.

       Mr. *Dryden.*

Sic ubi fœcundâ reparavit morte juventam,
Et patrios idem cineres, collectaque portat
Unguibus offa piis, Nilique ad littora tendens
Unicus extremo Phœnix procedit ab Euro:
Conveniunt Aquilæ, cunctæque ex orbe volucres.
Ut Solis mirentur avem——Claud. de laud. Stil. L. 2.

So when his parent's pile hath ceas'd to burn,
Tow'rs the young *Phœnix* from the teeming urn :
And from the purple eaft, with pious toil
Bears the dear reliques to the diftant *Nile*;
Himfelf a fpecies! Then, the bird of *Jove,*
And all his plumy nation quit the grove ;
The gay harmonious train delighted gaze,
Crowd the proceffion, and refound his praife.

The radiated head of the *Phœnix* gives us the meaning
of a paffage in *Aufonius*, which I was formerly furprized to meet with in the defcription of a Bird. But
at prefent I am very well fatisfied the Poet muft have
had his eye on the figure of this Bird in ancient fculpture and painting, as indeed it was impoffible to take it
from the life.

 Ter nova Neftoreos implevit purpura fufos,
 Et toties terno cornix vivacior ævo,

         Quam.

Quam novies terni glomerantem secula tractûs
Vincunt œripides ter terno Nestore cervi,
Tres quorum ætates superat Phœbeijus oscen,
Quem novies senior Gangeticus anteit ales,
Ales cinnameo radiatus tempora nido.

Auson. Eidyll. 11.

Arcanum radiant oculi jubar, igneus ora
Cingit honos, rutilo cognatum vertice sidus
Attollit cristatus apex, tenebrasque serenâ
Luce secat——— Claud. de Phœn.

His fiery eyes shoot forth a glitt'ring ray,
And round his head ten thousand glories play :
High on his crest, a Star celestial bright
Divides the darknefs with its piercing light.

———Procul ignea lucet
Ales, odorati redolent cui cinnama busti.

Cl. de laud. Stil. L. 2.

If you have a mind to compare this scale of Beings
with that of *Hesiod*, I shall give it you in a translation
of that Poet.

Ter binos deciesque novem super exit in annos
Justa senescentem quos implet vita virorum.
Hos novies superat vivendo garrula Cornix :
Et quater aggreditur cornicis sæcula cervus.
Alipedem cervum ter vincit Corvus : at illum
Multiplicat novies Phænix, reparabilis ales.
Quam vos perpetuo decies prævertitis ævo
Nymphæ Hamadryades, quarum longissima vita est :
Hi cohibent fines vivacia fata animantum.

Auson. Eidyl. 18.

The utmost age to man the Gods assign
Are winters three times two, and ten times nine:
Poor man nine times the prating Daws exceed :
Three times the Daw's the Deer's more lasting breed :
The Deer's full thrice the raven's race outrun :
Nine times the Raven *Titan*'s feather'd son :
Beyond his age, with youth and beauty crown'd,
The *Hamadryades* shine ten ages round :
Their breath the longest is the Fates bestow ;
And such the bounds to mortal lives below.

A

A man had need be a good Arithmetician, says *Cyn-thio*, to understand this Author's works. His description runs on like a Multiplication Table. But methinks the Poets ought to have agreed a little better in the calculations of a Bird's life that was probably of their own creation.

Fig 14. We generally find a great confusion in the traditions of the Ancients, says *Philander*. It seems to me, from the next Medal, it was an opinion among them, that the *Phœnix* renewed her self at the beginning of the great year, and the return of the Golden Age. This opinion I find touched upon in a couple of lines in *Claudian*.

> *Quicquid ab externis ales longæva colonis*
> *Colligit, optati referens exordia sæcli.*
>
> Claud. de rapt. Prof. Li. 2.

The person in the midst of the circle is supposed to be *Jupiter*, by the Author that has published this Medal, but I should rather take it for the figure of Time. I remember I have seen at *Rome* an antique Statue of Time, with a wheel or hoop of marble in his hand, as *Seneca* describes him, and not with a serpent as he is generally represented.

> ————*properat cursu*
> *Vita citato, volucrique die*
> *Rota præcipitis volvitur anni.*   Herc. fur. Act. 1.

> Life posts away,
> And day from day drives on with swift carreer
> The wheel that hurries on the headlong year.

As the circle of marble in his hand represents the common year, so this that encompasses him is a proper representation of the great year, which is the whole round and comprehension of Time. For when this is finished, the heavenly bodies are supposed to begin their courses anew, and to measure over again the several periods and divisions of years, months, days, &c. into which the great year is distinguished.

> ————*consumto, Magnus qui dicitur, anno*
> *Rursus in antiquum venient vaga sidera cursum:*
> *Qualia disposti steterant ab origine mundi.* Auf. Eid. 18.

When

When round the great Platonick year has turn'd,
In their old ranks the wandring ftars fhall ftand,
As when firft marfhal'd by the Almighty's hand.

To fum up therefore the thoughts of this Medal.
The infcription teaches us that the whole defign muft
refer to the Golden Age which it lively reprefents, if
we fuppofe the circle that encompaffes *Time,* or (if
you pleafe) *Jupiter,* fignifies the finifhing of the great
year ; and that the *Phœnix* figures out the beginning
of a new feries of time. So that the compliment on
this Medal to the Emperor *Adrian,* is in all refpects
the fame that *Virgil* makes to *Pollio*'s fon, at whofe
birth he fuppofes the *annus magnus* or Platonical year
run out, and renewed again with the opening of the
Golden Age.

Magnus ab integro fæclorum nafcitur ordo ;
Jam redit et Virgo, redeunt Saturnia regna :
Et nova progenies cœlo demittitur alto. Virg. Ec. 4.

The time is come the *Sibyls* long foretold,
And the bleft maid reftores the Age of Gold ;
In the great wheel of *Time* before enroll'd.
Now a great progeny from Heav'n defcends.
Ld. *Lauderdale.*

————*nunc adeft mundi dies*
Supremus ille, qui premat genus impium
Cæli ruinâ ; rurfus ut ftirpem novam
Generet renafcens melior : ut quondam tulit
Juvenis tenente regna Saturno poli. Sen. Oet. Act. 2.

————The laft great day is come,
When earth and all her impious fons fhall lie
Crufht in the ruines of the falling fky,
Whence frefh fhall rife, her new-born realms to grace,
A pious offspring and a purer race,
Such as e'erwhile in golden ages fprung,
When *Saturn* govern'd, and the world was young.

You may compare the defign of this reverfe, if you
pleafe, with one of *Conftantine,* fo far as the *Phœnix* is
concerned in both. As for the other figure, we may
have occafion to fpeak of it in another place. *Vid.* 15
figure. King of *France*'s Medalions.

Fig. 16.

Fig. 16 The next figure shadows out *Eternity* to us, by the Sun in one hand and the Moon in the other, which in the language of sacred poetry is *as long as the Sun and Moon endureth*. The heathens made choice of these Lights as apt symbols of *Eternity*, because contrary to all sublunary Beings, though they seem to perish every night, they renew themselves every morning.

Soles occidere et redire possunt;
Nobis cum semel occidit brevis lux,
Nox est perpetua una dormienda.   Catul.

The Suns shall often often fall and rise :
But when the short-liv'd mortal dies
A night eternal seals his eyes.

Horace, whether in imitation of *Catullus* or not, has applied the same thought to the Moon : and that too in the plural number.

Damna tamen celeres reparant cælestia lunæ :
   Nos ubi decidimus
Quò pius Æneas, quò Tullus dives, et Ancas,
   Pulvis et umbra sumus.   Hor. Od. 7. Lib. 4.

Each loss the hastning Moon repairs again.
But we, when once our race is done,
With *Tullus* and *Anchises'* son,
(Tho' rich like one, like t'other good)
To dust and shades, without a Sun,
  Descend, and sink in dark oblivion's flood.
           Sir *W. Temple.*

Fig. 17. In the next figure *Eternity* sits on a globe of the heavens adorned with stars. We have already seen how proper an emblem of *Eternity* the globe is, and may find the duration of the stars made use of by the Poets, as an expression of what is never like to end.

————*Stellas qui vividus æquas*
Durando————
————*Polus dum sidera pascet,*
Semper honos nomenque tuum laudesque manebunt.
           Virg. Æn. L. 1.
Lucida dum current annosi sidera mundi, &c. Sen. Med.
           Vid.

Vid Fig. 13. I might here tell you that *Eternity* has a covering on her head, becaufe we can never find out her beginning ; that her legs are bare, becaufe we fee only thofe parts of her that are actually running on ; that fhe fits on a globe and bears a fcepter in her hand, to fhew fhe is fovereign Miftrefs of all things : but for any of thefe affertions I have no warrant from the Poets.

Fig. 18. You muft excufe me, if I have been longer than ordinary on fuch a fubject as *Eternity.* The next you fee is *Victory,* to whom the Medallifts as well as Poets never fail to give a pair of wings.

Adfuit ipfa fuis Ales Victoria————
Claud de 6. Conf. Honor.

————*dubiis volitat Victoria pennis.*   Ov.

————*niveis Victoria concolor alis.*   Sil. It.

The palm branch and lawrel were both the rewards of Conquerors, and therefore no improper ornaments for *Victory.*

————*lentæ Victoris præmia palmæ.*   Ov. Met.

Et palmæ pretium Victoribus.   Virg. Æn. 5.

Tu ducibus lætis aderis cum læta triumphum
Vox canet, et longas vifent capitolia pompas.
Apollo ad Laurum. Ov. Met.

Thou fhalt the *Roman* feftivals adorn ;
Thou fhalt returning *Cæfar*'s triumphs grace,
When pomps fhall in a long proceffion pafs. *Dryden.*

By the way you may obferve the lower plaits of the Drapery that feem to have gathered the wind into them. I have feen abundance of antique figures in Sculpture and Painting, with juft the fame turn in the lower foldings of the Veft, when the perfon that wears it is in a pofture of tripping forward.

Obviaque adverfas vibrabant flamina Veftes.
Ov. Met. Lib. 1.

————As fhe fled, the wind
Increafing, fpread her flowing hair behind ;
And left her legs and thighs expos'd to view. *Dryden.*

————*tenues finuantur flamine veftes.* Id. Lib. 2.

It

It is worth while to compare this figure of *Victory* with her Statues as it is described in a very beautiful passage of Prudentius.

> *Non aris non farre molæ Victoria felix*
> *Exorata venit: labor impiger, aspera virtus,*
> *Vis animi, excellens ardor, violentia, cura,*
> *Hanc tribuunt, durum tractandis robur in armis.*
> *Quæ si defuerint bellantibus, aurea quamvis*
> *Marmoreo in templo rutilas Victoria pinnas*
> *Explicet, et multis surgat formata talentis:*
> *Non aderit vestisque offensa videbitur hastis.*
> *Quid miles propriis diffisus viribus optas*
> *Irrita fœmineæ tibimet solatia formæ?*
> *Nunquam pennigeram legio ferrata puellam*
> *Vidit anhelantum regeret quæ tela virorum.*
> *Vincendi quæris dominam? sua dextra cuique est,*
> *Et Deus omnipotens. Non pexo crine virago,*
> *Nec nudo suspensa pede, strophioque revincta,*
> *Nec tumidas fluitante sinu vestita papillas.*

Prudentius contra Symm. Lib. 2.

Shall *Victory* intreated lend her aid
For cakes of flower on smoaking Altars laid?
Her help from toils and watchings hope to find,
From the strong body, and undaunted mind:
If these be wanting on th' embattel'd plain,
Ye sue the unpropitious maid in vain.
Though in her marble temples taught to blaze
Her dazling wings the golden dame displays,
And many a talent in due weight was told
To shape her God-head in the curious mould,
Shall the rough soldier of himself despair,
And hope for female visions in the air?
What legion sheath'd in iron e'er survey'd
Their darts directed by this winged maid!
Do'st thou the power that gives success demand?
'Tis He th' Almighty, and thy own right hand;
Not the smooth Nymph, whose locks in knots are twin'd,
Who bending shows her naked foot behind,

Who

Who girds the virgin zone beneath her breaſt,
And from her boſom heaves the ſwelling veſt.

Fig. 19. You have here another *Victory*, that I fancy *Claudian* had in his view when he mentions her wings, palm and trophy in the following deſcription. It ap- pears on a Coin of *Conſtantine* who lived about an age before *Claudian*, and I believe we ſhall find that it is not the only piece of antique ſculpture that this Poet has copied out in his deſcriptions.

―――――*cum totis exurgens ardua pennis*
Ipſa duci ſacras Victoria panderet ædes,
Et palma viridi gaudens, et amicta trophæis.

Claud. de Lau. Stil. Li. 3.

On all her plumage riſing when ſhe threw
Her ſacred ſhrines wide-open to thy view,
How pleas'd for thee her emblems to diſplay,
With palms diſtinguiſh'd, and with trophies gay.

Fig. 20. The laſt of our imaginary Beings is *Liberty.* In her left hand ſhe carries the wand that the *Latins* call the *Rudis* or *Vindicta,* and in her right the cap of Liberty. The Poets uſe the ſame kinds of metaphors to expreſs Liberty. I ſhall quote *Horace* for the firſt whom *Ovid* has imitated on the ſame occaſion, and for the latter *Martial.*

―――――*donatum jam rude quæris*
Mecænas iterum antiquo me includere ludo.

Hor. Lib. 1. Epiſt. 1.

―――――*tardâ veres minuente ſenectâ*
Me quoque donari jam rude tempus erat.

Ov. de Tr. Lib. 4. El. 8.

Since bent beneath the load of years I ſtand,
I too might claim the freedom-giving wand.

Quod te nomine jam tuo ſaluto
Quem regem, et dominum priùs vocabam,
Nè me dixeris eſſe contumacem
Totis pilea ſarcinis redemi. Mar. Lib. 2. Epig. 68.

By thy plain name though now addreſt,
Though once my King and Lord confeſt,
Frown not: with all my goods I buy
The precious Cap of Liberty.

I cannot forbear repeating a paffage out of *Perfius,* fays *Cynthio,* that in my opinion turns the ceremony of making a Freeman very handfomely into ridicule.   It feems the clapping a Cap on his head and giving him a Turn on the heel were neceffary circumftances.   A Slave thus qualified became a Citizen of *Rome,* and was honoured with a name more than belonged to any of his Forefathers, which *Perfius* has repeated with a great deal of humour.

—*Heu fteriles veri, quibus una Quiritem*
Vertigo facit! hic Dama eft, non treffis agafo,
Vappa, et lippus, et in tenui farragine mendax.
Verterit hunc dominus, momento turbinis exit
Marcus Dama.   Papæ! Marco fpondente, recufas
Credere tu nummos? Marco fub Judice palles?
Marcus dixit, ita eft: affigna, Maree, tabellas.
Hæc mera libertas: hanc nobis pilea donant.

Perf.Sat. 5.

That falfe Enfranchifement with eafe is found:
Slaves are made Citizens by turning round.
How! replies one, can any be more free?
Here's *Dama,* once a Groom of low degree,
Not worth a farthing, and a Sot befide;
So true a Rogue, for lying's fake he ly'd:
But, with a Turn, a Freeman he became;
Now *Marcus Dama* is his Worfhip's name.
Good Gods! who wou'd refufe to lend a fum,
If wealthy *Marcus* furety wou'd become!
Marcus is made a Judge, and for a proof
Of certain truth, *he faid it,* is enough.
A Will is to be prov'd; put in your claim;
'Tis clear, if *Marcus* has fubfcrib'd his name.
This is true liberty, as I believe;
What farther can we from our Caps receive,
Than as we pleafe without controul to live?

Mr. D*ryden.*

Since you have given us the ceremony of the Cap, fays *Eugenius,* I'll give you that of the Wand, out of *Claudian.*
Te faftos ineunte quater, follennia ludit
Omina libertas, deductum Vindice morem

Lex

Lex celebrat, famulofque jugo laxatus berili
Ducitur, et grato remeat fecurior ictu.
Triftis conditio pulfata fronte recedit:
In civem rubuere genæ, tergoque removit
Verbera promiffi felix injuria voti.

Claud. de 4. Conf. Hon.

The *Grato ictu* and the *felix injuria*, fays *Cynthio*, would have told us the name of the Author, though you had faid nothing of him. There is none of all the Poets that delights fo much in thefe pretty kinds of contradictions as *Claudian*. He loves to fet his Epithet at variance with its fubftantive, and to furprize his Reader with a feeming abfurdity. If this Poet were well examined, one would find that fome of his greateft beauties as well as faults arife from the frequent ufe of this particular figure.

I queftion not, fays *Pilander*, but you are tired by this time with the company of fo myfterious a fort of Ladies as thofe we have had before us. We will now, for our diverfion entertain our felves with a fett of Riddles, and fee if we can find a key to them among the ancient Poets. The firft of them, fays *Cynthio*, is a Ship under fail, I fuppofe it has at leaft a metaphor or moral precept for its cargo. This, fays *Philander*, is an emblem of Happinefs, as you may fee by the infcription it carries in its fails. We find the fame Device to exprefs the fame thought in feveral of the Poets: as in *Horace*, when he fpeaks of the moderation to be ufed in a flowing fortune, and in *Ovid* when he reflects on his paft happinefs. *Second Series.* *Fig.* 1.

Rebus anguftis animofus atque
Fortis appare: fapienter idem
Contrahes vento nimium fecundo
   Turgida vela.   Hor. Od. 10. Lib. 2.

When *Fortune* fends a ftormy wind,.
Then fhew a brave and prefent mind;
And when with too indulgent gales
She fwells too much, then furl thy fails. Mr. *Creech.*

Nominis et famæ quondam fulgore trahebar,
   Dum tulit antennas aura fecunda meas.

Ov. de Trif. Lib. 5. El. 12.

    En

En ego, non paucis quondam munitus amicis,
  Dum flavit velis aura secunda meis.
                    Id. Epift. ex Ponto 3. Lib. 2.

I liv'd the darling Theme of ev'ry tongue,
The golden Idol of 'th' adoring throng;
  Guarded with friends, while *Fortune's* balmy gales
  Wanton'd aufpicious in my fwelling fails.

You fee the Metaphor is the fame in the Verfes as in the
Medal, with this diftinction only, that the one is in
words and the other in figures. The Idea is alike in
both, though the manner of reprefenting it is different.
If you would fee the whole Ship made ufe of in the
fame fenfe by an old Poet, as it is here on the Medal,
you may find it in a pretty Allegory of *Seneca*.

Fata fi liceat mihi
Fingere arbitrio meo,
Temperem zephyro levi
Vela, nè preffæ gravi
Spiritu antennæ tremant.
Lenis et modicè fluens
Aura, nec vergens latus,
  Ducat intrepidam ratem.   Sen. OEdip. Chor. Act. 4.

My fortune might I form at will,
My canvas Zephyrs foft fhould fill
With gentle breath, left ruder gales
Crack the main-yard, or burft the fails.
By winds that temperately blow
The Barque fhould pafs fecure and flow,
Nor fcar me leaning on her fide:
But fmoothly cleave th' unruffled tide.

After having confidered the Ship as a Metaphor, we may
now look on it as a Reality, and obferve in it the Make of
the old *Roman* veffels, as they are defcribed among the
Poets. It is carried on by oars and fails at the fame time.

Sive opus eft velis minimam bene currit ad auram,
  Sive opus eft remo remige carpit iter.
                    Ov. Tr. Li. 1. El. 10.

The Poop of it has the bend that *Ovid* and *Virgil*
mention.

——*pup*-

—————————*puppique recurvæ.* Ibid. Li. 1. El. 3.

—————————*littora curvæ*

Prætexunt puppes——————— Virg.

You fee the defcription of the Pilot, and the place he
fits on, in the following quotations.

Ipfe gubernator puppi Palinurus ab alta. Virg. Æn. Li. 5.
Ipfius ante oculos ingens à vertice pontus
In puppim ferit : excutitur, pronufque magifter
Volvitur in caput.——————— Id. Æn. Li. 1.

Orontes' bark, that bore the *Lycian* crew,
(A horrid fight) ev'n in the Hero's view,
From ftem to ftern, by waves was overborn ;
The trembling Pilot, from his rudder torn,
Was headlong hurl'd ;——————— Mr. Dryden.

——————————*Segnemque Menœten,*
Oblitus decorifque fui fociumque falutis,
In mare præcipitem puppi deturbat ab altâ :
Ipfe gubernaclo rector fubit. Id. Æn. Li. 5.

Mindlefs of others lives, (fo high was grown
His rifing rage,) and carelefs of his own :
The trembling dotard to the deck he drew,
And hoifted up, and overboard he threw ;
This done, he feiz'd the helm——————— Mr. Dryden.

I have mentioned thefe two laft paffages of *Virgil*, becaufe I think we cannot have fo right an idea of the
Pilot's misfortune in each of them, without obferving
the fituation of his poft, as appears in ancient Coins.
The figure you fee on the other end of the fhip is a
Triton, a man in his upper-parts, and a fifh below
with a trumpet in his mouth. *Virgil* defcribes him in
the fame manner on one of *Æneas's* fhips. It was
probably a common figure on their ancient veffels, for
we meet with it too in *Silius Italicus.*

Hunc vehit immanis Triton, et cærula conchâ
Exterrens freta : cui laterum tenus hifpida nanti
Frons hominem præfert, in priftim definit alvus ;
Spumea femifero fub pectore murmurat unda.

Vir. Æn. Li. 10.

The *Triton* bears him ; he, whofe trumpet's found
Old Ocean's waves from fhore to fhore rebound.

A hairy

A hairy man above the wafte he fhews,
A Porpoife tail down from his belly grows,
The billows murmur, which his breaft oppofe.

Ld. *Lauderdale.*

Ducitur et Libyæ puppis fignata figuram
Et Triton captivus. —————— Sil. It. Lib. 14.

I am apt to think, fays *Eugenius*, from certain paffages
of the Poets, that feveral fhips made choice of fome God
or other for their guardians, as among the *Roman* Ca-
tholics every veffel is recommeded to the patronage of
fome particular faint to give an inftance of two
or three.

Eft mihi fitque precor flavæ tutela Minervæ
Navis——————— Ov. de Trift. Lib. 1. El. 10.
Numen erat celfæ puppis vicina Dione. Sil. It. Lib. 14.
Hammon numen erat Libycæ gentile carinæ,
Cornigeráque fedens fpectabat cærula fronte. Ibid.

The poop great *Ammon Libya*'s god difplay'd,
Whofe horned front the nether flood furvey'd.

The figure of the Deity was very large, as I have feen it
on other Medals as well as this you have fhown us, and
ftood on one end of the veffel that it patronifed. This
may give us an image of a very beautiful circumftance
that we meet with in a couple of wrecks defcribed by
Silius Italicus and *Perfius.*

——————————*Subito cum pondere victus*
Infiliente mari fubmergitur alveus undis.
Scuta virûm criftæque, et inerti fpicula ferro
Tutelæque Deûm fluitant.——————— Sil. It. Lib. 14.

Sunk by a weight fo dreadful down fhe goes,
And o'er her head the broken billows clofe,
Bright fhields and crefts float round the whirling floods
And ufelefs fpears confus'd with tutelary Gods.

——————————*trabe ruptâ Bruttia faxa*
Prendit amicus inops, remque omnem furdaque vota.
Condidit: Ionio jacet ipfe in littore, et unà
Ingentes de puppe Dei, jamque obvia mergis
Cofta ratis laceræ.——————— Perf. Sat. 6.

My friend is fhipwreck'd on the *Brutian* ftrand,
His riches in th' *Ionian* main are loft;

And

And he himſelf ſtands ſhiv'ring on the coaſt.
Where, deſtitute of help, forlorn and bare,
He wearies the deaf Gods with fruitleſs pray'r.
Their images, the relicks of the wrack,
Torn from their naked poop, are tided back
By the wild waves ; and rudely thrown aſhore,
Lie impotent, nor can themſelves reſtore.
The veſſel ſticks, and ſhews her open'd ſide,
And on her ſhatter'd maſt the Mews in triumph ride.
Mr. *Dryden.*

You will think perhaps I carry my conjectures too far, if
I tell you that I fancy they are theſe kind of Gods that
Horace mentions in his Allegorical veſſel which was ſo
broken and ſhattered to pieces ; for I am apt to think
that *integra* relates to the Gods as well as the *Lintea.*

————*non tibi ſunt integra lintea,*
Non Dii, quos iterum preſſa voces malo.
Hor. Od. 14. Lib. 1.

Thy ſtern is gone, thy Gods are loſt.
And thou haſt none to hear thy cry,
Which thou on dang'rous ſhelves are toſt,
When billows rage, and winds are high.
Mr. *Creech.*

Fig. 2. Since we are engaged ſo far in the *Roman*
ſhipping, ſays *Philander,* I'll here ſhow you a Medal
that has on its reverſe a *Roſtrum* with three teeth to it :
whence *Silius's trifidum roſtrum* and *Virgil's roſtriſque tri-*
dentibus, which in ſome editions is *ſtridentibus,* the Edi-
tor chuſing rather to make a falſe quantity than to inſert
a word that he did not know the meaning of. *Flaccus*
gives us a *Roſtrum* of the ſame make:

————*volat immiſſis cava pinus habenis*
Infinditque ſalum, et ſpumas vomit ære tridenti.
Val. Flac. Argon. Lib. 1.

A Ship-carpenter of old *Rome,* ſays *Cynthio,* could not
have talked more judiciouſly. I am afraid, if we let you
alone, you will find out every plank and rope about the
veſſel among the *Latin* Poets. Let us now, if you pleaſe,
go to the next Medal.

H 4

Fig. 3.

Fig. 3. The next, says *Philander*, is a pair of Scales,. which we meet with on several old Coins. They are commonly interpreted as an emblem of the Emperor's Justice. But why may not we suppose that they allude sometimes to the Balance in the Heavens, which was the reigning constellation of *Rome* and *Italy?* Whether it be so or no, they are capable methinks of receiving a nobler interpretation than what is commonly put on them, if we suppose the thought of the reverse to be the same as that in *Manilius.*

Hesperiam sua libra tenet, quâ condita Roma
Et propriis frænat pendentem nutibus orbem,
Orbis et imperium retinet, discrimina rerum
Lancibus, et positas gentes tollitque premitque :
Qua genitus cum fratre Remus hanc condidit urbem.

Manil. Lib. 4.

The Scales rule *Italy*, where *Rome* commands,
And spreads its empire wide to foreign lands :
They hang upon her nod, their fates are weigh'd.
By her, and laws are sent to be obey'd :
And as her pow'rful favour turns the poize,
How low some nations sink and others rise !
Thus guide the Scales, and then to fix our doom,
They gave us**Cæsar founder of our *Rome*. Mr. *Creech.*

Fig. 4. The Thunderbolt is a reverse of *Augustus.* We see it used by the greatest Poet of the same age to express a terrible and irresistible force in battle, which is probably the meaning of it on this Medal, for in another place the same Poet applies the same metaphor to *Augustus's* person.

————*duo Fulmina belli*
Scipiadas————   Virg. Æn. Lib. 6.
————Who can declare
The *Scipio's* worth, those Thunderbolts of war? Mr. *Dryd.*
————*dum Cæsar ad altum*
Fulminat Euphratem bello————   Id. Georg. Lib. 4.
While mighty *Cæsar*, thund'ring from afar,
Seeks on *Euphrates'* banks the spoils of war. Mr. *Dryden.*

I have

---

* *So* Vossius *reads it.*

I have fometimes wondered, fays *Eugenius*, why the *Latin* Poets fo frequently give the Epithets of *trifidum* and *trifulcum* to the Thunderbolt. I am now perfuaded they took it from the fculptors and painters that lived before them, and had generally given it three forks as in the prefent figure. *Virgil* infifts on the number three in its defcription, and feems to hint at the wings we fee on it. He has worked up fuch a noife and terror in the compofition of his Thunderbolt as cannot be exprefled by a pencil or graving-tool.

Tres imbris torti radios, tres nubis aquofæ
Addiderant, rutili tres ignis, et Alitis Auftri.
Fulgores nunc terrificas fonitumque metumque
Mifcebant operi, flammifque fequacibus iras.

Virg. Æn. Lib. 8.

Three rays of writhen rain, of fire three more,
Of winged fouthern winds, and cloudy ftore
As many parts, the dreadful mixture frame,
And fears are added, and avenging flame. Mr. *Dryd.*

Fig. 5. Our next reverfe is an Oaken Garland, which we find on abundance of imperial Coins. I fhall not here multiply quotations to fhow that the garland of Oak was the reward of fuch as had faved the life of a citizen, but will give you a paffage out of *Claudian*, where the compliment to *Stilico* is the fame that we have here on the Medal. I queftion not but the old Coins gave the thought to the Poet.

Mos erat in veterum caftris, at tempora quercu
Velaret, validis qui fufo viribus hofte
Cafurum potuit morti fubducere civem.
At tibi quæ poterit pro tantis civica reddi
Mœnibus? aut quantæ penfabunt faſta coronæ?

Claud. de Lau. Stil. Lib. 3.

Of old, when in the war's tumultuous ftrife
A *Roman* fav'd a brother *Roman*'s life,
And foil'd the threatning foe, our Sires decreed
An Oaken Garland to the viſtor's meed.
Thou, who haft fav'd whole crowds, whole towns fet free
What groves, what Woods, fhall furnifh crowns for thee? H 5 *It*

It is not to be suppofed that the Emperor had actually covered a *Roman* in battle. It is enough that he had driven out a tyrant, gained a victory, or reftored Juftice. For in any of thefe or the like cafes he may very well be faid to have faved the life of a citizen; and by confequence entitled to the reward of it. Accordingly we find *Virgil* diftributing his Oaken garlands to thofe that had enlarged or ftrength'ned the dominions of *Rome*; as we may learn from *Statius* that the ftatue of *Curtius*, who had facrificed himfelf for the good of the people, had the head furrounded with the fame kind of ornament.

Atque umbrata gerunt civili tempora quercu.
Hi tibi Nomentum, et Gabios, urbemque Fidenam,
Hi Collatinas imponent montibus arces. Virg. Æn. Lib. 6.
But they, who crown'd with Oaken wreaths appear,
Shall *Gabian* walls and ftrong *Fidena* rear:
Nomentum, Bola, with *Pometia,* found;
And raife *Colatian* tow'rs on rocky ground.
Mr. Dryden.

Ipfe loci cuftos, cujus facrata vorago;
Famofufque lacus nomen memorabile fervat;
Innumeros æris fonitus, et verbere crudo
Ut fenfit mugire forum, movet horrida fancto
Ora fitu, meritaque caput venerabile quercu.
Statius Sylv. Lib. 1.
The Guardian of that Lake, which boafts to claim
A fure memorial from the *Curtian* name;
Rous'd by th' artificers, whofe mingled found
From the loud *Forum* pierc'd the fhades profound,
The hoary vifion rofe confefs'd in view,
And fhook the Civic wreath that bound his brow.
Fig. 6. The two horns that you fee on the next Medal are emblems of *Plenty.*
————*apparetque beata pleno*
Copia Cornu.   Hor. Car. Sæc.
Your Medallifts tell us that two Horns on a Coin fignify an extraordinary Plenty. But I fee no foundation for this conjecture. Why fhould they not as well have ftamped two Thunderbolts, two *Caduceus's,* or two
Ships,

Ships, to reprefent an extraordinary force, a lafting peace, of an unbounded happinefs. I rather think that the double *Cornu-copia* relates to the double tradition of its original. Some reprefenting it as the horn of *Achelous* broken off by *Hercules*, and others as the horn of the Goat that gave fuck to *Jupiter.*

—————rigidum fera dextera cornu
Dum tenet, infregit; truncâque à fronti revellit.
Naiades hoc, pomis et odoro flore repletum,
Sacrârunt; divefque meo bona Copia cornu eft.
Dixerat: at Nymphe ritu fuccinĉta Dianæ
Una miniftrarum, fufis utrinque capillis,
Inceffit, totumque tulit prædivite cornu
Autumnum, et menfas felicia poma fecundas.
           De Acheloi Cornu. Ov. Met. Lib. 9.

Nor yet his fury cool'd; 'twixt rage and fcorn
From my maim'd front he bore the ftubborn horn:
This, heap'd with flowers and fruits the *Naiads* bear,
Sacred to Plenty and the bounteous year.
   He fpoke; when lo, a beauteous Nymph appears,
Girt like *Diana*'s train, with flowing hairs;
The horn fhe brings, in which all Autumn's ftor'd;
And ruddy apples for the fecond board.   Mr. *Gay.*

Lac dabat illa Deo: fed fregit in arbore cornu:
   Truncaque dimidiâ parte decoris erat.
Suftulit hoc Nymphe; cinĉtumque recentibus herbis,
   Et plenum pomis ad Jovis ora tulit.
Ille, ubi res cæli tenuit, folioque paterno
   Sedit, et inviĉto nil Jove majus erat,
Sidera nutricem, nutricis fertile cornu
   Fecit; quod dominæ nunc quoque nomen habet.
         De Cornu Amaltheæ. Ov. de Faft. Lib. 5.

The God fhe fuckled of old *Rhea* born;
And in the pious office broke her horn,
As playful in a rifted Oak fhe toft
Her heedlefs head, and half its honours loft.
Fair *Amalthæa* took it off the ground,
With apples fill'd it and with garlands bound,
Which to the fmiling infant fhe convey'd.
He, when the fceptre of the Gods he fway'd,

                              When.

When bold he seiz'd his father's vacant throne,
And reign'd the tyrant of the skies alone,
Bid his rough nurse the starry Heavens adorn,
And grateful in the Zodiac fix'd her Horn.

Betwixt the double *Cornu-copia* you see *Mercury's* rod.

Cyllenes cœlique decus, facunde minister,
  Aurea cui torto virgo dracone viret. Mar. L. 7. Epig. 74.

Descend, *Cyllene's* tutelary God,
With serpents twining round thy golden rod.

It stands on old Coins as an emblem of Peace, by reason
of its stupifying quality that has gained it the title of *Virga somnifera.* It has wings for another quality that *Virgil* mentions in his description of it.

———————*hac fretus ventos et nubila tranat.*   Virg.

Thus arm'd, the God begins his airy race,
And drives the racking clouds along the liquid space.
                                             Mr. Dryden.

The two heads over the two *Cornu-copiæ* are of the
Emperor's children, who are sometimes called among
the Poets the pledges of Peace, as they took away the
occasions of war in cutting off all disputes to the succession.

———————*tu mihi primum*
Tot natorum memoranda parens, ———————
Utero toties enixa gravi
  Pignora pacis.   Sen. Octav. Act. 5.

Thee first kind author of my joys,
Thou source of many smiling boys,
Nobly contented to bestow
A pledge of peace in every throe.

This medal therefore compliments the Emperor on his
two children, whom it represents as public blessings
that promise Peace and Plenty to the Empire.

Fig. 7. The two hands that joyn one another are Emblems of *Fidelity.*

Inde Fides dextræque datæ——————— Ov. Met. L. 14.

Sociemus animos, pignus hoc fidei cape,
Continge dextram——————— Sen. Herc. Fur. Act. 2.

———————*en dextra fidesque*
Quem secum patrios aiunt portare penates!
                                         Virg. Æn. Lib. 5.

See

See now the promis'd faith, the vaunted name,
The picus man, who, rushing thro' the flame,
Preferv'd his Gods—————. Mr. *Dryden.*

By the infcription we may fee that they reprefent in
this place the Fidelity or Loyalty of the public towards
their Emperor. The *Caduceus* rifing between the hands
fignifies the Peace that arifes from fuch. an union with
their Prince, as the fpike of Corn on each fide fhadows
out the Plenty that is the fruit of fuch a peace.

Pax Cererem nutrit, pacis alumna Ceres.
.Ov. de Faft. Lib. 1.

Fig. 8 The giving of a hand, in the reverfe of *Claudius*, is a token of good will. For when, after the death
of his nephew *Caligula, Claudius* was in no fmall ap-
prehenfion for his own life, he was, contrary to his expectation, well received among the *Prætorian* guards,
and afterwards declared their Emperor. His reception
is here recorded on a Medal, in which one of the En-
figns prefents him his hand, in the fame fenfe as *Anchifes* gives it in the following verfes.

*Ipfe pater dextram Anchifes haud multa moratus
Dat juveni, atque animum præfenti munere firmat.*
Virg. Æn. Lib. 3.

The old weather-beaten foldier that carries in his hand
the *Roman* Eagle, is the fame kind of officer that you
meet with in *Juvenal*'s fourteenth Satire.

*Dirue Maurorum attegias, caftella Brigantum,
Ut locupletem Aquilam tibi fexagefimus annus
Afferat*———— Juv. Sat. 14.

I remember in one of the Poets the *Signifer* is defcribed
with a Lion's fkin over his head and fhoulders, like this
we fee in the Medal, but at prefent I cannot recollect the
paffage. *Virgil* has given us a noble defcription of a warrior making his appearance under a Lion's fkin.

————*tegmen torquens immane Leonis .
Terribili impexum fetâ, cum dentibus albis
Indutus capiti, fic regia tecta fubibat
Horridus, Herculeoque humeros indutus amictu.*
Virg. Æn. Lib. 7.

-Like *Hercules* himfelf his Son appears,
In favage pomp : a Lion's hide he wears ; **About**

About his shoulders hangs the shaggy skin,
The teeth, and gaping jaws severely grin.
' Thus like the God his father, homely drest,
He strides into the hall, a horrid guest? Mr. *Dryden.*
Since you have mentioned the dress of your Standard-
bearer, says *Cynthio,* I cannot forbear remarking that
of *Claudius,* which was the usual *Roman* habit. One
may see in this Medal, as well as in any antique Statues, that the old *Romans* had their necks and arms
bare, and as much exposed to view as our hands and
faces are at present. Before I had made this remark,
I have sometimes wondred to see the *Roman* Poets, in
their descriptions of a beautiful man, so often mentioning the Turn of his Neck and Arms, that in our
modern dresses lie out of sight, and are covered under
part of the cloathing. Not to trouble you with many
quotations, *Horace* speaks of both these parts of the
body in the beginning of an Ode, that in my opinion
may be reckoned among the finest of his book, for the
naturalness of the thought, and the beauty of the expression.

> *Dum tu Lydia Telephi*
> *Cervicem roseam, et cerea Telephi*
> *Laudas brachia, væ meum*
> *Fervens difficili bile tumet jecur.*

When *Telephus* his youthful charms,
His rosy neck, and winding arms,
With endless rapture you recite,
And in that pleasing name delight;
My heart, inflam'd by jealous heats,
With numberless resentments beats;
From my pale cheek the colour flies,
And all the Man within me dies.

It was probably this particular in the *Roman* habit that
gave *Virgil* the thought in the following verse, where
Romulus, among other reproaches that he makes the
Trojans for their softness and effeminacy, upbraids them
with the Make of their *Tunica's,* that had sleeves to them,
and did not leave the arms naked and exposed to the
weather like that of the *Romans.*

Et

Et tunicæ manicas, et habent redimicula mitræ.

Virgil lets us know in another place, that the *Italians* preferved their old language and habits, notwithftanding the *Trojans* became their Mafters, and that the *Trojans* themfelves quitted the drefs of their own country for that of *Italy*. This he tells us was the effect of a prayer that *Juno* made to *Jupiter*.

Illud te, nullâ fati quod lege tenetur,
Pro Latio obteftor, pro majeftate tuorum :
Cum jam connubiis pacem felicibus (efto ;)
Component, cum jam leges et fædera jungent ;
Nè vetus indigenas nomen mutare Latinos,
Neu Troas fieri jubeas, Teucrofque vocari ;
Aut vocem mutare viros, aut vertere veftes:
Sit Latium, fint Albani per fecula reges,
Sit Romana potens Italâ virtute propago :
Occidit, occideritque finas cum nomine Troja. Æn. Lib. 1 2.

This let me beg (and this no Fates withftand)
Both for my felf, and for your father's land,
That when the nuptial bed fhall bind the peace,
(Which I, fince you ordain, confent to blefs)
The laws of either nation be the fame ;
But let the *Latins* ftill retain their name :
Speak the fame language which they fpoke before,
Wear the fame habits, which their Grandfires wore.
Call them not *Trojans* : perifh the renown
And name of *Troy*, with that detefted town.
Latium be *Latium* ftill : let *Alba* reign,
And *Rome*'s immortal Majefty remain.   Mr. D*ryden*.

By the way, I have often admired at *Virgil* for reprefenting his *Juno* with fuch an impotent kind of revenge as what is the fubject of this fpeech. You may be fure, fays *Eugenius*, that *Virgil* knew very well this was a trifling kind of requeft for the Queen of the Gods to make, as we may find by *Jupiter*'s way of accepting it.

Olli fubridens hominum rerumque repertor :
Et germana Jovis, Saturnique altera proles :
Irarum tantos volvis fub pectore fluctus?
Verum age, et inceptum fruftrà fubmitte furorem.
Do, quod vis ; et me victufque volenfque remitto.

Sermonem Ausonii patrium moresque tenebunt.
Utque est, nomen erit: commixti corpore tantùm
Subsident Teucri: morem ritusque sacrorum
Adjiciam, faciamque omnes uno ore Latinos, &c.

Æn. Lib. 12.

Then thus the founder of mankind replies.
(Unruffled was his front, serene his eyes,)
Can *Saturn*'s issue, and Heav'ns other Heir,
Such endless anger in her bosom bear?
Be Mistress, and your full desires obtain;
But quench the choler you foment in vain.
From ancient blood th' *Ausonian* people sprung,
Shall keep their name, their habit, and their tongue.
The *Trojans* to their customs shall be ty'd,
I will my self their common rites provide; }
The natives shall command, the foreigners subside: }
And shall be *Latium*; *Troy* without a name:
And her lost sons forget from whence they came.

Mr. Dryden.

I am apt to think *Virgil* had a further view in this request
of *Juno* than what his Commentators have discovered
in it. He knew very well that his *Æneid* was founded
on a very doubtful story, and that *Æneas*'s coming into
Italy was not universally received among the *Romans*
themselves. He knew too that a main objection to this
story was the great difference of Customs, Language and
Habits among the *Romans* and *Trojans*. To obviate
therefore so strong an objection, he makes this difference
to arise from the forecast and præ-determination of the
Gods themselves. But pray what is the name of the
Lady in the next Medal? Methinks she is very particular
in her Quoiffure.

Fig. 9. It is the emblem of fruitfulness, says *Philander*, and was designed as a compliment to *Julia* the
wife of *Septimius Severus*, who had the same number of
children as you see on this Coin. Her head is crowned
with towers in allusion to *Cybele* the mother of the Gods,
and for the same reason that *Virgil* compares the city of
Rome to her.

Felix

Felix prole virûm, qualis Berecynthia mater
Invehitur curru Phrygias turrita per urbes,
Læta Deûm partu——— Virg. Æn. Lib. 6.

High as the mother of the Gods in place,
And proud, like her, of an immortal race.
Then when in pomp she makes a *Phrygian*-round,
With golden turrets on her temples crown'd.
Mr. *Dryden.*

The Vine iffuing out of the Urn fpeaks the fame fenfe as that in the Pfalmift. *Thy wife fhall be as the fruitful vine on the walls of thy houfe.* The four ftars overhead, and the fame number on the Globe, reprefent the four children. There is a Medal of *Romulus* and *Remus* fucking the wolf, with a Star over each of their heads, as we find the *Latin* Poets fpeaking of the children of Princes under the fame metaphor.

Utque tui faciunt fidus juvenile nepotes,
  Per tua perque fui facta parentis eant.
Ov. de Trift. Lib. 2. El. 1.

———*Tu quoque extinctus jaces,*
Deflende nobis femper, infelix puer,
Modo fidus orbis, columen augustæ domûs,
Britannice——— ——— Sen. Octav, Act. 1.

Thou too dear youth, to afhes turn'd,
Britannicus, for ever mourn'd !
Thou Star that wont this Orb to grace !
Thou pillar of the *Julian*-race !

———*Maneas hominum contentus habenis,*
*Undarum terræq; potens, et fidera dones.*Stat.Theb.l.1.

———Stay, great *Cæfar,* and vouchfafe to reign
O'er the wide earth, and o'er the wat'ry main ;
Refign to *Jove* his Empire of the fkies,
And people Heav'n with *Roman* Deities. Mr. *Pope.*

I need not mention *Homer's* comparing *Aftyanax* to the Morning-ftar, nor *Virgil's* imitation of him in his defcription of *Afcanius.*

Fig. 10. The next Medal was ftampt on the marriage of *Nero* and *Octavia;* you fee the Sun over the head of *Nero,* and the Moon over that of *Octavia.* They
face

face one another according to the situation of these two
Planets in the Heavens.

————*Phœbeis obvia flammis*
Demet nocti Luna timores.. Sen. Thyeft. Act. 4.

And to shew that *Octavia* derived her whole lustre from
the friendly aspect of her husband.

Sicut Luna suo tunc tantum deficit orbe,
Quum Phœbum adversis currentem non vidit astris.
           Manil. Lib. 4.

Because the Moon then only feels decay,
 When opposite unto her brother's ray.. Mr. *Creech.*

But if we consider the history of this Medal, we shall
find more Fancy in it than the Medallists have yet difcovered. *Nero* and *Octavia* were not only husband and
wife, but brother and sister, *Claudius* being the father
of both. We have this relation between them marked
out in the Tragedy of *Octavia,* where it speaks of her
marriage with *Nero.*

Fratris thalamos fortita tenet
Maxima Juno: soror Augusti
Sociata toris, cur à patriâ
Pellitur Aulâ ?————   Sen Oct. 8. Act. 1.

To *Jove* his sister consort wed,
Uncensur'd shares her brother's bed :
Shall *Cæsar's* wife and sister wait,
An Exile at her husband's gate ?

Implebit aulam stirpe cælesti tuam
Generata divo, Claudiæ gentis decus,
Sortita fratris, more Junonis, toros. Ibid. Act. 2.

Thy sister, bright with ev'ry blooming grace,
Will mount thy bed t'inlarge the *Claudian* race :
And proudly teeming with fraternal love,
Shall reign a *Juno* with the *Roman Jove.*

They are therefore very prettily represented by the Sun
and Moon, who as they are the most glorious parts of
the universe, are in poetical genealogy brother and sister.
Virgil gives us a sight of them in the same position that
they regard each other on this Medal.

Nec Fratris radiis obnoxia surgere Luna. Vir. Geor. 1.

Fig.

Fig. 11.   The flattery on the next Medal is in the
same thought as that of *Lucretius.*

Ipse Epicurus obit decurso lumine vitæ,
Qui genus humanum ingenio superavit, et omneis
*Præstrinxit, stellas exortus uti ætherius sol.*Lucr.lib.3.
Nay, *Epicurus*'s race of life is run;
That man of wit, who other men outshone;
As far as meaner stars the mid day Sun.

Mr. C*reech.*

The Emperor appears as the rising Sun, and holds a
Globe in his hand, to figure out the Earth that is en-
lightned and actuated by his beauty.

Sol qui terrarum flammis opera omnia lustras.   Virg.
————*ubi primos crastinus ortus*
Extulerit Titan, radiisque retexerit orbem.   Id.
When next the Sun his rising light displays,
And gilds the world below with purple rays.

Mr. D*ryden.*

On his head you see the rays that seem to grow out
of it.   *Claudian* in the description of his infant *Titan*
descants on this glory about his head, but has run his
description into most wretched fustian.

Invalidum dextro portat Titana lacerto,
Nondum luce gravem, nec pubescentibus altè
Cristatum radiis; primo clementior ævo
Fingitur, et tenerum vagitu despuit ignem.

Claud. de rapt. Prof. Lib. 2.

An infant *Titan* held she in her arms;
Yet sufferably bright, the eye might bear
The ungrown glories of his beamy hair.
Mild was the babe, and from his cries there came
A gentle breathing and a harmless flame.

Fig. 12.   The Sun rises on a medal of *Commodus,* as
Ovid describes him in the story of *Phaeton.*

Ardua prima via est et quà vix manè recentes
Enituntur equi————   Ov. Met. Lib. 2.
You have here too the four horses breaking through the
clouds in their morning passage,

————*Pyroëis, et Eous, et Æthon,*
Solis equi, quartusque Phlegon————   Ibid.

C*orri-*

Corripuere viam, pedibusque per aëra motis
Obstantes scindunt nebulas————————   Ibid.

The woman underneath represents the Earth, as *Ovid*
has drawn her fitting in the same figure.

Sustulit omniferos collo tenus arida vultus;
Oppofuitque manum fronti, magnoque tremore
Omnia concutiens paulum subfedit.   Ibid.

The Earth at length ————————
Uplifted to the heav'ns her blasted head,
And clapt her hands upon her brows, and said,
(But first, impatient of the sultry heat,
Sunk deeper down, and fought a cooler feat.)

The *Cornu-copiæ* in her hand is a type of her fruitfulness,
as in the speech she makes to *Jupiter*.

Hosne mihi fructus, hunc fertilitatis honorem,
Officiique refers? quod adunci vulnera aratri
Rastrorumque fero, totoque exerceor anno?
Quod pecori frondes alimentaque mitia fruges
Humano generi, vobis quoque thura ministro?   Ibid.

And does the plow for this my body tear?
This the reward for all the fruits I bear,
Tortur'd with rakes, and harrafs'd all the year?
That herbs for cattel daily I renew,
And food for man, and frankincenfe for you?

So much for the defigning part of the Medal; as for
the thought of it, the Antiquaries are divided upon it.
For my part I cannot doubt but it was made as a compliment to *Commodus* on his fkill in the chariot-race.
It is fuppofed that the fame occafion furnifhed *Lucan*
with the fame thought in his addrefs to *Nero*.

Seu te flammigeros Phœbi confcendere currus,
Telluremque, nihil mutato fole, timentem
Igne vago luftrare juvet———— Luc.Lib. 1.adNeronem.

Or if thou chufe the empire of the day,
And make the Sun's unwilling fteeds obey;
Aufpicious if thou drive the flaming team,
While earth rejoyces in thy gentler beam————
                                            Mr. *Rowe.*

This is fo natural an allufion, that we find the courfe of
the Sun defcribed in the Poets by metaphors borrowed
on the *Circus.*
                                            Quum

Quum suspensus eat Phœbus, currumque reflectat
Huc illuc agiles, et servet in æthere metas, Manil. l. 1.
————*Hesperio positas in littore metas.* Ov. Met. l. 2.
Et Sol ex æquo metâ distabat utrâque. Idem.

However it be, we are sure in general it is a comparing of *Commodus* to the Sun, which is a simile of as long standing as poetry, I had almost said, as the Sun it self.

I believe, says *Cynthio*, there is scarce a great man he ever shone upon that has not been compared to him. I look on similes as a part of his productions. I do not know whether he raises fruits or flowers in greater number. *Horace* has turn'd this comparison into ridicule seventeen hundred years ago.

————*laudat Brutum, laudatque cohortem,*
Solem Asiæ Brutum appellat—— Hor. Sat. 7. Lib. 1.
He praiseth *Brutus* much and all his train ;
He calls him *Asia*'s Sun———— Mr. *Creech.*

You have now shown us persons under the disguise of Stars, Moons and Suns. I suppose we at last have done with the cœlestial bodies.

Fig. 13. The next figure you see, says *Philander*, had once a place in the heavens, if you will believe ecclesiastical story. It is the sign that is said to have appeared to *Constantine* before the battle with *Mexentius.* We are told by a Christian Poet, that he caus'd it to be wrought on the military Ensign that the *Romans* call their *Labarum.* And it is on this Ensign that we find it in the present Medal.

Christus purpureum gemmanti, textus in auro
Signabat Labarum————
Prudent. contra Symm. Lib. 1.
A Christ was on th'Imperial standard born,
That Gold embroiders, and that Gemms adorn.

By the word *Christus* he means without doubt the present figure, which is composed out of the two Initial letters of the name.

Fig. 14. He bore the same sign in his standards, as you may see in the following Medal and verses.

Ag-

Agnoscas Regina, libens mea signa necesse est:
In quibus Effigies Crucis aut gemmata refulget,
Aut longis solido ex auro præ fertur in hastis.

Conſtantinus Romam alloquitur. Ibid.

My Enſign let the Queen of nations praiſe,
That rich in gemms the Chriſtian Croſs diſplays:
There rich in gemms; but on my quiv'ring ſpears
In ſolid gold the ſacred mark appears.

Vexillumque Crucis ſummus dominator adorat.

Id. in Apotheoſi.

See there the Croſs he wav'd on hoſtile ſhores,
The Emperor of all the world adores,

Fig. 15. But to return to our *Labarum*; if you have a mind
to ſee it in a ſtate of Paganiſm you have it on a Coin of
Tiberius. It ſtands between two other Enſigns, and is the
mark of a *Roman* Colony where the Medal was ſtamped. By the way you muſt obſerve, that where-ever
the *Romans* fixed their ſtandards they looked on that
place as their country, and thought themſelves obliged to defend it with their lives. For this reaſon
their ſtandards were always carryed before them when
they went to ſettle themſelves in a Colony. This
gives the meaning of a couple of verſes in *Silius Itali-*
cus, that make a very far-fetcht compliment to *Fa-*
bius.

Ocyus huc Acquilas ſervataque ſigna referte,
Hic patria eſt, murique urbis ſtant pectore in uno.

Sil. It. Li. 7.

Fig. 16. The following Medal was ſtamped on *Trajan*'s
victory over the *Daci,* you ſee on it the figure of *Trajan*
preſenting a little *Victory* to *Rome.* Between them lies
the conquered province of *Dacia.* It may be worth
while to obſerve the particularities in each figure. We
ſee abundance of perſons on old Coins that hold a
little *Victory* in one hand, like this of *Trajan,* which
is always the ſign of a conqueſt. I have ſometimes
fancied *Virgil* alludes to this cuſtom in a verſe that *Tur-*
nus ſpeaks.

Non adeo has exoſa manus Victoria fugit.

Virg. Æn. Li. 11.

IF

If you confent, he fhall not be refus'd,
Nor find a hand to Victory unus'd.   Mr. *Dryden.*

The Emperor's ftanding in a Gown, and making a
prefent of his *Dacian* victory to the city of *Rome,* agrees
very well with *Claudian's* character of him.

—————————*victura feretur*
Gloria Trajani ; non tam quod, Tigride victo,
Noftra triumphati fuerint provincia Parthi,
Alta quod invectus ftratis capitolia Dacis :
Quam patriæ quod mitis erat—————————
Claud. de 4to Conf. Honor.

Thy glory, *Trajan,* fhall for-ever live :
Not that thy arms the *Tigris* mourn'd, o'ercome,
And tributary *Parthia* bow'd to *Rome,*
Not that the Capitol receiv'd thy train
With fhouts of triumph for the *Daci* flain :
But for thy mildnefs to thy country fhown.

The city of *Rome* carries the Wand in her hand that
is the fymbol of her Divinity.

Delubrum Romæ (colitur nam fanguine et ipfa
More Deæ)—————   Prudent. cont. Sym. Lib. 1.
For *Rome,* a Goddefs too can boaft her fhrine,
With victims ftain'd, and fought with rites divine.

As the Globe under her feet betokens her dominion
over all the nations of the earth.

Terrarum Dea, Gentiumque Roma ;
Cui par eft nihil, et nihil fecundum.
Mart. Lib. 12. Epig. 8.

O *Rome,* thou Goddefs of the earth !
To whom no rival e'er had birth ;
Nor fecond e'er fhall rife.

The heap of arms fhe fits on fignifies the Peace that
the Emperor had procured her. On old Coins we
often fee an Emperor, a *Victory,* the city of *Rome,* or
a flave, fitting on a heap of arms, which always marks
out the Peace that arofe from fuch an action as gave
occafion to the Medal. I think we cannot doubt but
Virgil copied out this circumftance from the ancient
Sculptors, in that inimitable defcription he has given

us

us of *Military Fury* shut up in the Temple of *Janus* and loaden with chains.

> *Claudentur belli portæ : Furor impius intus*
> *Sæva sedens super arma, et centum vinctus ahenis*
> *Post tergum nodis, fremet horridus ore cruento.*
>
> Virg. Æn. Li. 1.

Janus himself before his fane shall wait,
And keep the dreadful issues of his gate,
With bolts and iron bars : within remains
Imprison'd *Fury*, bound in brazen chains:
High on a Trophy rais'd of useless arms
He sits, and threats the world with dire alarms.

Mr. Dryden.

We are told by the old Scholiast, says *Eugenius*, that there was actually such a statue in the Temple of *Janus* as that *Virgil* has here described, which I am almost apt to believe, since you assure us that this part of the design is so often met with on ancient Medals. But have you nothing to remark on the figure of the Province? Her posture, says *Philander*, is what we often meet with in the slaves and captives of old Coins: among the Poets too, sitting on the ground is a mark of Misery or Captivity.

> *Multos illa dies incomtis mæsta capillis*
> *Sederat*———   Propert. Li. 1,
> *O utinam ante tuos sedeam captiva penates.* Id. L. 4.

O might I sit a captive at thy gate!

Fig. 17. You have the same posture in an old Coin that celebrates a victory of *Lucius Verus* over the *Parthians*. The captive's hands are here bound behind him, as a farther instance of his slavery.

> *Ecce manus juvenem interea post terga revinctum,*
> *Pastores magno ad Regem clamore ferebant.*
>
> Virg. Æn. L. 2.

Mean while, with shouts, the *Trojan* shepherds bring
A captive *Greek* in bands before the King.

Mr. Dryden.

> *Cui dedit invitas victa noverca manus.*   Ov. de Fast.
> *Cum rudis urgenti brachia victa dedi.*   Propert. Li. 4.

We

We may learn from *Ovid* that it was fometimes the cuftom to place a flave with his arms bound at the foot of
the Trophy, as in the figure before us.

Stentque fuper vinctos trunca trophæa viros.

Ov. Ep. ex Ponto. Lib. 4.

You fee on his head the cap which the *Parthians*, and
indeed moft of the eaftern nations, wear on Medals.
They had not probably the ceremony of veiling the
Bonnet in their falutations, for in Medals they ftill have
it on their heads, whether they are before Emperors
or Generals, kneeling, fitting, or ftanding, *Martial* has
diftinguifhed them by this cap as their chief characte-
riftic.

Fruftra blanditiæ venitis ad me
Attritis miferabiles labellis,
Dicturus dominum, deumque non fum :
Jam non eft locus hâc in urbe vobis.
Ad Parthos procul ite pileatos,
Et turpes, humilefque fupplicefque
Pictorum fola bafiate regum. Mart. Epig. 72. Li. 10.

In vain, mean flatteries, ye try,
To gnaw the lip, and fall the eye :
No man a God or Lord I name :
From *Romans* far be fuch a fhame !
Go teach the fupple *Parthian* how
To veil the Bonnet on his brow :
Or on the ground all proftrate fling
Some *Pict*, before his barb'rous King.

I cannot hear, fays *Cynthio*, without a kind of Indignation, the fatyrical reflections that *Martial* has made
on the memory of *Domitian*. It is certain fo ill an
Emperor deferved all the reproaches that could be
heaped upon him, but he could not deferve them of
Martial. I muft confefs I am lefs fcandalifed at the
flatteries the Epigrammatift paid him living, than the
ingratitude he fhowed him dead. A man may be betrayed into the one by an over-ftrained complaifance,
or by a temper extremely fenfible of favours and obli-
gations : whereas the other can arife from nothing

I   but

but a natural baseness and villany of soul. It does not
always happen, says *Philander*, that the Poet and the
honest man meet together in the same person. I think
we need enlarge no farther on this Medal, unless you
have a mind to compare the Trophy on it with that of
Mezentius in *Virgil*.

> *Ingentem quercum decisis undique ramis*
> *Constituit tumulo, fulgentiaque induit arma,*
> *Mezenti ducis exuvias; tibi, magne, tropæum,*
> *Bellipotens: aptat rorantes sanguine cristas.*
> *Telaque trunca viri, et bis sex thoraca petitum*
> *Perfossumque locis; clypeumque ex ære sinistræ*
> *Subligat, atque ensem collo suspendit eburnum.*
>
> Virg. Æn. Lib. 11.

He bar'd an ancient Oak of all her boughs,
Then on a rising ground the trunk he plac'd;
Which with the spoils of his dead foe he grac'd.
The coat of arms by proud *Mezentius* worn,
Now on a naked Stag in triumph born,
Was hung on high; and glitter'd from afar:
A trophy sacred to the God of war.
Above his arms, fix'd on the leafless wood,
Appear'd his plumy crest, besmear'd with blood;
His brazen buckler on the left was seen;
Trunchions of shiver'd lances hung between:
And on the right was plac'd his Corslet, bor'd,
And to the neck was ty'd his unavailing sword.

Mr. *Dryden*.

Fig. 18. On the next Medal you see the Peace that
Vespasian procured the Empire after having happily finished all its wars both at home and abroad. The woman
with the olive-branch in her hand is the figure of *Peace*.

> ————*pignora pacis*
> *Prætendens dextrâ ramum canentis olivæ.*Sil.It.Lib 3.

With the other hand she thrusts a lighted torch under
a heap of armour that lies by an Altar. This alludes to
a custom among the ancient *Romans* of gathering up the
armour that lay scattered on the field of battle, and burning it as an offering to one of their Deities. It is to this
custom that *Virgil* refers, and *Silius Italicus* has described
at large. *Qualis*

Qualis eram cùm primam aciem Præneste sub ipsâ
Stravi, scutorumque incendi victor acervos.

Virg. Æn. Lib. 8

Such as I was beneath *Præneste*'s walls ;
Then when I made the foremost foes retire,
And set whole heaps of conquer'd shields on fire.

Mr. Dryden.

Ast tibi, Bellipotens, Sacrum, constructus acervo
Ingenti mons armorum consurgit ad astra :
Ipse manu celsam pinum, flammâque comantem
Attollens, ductor Gradivum in vota ciebat :
Primitias pugnæ, et læti libamina belli,
Hannibal Ausonio cremat hæc de nomine victor.
Et tibi, Mars genitor, votorum haud surde meorum,
Arma electa dicat spirantum turba virorum.
Tum face conjectâ, populatur fervidus ignis
Flagrantem molem; et ruptâ caligine, in auras
Actus apex claro perfundit lumine campos. Sil. It. Li. 10.

To thee the Warrior-God, aloft in air ·
A mountain pile of *Roman* arms they rear:
The Gen'ral grasping in his Victor hand
A pine of stately growth, he wav'd the brand,
And cry'd, O *Mars !* to thee devote I yield
These choice first-fruits of Honour's purple field. ·
Join'd with the partners of my toil and praise,
Thy *Hannibal* this vow'd oblation pays ;
Grateful to thee for *Latian* laurels won :
Accept this homage, and absolve thy son.——
Then, to the pile the flaming torch he tost ;
In smould'ring smoke the light of Heav'n is lost :
But when the fire increase of fury gains,
The blaze of Glory gilds the distant plains.

Fig. 19, 20. As for the heap of Arms, and mountain
of Arms, that the Poet mentions, you may see them on
two Coins of *Marcus Aurelius.* DE SARMATIS and DE
GERMANIS allude perhaps to the form of words that
might be used at the setting fire to them——*Ausonio*
de nomine. Those who will not allow of the interpretation I have put on these two last Medals may think it

I 2

an

an objection that there is no torch or fire near them to fignify any fuch allufion.   But they may confider that on feveral Imperial Coins we meet with the figure of a funeral pile, without any thing to denote the burning of it, though indeed there is on fome of them a Flambeau fticking out on each fide, to let us know it was to be confumed to afhes.

You have been fo intent on the burning of the Arms, fays *Cynthio*, that you have forgotten the Pillar on your 18th Medal.   You may find the hiftory of it, fays *Philander*, in *Ovid de Faftis*.   It was from this Pillar that the fpear was toffed at the opening of a war, for which reafon the little figure on the top of it holds a fpear in its hand, and *Peace* turns her back upon it.

Profpicit à templo fummum brevis area Circum :
  Eft ibi non parvæ parva columna notæ :
Hinc folet hafta manu, belli prænuncia, mitti ;
  In regem et gentes cùm placet arma capi.

Ov. de faft. Lib. 6.

Where the high Fane the ample Cirque commands,
A little, but a noted pillar ftands,
From hence, when *Rome* the diftant Kings defies,
In form the war-denouncing Javelin flies.

Fig. 21.   The different interpretations that have been made on the next Medal feem to be forced and unnatural.   I will therefore give you my own opinion of it. The veffel is here reprefented as ftranded.   The figure before it feems to come into its affiftance, and to lift it off the fhallows : for we fee the water fcarce reaches up to the knees, though it is the figure of a man ftanding on firm ground.   His attendants, and the good office he is employed upon, refemble thofe the Poets often attribute to *Neptune*.   *Homer* tells us, that the Whales leaped up at their God's approach, as we fee in the Medal.   The two fmall figures that ftand naked among the waves are Sea-Deities of an inferiour rank, who are fuppofed to affift their Sovereign in the fuccour he gives the diftreffed veffel.

Cymo-

Cymothoë, fimul et Triton adnixus acuto
Detrudunt naves scopulo ; levat ipse tridenti,
Et vaftas aperit fyrtes, et temperat æquor.
Virg. Æn. Lib. 1.

Cymothoë, Triton, and the fea-green train
Of beauteous Nymphs, the daughter's of the main,
Clear from the rocks the veffels with their hands ;
The God himfelf with ready trident ftands,
And opes the deep, and fpreads the moving fands.
Mr. *Dryden:*

Jam placidis ratis extat aquis, quam gurgite ab imo
Et Thetis, et magnis Nereus focer erigit ulnis.
Val. Flac. Lib. 1.

The interpreters of this Medal have miftaken thefe two
figures for the reprefentation of two perfons that are
drowning. But as they are both naked and drawn in
a pofture rather of triumphing o'er the waves than
of finking under them, fo we fee abundance of Wa-
ter-Deities on other Medals reprefented after the fame
manner.

Ite Deæ virides, liquidofque advertite vultus,
Et vitreum teneris crinem redimite corymbis,
Vefte nihil tectæ : quales emergitis altis
Fontibus, et vifu Satyros torquetis amantes.
Statius de Balneo Etrufci. Lib. 1.

Hafte, hafte, ye *Naiads !* with attractive art
New charms to ev'ry native grace impart :
With op'ning flourets bind your fea-green hair,
Unveil'd ; and naked let your limbs appear :
So from the fprings the *Satyrs* fee you rife,
And drink eternal paffion at their eyes.

After having thus far cleared our way to the Medal, I
take the thought of the reverfe to be this. The ftranded
veffel is the Commonwealth of *Rome,* that by the tyranny
of *Domitian,* and the infolence of the *Prætorian* Guards
under *Nerva,* was quite run aground and in danger of
perifhing. Some of thofe embarked in it endeavour at
her recovery, but it is *Trajan* that by the adoption of
Nerva ftems the tide to her relief, and like another *Nep-*
tune fhoves her off the quick-fands. Your Device, fays
Eugenius,

Eugenius, hangs very well together; but is not it liable
to the same exceptions that you made us last night to
such explications as have nothing but the writers imagination to support them ? To shew you, says *Philander*,
that the construction I put on this Medal is conformable to the fancies of the old *Romans*, you may observe, that *Horace* represents at length the Commonwealth of *Rome* under the figure of a ship, in the Allegory that you meet with in the fourteenth Ode of
his first book.

> *O Navis, referent in mare te novi*
> *Flactus.* ———————

And shall the raging waves again
Bear thee back into the main ?   Mr. *Creech.*

Nor was any thing more usual than to represent a God in
the shape and dress of an Emperor.

> ———— *Apelleæ cuperent te scribere ceræ,*
> *Optassetque novo similem te ponere templo*
> *Atticus Elei senior Jovis ; et tua mitis*
> *Ora Taras : tua sidereas imitantia flammas*
> *Lumina, contempto mallet Rhodos aspera Phœbo.*
>
>   Statius de Equo Domitiani Syl. 1.

Now had *Apelles* liv'd, he'd sue to grace
His glowing Tablets with thy godlike face:
Phidias, a Sculptor for the Pow'rs above !
Had wish'd to place thee with his Iv'ry *Jove.*
Rhodes, and *Tarentum*, that with Pride survey,
The Thund'rer This, and That the God of day ;
Each fam'd *Colossus* wou'd exchange for Thee,
And own thy form the loveliest of the three.

For the thought in general, you have just the same me-
taphorical compliment to *Theodosius* in *Claudian*, as the
Medal here makes to *Trajan*.

> *Nulla relicta foret Romani nominis umbra,*
> *Ni pater ille tuus jamjam ruitura subisset*
> *Pondera, turbatamque ratem, certâque levasset*
> *Naufragium commune manu.* ————
>
>   Claudian. de 4to Consf. Honorii.

Had not thy Sire deferr'd th' impending fate,
And with his solid virtue prop'd the state ;

                                                  Sunk.

Sunk in Oblivion's fhade, the name of *Rome*,
An empty name! had fcarce furviv'd her doom:
Half-wreck'd fhe was, 'till his aufpicious hand
Refum'd the rudder, and 1egain'd the land.

I fhall only add, that this Medal was flamped in honour of *Trajan*, when he was only *Cæfar*, as appears by the face of it —— SARI TRAIANO.

Fig. 22. The next is a reverfe of *Marcus Aurelius.* We have on it a *Minerva* mounted on a monfter, that *Aufonius* defcribes in the following verfes.

Illa etiam Thalamos per trina ænigmata quærens
Qui bipes, et quadrupes foret, et tripes omnia folus;
Terruit Aoniam Volucris, Leo, Virgo; triformis
Sphinx, volucris pennis, pedibus fera, fronte puella.

To form the monfter *Sphinx*, a triple kind,
Man, bird, and beaft, by nature were combin'd:
With feather'd fans fhe wing'd th' aerial fpace;
And on her feet the Lion claws difgrace
The bloomy features of a Virgin-face.
O'er pale *Aonia* pannic horror ran,
While in myfterious fpeech fhe thus began:
" What Animal when yet the Morn is new,
" Walks on Four legs infirm; at Noon on Two:
" But day declining to the weftern fkies,
" He needs a Third; a Third the Night fupplies?

The monfter, fays *Cynthio*, is a Sphinx, but for her meaning on this Medal, I am not *OEdipus* enough to unriddle it. I muft confefs, fays *Philander*, the Poets fail me in this particular. There is however a paffage in *Paufanias* that I will repeat to you, though it is in profe, fince I know no body elfe that has explained the Medal by it. The *Athenians*, fays he, drew a Sphinx on the armour of *Pallas*, by reafon of the ftrength and fagacity of this animal. The Sphinx therefore fignifies the fame as *Minerva* herfelf, who was the Goddefs of arms as well as wifdom, and defcribes the Emperor as one of the Poets expreffes it, ——

—— *Studiis florentem utriufque Minervæ.*
Whom both *Minerva*'s boaft t' adopt their own.
The *Romans* joined both devices together, to make

I 4.   the

the emblem the more significant, as indeed they could not too much extol the learning and military virtues of this excellent Emperor, who was the best Philosopher and the greatest General of his Age.

Fig. 23. We will close up this Series of Medals with one that was stamped under *Tiberius* to the memory of *Augustus.* Over his head you see the star that his father *Julius Cæsar* was supposed to have been changed into.

Ecce Dionæi processit Cæsaris astrum. Virg. Ecl. 9.

See, *Cæsar's* lamp is lighted in the skies. Mr.*Dryden.*

————————*micat inter omnes*
Julium sidus, velut inter ignes
   Luna minores.   Hor.

————————*Julius Cæsar's* light appears
As, in fair nights and smiling skies,
The beauteous *Moon* amidst the meaner stars.

                          Mr. *Creech.*

Vix ea fatus erat, mediâ cùm sede senatûs
Constitit alma Venus, nulli cernenda, suique
Cæsaris eripuit membris, nec in aëra solvi
Passa recentem animam, cælestibus intulit astris.
Dumque tulit lumen capere atque ignescere sensit,
Emisitque sinu: Lunâ evolat altius illa,
Flammiferumque trahens spatioso limite crinem,
Stella micat.————————   Ov. Met. Lib. 15.

  This spoke; the Goddess to the Senate flew;
Where, her fair form conceal'd from mortal view,
Her *Cæsar's* heav'nly part she made her care,
Nor left the recent Soul to waste to air ;
But bore it upwards to its native skies :
Glowing with new-born fires she saw it rise;
Forth springing from her bosom up it flew,
And kindling, as it soar'd, a Comet grew ;
Above the lunar Sphere it took its flight,
And shot behind it a long trail of light. Mr. *Welsted:*
Virgil draws the same figure of *Augustus* on *Æneas's* shield as we see on this Medal. The Commentators tell us, that the star was engraven on *Augustus* helmet, but we may be sure *Virgil* means such a figure

                                  of

of the Emperor as he ufed to be reprefented by in the *Roman* fculpture, and fuch a one as we may fuppofe this to be that we have before us.

Hinc Auguftus agens Italos in prælia Cæfar,
Cum patribus, populoque, Penatibus, et magnis Diis,
Stans celfâ in puppi; geminas cui tempora flammas
Læta vomunt, patriumque aperitur vertice fidus.
Virg. Æn. Lib. 8.

Young *Cæfar* on the ftern in armour bright,
Here leads the *Romans*, and the Gods, to fight:
His beamy temples fhoot their flames afar:
And o'er his head is hung the *Julian* ftar.
Mr. *Dryden.*

The thunderbolt that lies by him is a mark of his Apotheofis, that makes him as it were a companion of *Jupiter.* Thus the Poets of his own age that deified him living.

Divifum Imperium cum Jove Cæfar habet.   Virg.
Hic focium fummo cum Jove numen habet.   Ov.
———*regit Auguftus focio per figna Tonante.*
Manil. Lib. 1.

Sed tibi debetur cœlum, te fulmine pollens,
Accipiet cupidi Regia magna Jovis.
Ov. de Auguflo ad Liviam.

He wears on his head the *Corona Radiata*, which at that time was another type of his Divinity. The fpikes that fhoot out from the crown were to reprefent the rays of the Sun. There were twelve of them, in allufion to the Signs of the *Zodiac*. It is this kind of crown that *Virgil* defcribes.

———*ingenti mole Latinus*
Quadrijugo vehitur curru, cui tempora circum
Aurati bis fex radii fulgentia cingunt,
Solis avi fpecimen———   Virg. Æn. Lib. 12.

Four fteeds the chariots of *Latinus* bear:
Twelve golden beams around his temples play,
To mark his lineage from the God of day.
Mr. *Dryden.*

Fig. 24. If you would know why the *corona radiata* is a reprefentation of the Sun, you may fee it in the figure of *Apollo* on the next reverfe, where his head

L 5

is encompassed with such an arch of glory as Ovid and Statius mention, that might be put on and taken off at pleasure.

——*at genitor circum caput omne micantes*
Deposuit radios——   Ovid. Met. Lib. 2.

The tender Sire was touch'd with what he said,
And flung the blaze of glories from his head.

Imposuitque comæ radios——   Ibid.

Then fix'd his beamy circle on his head.

——*licet ignipedum frænator equorum*
Ipse tuis alte radiantem crinibus arcum
Imprimat——

          Statius. Theb. Lib. 1. ad Domitian.

Tho' *Phœbus* longs to mix his rays with thine,
And in thy glories more serenely shine.   Mr. *Pope.*

In his right hand he holds the whip with which he is supposed to drive the horses of the Sun: as in a pretty passage of *Ovid*, that some of his editors must needs fancy spurious.

Colligit amentes, et adhuc terrore paventes,
Phœbus equos, stimuloque dolens et verbere sævit:
Sævit enim, natumque objectat, et imputat illis.

          Ov. Met. Lib. 2.

Prevail'd upon at length, again he took
The harness'd steeds that still with horrour shook,
And plies 'em with the lash, and whips 'em on,
And, as he whips, upbraids 'em with his son.

The double-pointed dart in his left hand is an emblem of his beams, that pierce through such an infinite depth of air, and enter into the very bowels of the earth. Accordingly *Lucretius* calls them the darts of the day, as *Ausonius* to make a sort of witticism has followed his example.

. *Non radii solis, neque lucida tela Diei.*   Lucr.

Exultant udæ super arida saxa rapinæ,
Luciferique pavent letalia tela Diei.

          De piscibus captis. Auf. Eid. 10.

Caligo terræ scinditur,
Percussa sola spiculo.   Prud. Hym. 2.

I have now given you a sample of such emblematical Medals as are unriddled by the *Latin* Poets, and have

have fhown feveral paffages in the *Latin* Poets that receive an illuftration from Medals. Some of the Coins we have had before us have not been explained by others, as many of them have been explained in a different manner. There are indeed others that have had very near the fame explication put upon them, but as this explication has been fupported by no authority, it can at beft be looked upon but as a probable conjecture. It is certain, fays *Eugenius*, there cannot be any more authentic illuftrations of *Roman* Medals, efpecially of thofe that are full of fancy, than fuch as are drawn out of the *Latin* Poets. For as there is a great affinity between Defigning and Poetry, fo the *Latin* Poets, and the Defigners of the *Roman* Medals, lived very near one another, were acquainted with the fame cuftoms, converfant with the fame objects, and bred up to the fame relifh for wit and fancy. But who are the Ladies that we are next to examine? Thefe are, fays *Philander*, fo many Cities, Nations and Provinces that prefent themfelves to you under the fhape of women. What you take for a fine Lady at firft fight, when you come to look into her will prove a town, a country, or one of the four parts of the world. In fhort, you have now *Afric*, *Spain*, *France*, *Italy*, and feveral other nations of the earth before you. This is one of the pleafanteft Maps, fays *Cynthio*, that I ever faw. Your Geographers now and then fancy a country like a Leg or a Head, a Bear or a Dragon, but I never before faw them reprefented like women. I could not have thought your mountains, feas and promontories could have made up an affembly of fuch well-fhaped perfons. This therefore, fays *Philander*, is a Geography peculiar to to the Medallifts. The Poets however have fometimes given into it, and furnifh us with very good lights for the explication of it. The *Third Series.* firft Lady you fee on the Lift is *Africa*. Fig. 1. She carries an Elephant's tooth by her fide.

Dentibus

Dentibus ex illis quos mittit porta Syenes,
Et Mauri celeres, et Mauro obscurior Indus :
Et quos deposuit Nabathæo bellua saltu,
Jam nimios, capitique graves———— Juv. Sat. 11.

She is always quoifl'd with the head of an Elephant,
to shew that this animal is the breed of that country, as
for the same reason she has a Dragon lying at her feet.

Huic varias pestes, diversaque membra ferarum,
Concessit bellis natura infesta futuris ;
Horrendos angues, habitataque membra veneno,
Et mortis partus, viventia crimina terræ ;
Et vastos Elephantes habet, sævosque Leones,
In pœnas fœcunda suas, parit horrida tellus.

                         Manil. Lib. 4. de Africâ.

Here Nature, angry with mankind, prepares
Strange monsters, instruments of future wars ;
Here Snakes, those Cells of poyson, take their birth,
Those living crimes and grievance of the earth ;
Fruitful in its own plagues, the desart shore
Hears Elephants, and frightful Lions roar. Mr. *Creech.*

Lucan in his description of the several noxious animals of
this country, mentions in particular the flying Dragon
that we see on this Medal.

Vos quoque, qui cunctis innoxia numina terris
Serpitis aurato nitidi fulgore dracones,
Pestiferos ardens facit Africa : ducitis altum
Aëra cum pennis, armentaque tota secuti
Rumpitis ingentes amplexi verbere tauros;
Nec tutus spatio est Elephas ; datis omnia letho :
Nec vobis opus est ad noxia fata veneno. Luc. Lib. 9.

And you, ye Dragōns 1 of the scaly race,
Whom glittering gold and shining armours grace,
In other nations harmless are you found,
Their guardian Genii and Protectors own'd ;
In *Afric* only are you fatal ; there,
On wide-expanded wings, sublime you rear
Your dreadful forms, and drive the yielding air,
The lowing Kine in droves you chace, and cull
Some master of the herd, some mighty Bull ;
Around his stubborn sides your tails you twist
By force compress, and burst his brawny chest.   Not

Not-Elephants are by their larger fize
Secure, but with the reft become your prize.
Refiftlefs in your Might, you all invade,
And for deftruction need not poifon's aid. Mr. *Rowe.*
The bull that appears on the other fide of the Dragon,
fhows us that *Africk* abounds in agriculture.

————————*tibi habe frumentum, Alledius inquit,*
O *Libye, disjunge boves, dum tubera mittas.* Juv. Sat. 5.
————————No more plough up the ground,
O *Libya,* where fuch mufhrooms can be found,
Alledius cries, but furnifh us with ftore
Of mufhrooms, and import thy corn no more.

Mr. Bowles.

This part of the world has always on Medals fomething
to denote her wonderful fruitfulnefs, as it was indeed the
great granary of *Italy.* In the two following figures,
the handful of wheat, the *Cornu-copiæ,* and bafket of
corn, are all emblems of the fame fignification.

Sed quâ fe campis fqualentibus Africa tendit,
Serpentum largo coquitur fœcunda veneno :
Felix quà pingues mitis plaga temperat agros ;
Nec Cerere Ennæà, Phario nec victa coluno. Sil. It. Li. 1.
Frumenti quantum metit Africa— Hor. Sat. 3. Lib. 2.
————*fegetes mirantur Iberas*
Horrea ; nec Libyæ fenferunt damna rebellis
Jam tranfalpinâ contenti meffe Quirites.

Claud. in Eutrop. Lib. 1.

Fig. 2. The Lion on the fecond Medal marks her out
for the

————*Leonum*
Arida nutrix. Hor.

Fig. 3. The Scorpion on the third is another of her
productions, as *Lucan* mentions it in particular, in the
long catalogue of her venomous animals.

————*quis fata putaret*
Scorpion, aut vires maturæ mortis habere ?
Ille minax nodis, et recto verbere fævus,
Tefte tulit cœlo victi decus Orionis. Luc. Lib. 9.
Who, that the Scorpion's infect form furveys,
Would think that ready Death his call obeys ?

Threat'-

Threat'ning he rears his knotty tail on high.
The vast *Orion* thus, he doom'd to die,
And fix'd him, his proud trophy, in the sky.   }

Mr. *Rowe.*

The three figures you have here shown us, says *Eugenius,*
give me an idea of a description or two in *Claudian,*
that I must confess I did not before know what to make
of. They represent *Africa* in the shape of a woman,
and certainly allude to the corn and head-dress that she
wears on old coins.

———*mediis apparet in astris*
Africa, rescissæ vestes, et spicea passim
Serta jacent, lacero crinales vertice dentes,
Et fractum pendebat ebur——   Claud. de Bel. Gild.

Next *Afric,* mounting to the blest Abodes,
Pensive approach'd the Synod of the Gods:
No arts of dress the weeping Dame adorn ;
Her garments rent, and wheaten garlands torn :
The fillets, grac'd with teeth in Ivory rows,
Broke and disorder'd dangle on her brows,

Tum spicis et dente comas illustris eburno,
Et calido rubicunda die, sic Africa satur.

Claud. de Conf. Stil. Lib. 2.

I think, says *Philander,* there is no question but the
Poet has copied out in his description the figure that
Africa made in ancient sculpture and painting. The
next before us is *Egypt.* Her basket of
Fig. 4.   wheat shows us the great fruitfulness of
the country, which is caused by the in-
undations of the *Nile.*

Syrtibus hinc Libycis tuta est Ægyptas : at inde
Gurgite septeno rapidus mare summovit amnis :
Terra suis contenta bonis, non indiga mercis,
Aut Jovis ; in solo tanta est fiducia Nilo.   Luc. Lib.8.

By nature strengthned with a dang'rous strand,
Her Syrts and untry'd channels guard the land.
Rich in the fatness of her plenteous soil,
She plants her only confidence in *Nile.*   Mr. *Rowe.*

The instrument in her hand is the *Sistrum* of the *Ægyp-*
tians, made use of in the worship of the Goddess *Isis.*

———*Nilo*

——*Nilotica fiftris*
Rica fonat—— Claud. de. 4*to* Conf. Honor.
On Medals you fee it in the hand of *Ægypt*, of *Ifis*, or
any of her. Worfhippers. The Poets too make the fame
ufe of it, as *Virgil* has placed. it .in *Cleopatria*'s hand, to
diftinguifh her from an *Egyptian.*
Regina in mediis patrio vocat agmina fiftro.
Virg. Æn. Lib..8.
The Queen her felf, amidft the loud alarms,
With Cymbals tofs'd, her fainting foldiers warms.
Mr. *Dryden.*

————*reftabant Actia bella*;
*Atque ipfa Ifiaco certârunt fulmina fiftro.*Manil.Lib.1..
————*imitataque Lunam*
Cornua fulferunt, crepuitque fonabile fiftrum.
De Ifide. Ov. Met. Lib. 9.
————The lunar horns, that bind
The brows of *Ifis*, caft a blaze around ;.
The trembling Timbrel made a murm'ring found.
Mr. *Dryden*

*Quid tua nunc Ifis tibi, Delia? quid mihi profunt
Illa tuâ toties æra repulfa manu?* Tib. Lib. 1. El..3.
*Nos in templa tuam Romana accepimus Ifin,
Semideofque canes, et fiftra jubentia luctus.* Luc. Lib. 8.
Have we with honours dead *Ofris* crown'd,
And mourn'd him to the Timbrel's tinkling found?
Receiv'd her *Ifis* to divine abodes,
And rank'd her dogs deform'd, with *Roman* Gods?
Mr. *Rowe.*

The bird before her is the *Egyptian Ibis.* This figure
however does not reprefent the living bird, but rather
an idol of it, as one may guefs by the pedeftal it ftands
upon, for the *Egyptians.* worfhipped it as a God.
*Quis nefcit, Volufi Bithynice, qualia demens·
Ægyptus portenta colat? crocodilon adorat
Pars hæc, illa pavet.faturam ferpentibus Ibin*:
Effigies facri nitet aurea-Circopitheci Juv..Sat. 15.
How *Egypt*, mad with fuperftition grown,.
Makes· Gods of monfters, but too .well is known :

One

One sect devotion to *Nile*'s serpent pays ;
Others to *Ibis*, that on serpents preys.
Where *Thebes*, thy hundred gates lie unrepair'd,
And where maim'd *Memnon*'s magic harp is heard,
Where these are mould'ring left, the sots combine
With pious care a Monkey to enshrine.   Mr. *Tate*.

Venerem precaris? comprecare et Simiam.
Placet sacratus. aspis Æsculapii?
Crocodilus, Ibis et Canes cur displicent?

Prudentius. Pas. 1. Romani.

Fig. 5. We have *Mauritania* on the fifth Medal, leading a horse with something like a thread, for where there is a bridle in old Coins you see it much more distinctly. In her other hand she holds a switch. We have the design of this Medal in the following descriptions that celebrate the *Moors* and *Numidians*, Inhabitants of *Mauritania*, for their horsemanship.

Hic passim exultant Numidæ, gens inscia fræni :
Queis inter geminas per ludum mobillis aures
Quadrupedum flectit non cedens virga lupatis :
Altrix bellorum bellatorumque virorum,
Tellus———— ————   Sil. It. Li. 4.

On his hot Steed unus'd to curb or rein,
The black *Numidian* prances o'er the plain :
A wand betwixt his ears directs the course,
And as a bridle turns th' obedient horse.

————an Mauri fremitum raucosque repulsus.
Umbonum et nostros passuri, comminus enses ?
Non contra clypeis tectos, galeisque micantes
Ibitis ; in solis longè fiducia telis.
Exarmatus erit, cum missile torserit, hostis.
Dextra movet jaculum, prætentat pallia lævâ;
Cætera nudus Eques ; sonipes ignarus habenæ :
Virga regit, non ulla fides non agminis ordo;
Arma oneri———— ————   Claud. de Bel. Gildon.

Can *Moors* sustain the press, in close-fought fields,
Of shorten'd Faulchions, and repelling shields?
Against a host of quiv'ring spears ye go,
Nor helm nor buckler guards the naked foe :

The

The naked foe, who vainly trufts his art,.
And flings away his armour in his dart :
His dart the right hand fhakes, the left uprears
His robe, beneath his tender fkin appears.
Their Steeds un-rein'd, obey the horfeman's wand, '
Nor know their legions when to march, or ftand :
In the war's dreadful laws untaught and rude,.
A mob of men, a martial multitude.

The horfe too may ftand as an emblem of the warlike genius of the people.

Bello armantur Equi, bella hæc armenta minantur. ‚
Virg. Æn. Lib. 3.

Fig. 6. From *Africa* we will crofs over into *Spain.*
There are learned Medallifts, that tell us, the Rabbet which you fee before her feet, may fignifie either the great multitude of thefe Animals that are found in *Spain,* or perhaps the feveral mines that are wrought within. the bowels of that country, the *Latin* word *Cuniculus* fignifying either a Rabbet or a Mine. But thefe Gentlemen do not confider, that it-is not the Word but the Figure that appears on the Medal. *Cuniculus* may ftand for a Rabbet or a Mine, but the picture of a Rabbet is not the picture of a Mine. A pun can be no more engraven than it can be tranflated. When the word is conftrued into its idea the double meaning vanifhes. The figure therefore before us means a real Rabbet, which is there found in vaft multitudes.

Cuniculofæ Celtiberiæ fili.   Catul. in Egnatium.

The Olive-branch tells us, it is a country that abounds in Olives, as it is for this reafon that *Claudian* in his defcription of *Spain* binds an Olive-branch about her head.

——*glaucis tum prima Minervæ*
Nexa comam foliis, fulváque intexta micantem
Vefte Tagum, tales profert Hifpania voces.
Claud. de Laud. Stil. Li. 2.

Thus *Spain,* whofe brows the olive wreaths infold,
And o'er her robe a *Tagus* ftreams in gold.

Martial has given us the like figure of one of the greateft rivers in *Spain.*
Bætus

Bætis oliv_iferâ crinem redimite coronà,
   Aurea qui nitidis vellera tingis aquis :
Quem Bromius quem Pallas amat.— Mar.l.12.Ep.99.
Fair *Bætis !* Olives wreath thy azure locks ;
In fleecy gold thou cloath'st the neighb'ring flocks :
Thy fruitful banks with rival bounty smile,
While *Bacchus* wine bestows, and *Pallas* oil.
And *Prudentius* of one of its eminent towns.

Tu decem sanctos revehes et octo,
Cæsar Augusta studiosa Christi,
Verticem flavis oleis revincta
   Pacis honore.   Prud. Hymn. 4.

Fig. 7. France, you see, has a sheep by her, not
only as a sacrifice, but to shew that the riches of the
country consisted chiefly in flocks and pasturage. Thus
Horace mentioning the commodities of different countries,

Quanquam nec Calabræ mella ferunt apes,
Nec Læstrigonià Bacchus in amphorà
Languescit mihi, nec pinguia Gallicis
   Crescunt vellera pascuis.   Hor. Od. 16. Li. 3.
Tho' no *Calabrian* Bees do give
Their grateful tribute to my hive ;
No wines, by rich *Campania* sent,
In my ignoble casks ferment ;
No flocks in *Gallic* plains grow fat ;— Mr. *Creech.*
She carries on her shoulders the *Sagulum* that *Virgil*
speaks of as the habit of the ancient *Gauls.*

Aurea cæsaries ollis, atque aurea vestis :
Virgatis lucent sagulis——   Virg. Æn. Lib. 8.
The gold dissembled well their yellow hair ;
And golden chains on their white necks they wear ;
Gold are their vests——   Mr. *Dryden.*
She is drawn in a posture of sacrificing for the safe arrival of the Emperor, as we may learn from the inscription. We find in the several Medals that were
struck on *Adrian*'s progress through the Empire, that at
his arrival they offered a sacrifice to the Gods for the
reception of so great a blessing. *Horace* mentions this
custom.

Tum

S

1

FELIX ADVENTAVGGNN

CIIII

P·E·N

3

AFRICA

R I C

S C A

S C

O S

5

MAVRETANIA

S C

C 4

Tum meæ (ʃi quid loquar audiendum)
Vocis accedet bona pars: et O S°l
Pulcher, ó laudande, canam, recepto
          Cæʃare felix.————
Te decem tauri, totidemque vaccæ;
Me tener ʃolvet vitulus————   Hor. Od. 2. Lib. 4.
And there, if any patient ear
My Muʃe's feeble ʃong will hear,
     My voice ʃhall ʃound thro' *Rome:*
Thee, Sun, I'll ʃing thee, lovely fair,
     Thee, thee I'll praiʃe, when *Cæʃar*'s come.————
Ten large fair bulls, ten luʃty cows,
Muʃt die, to pay thy richer vows;
     Of my ʃmall ʃtock of kine
A calf juʃt wean'd————   Mr. *Creech.*
Fig. 8. *Italy* has a *Cornu-copiæ* in her hand, to de-
note her fruitfulneʃs.
————*magna parens frugum Saturnia tellus.* Virg.Geor.3.
a crown of towers on her head, to figure out the many
towns and cities that ʃtand upon her. *Lucan* has given
her the like ornament, where he repreʃents her addreʃ-
ʃing her ʃelf to *Julius Cæʃar.*
     Inʒens viʃa duci patriæ trepidantis Imago:
     Clara per obʃcuram vultu mæʃtiʃʃima noctem,
     Turrigero canos effundens vertice crines,
     Cæʃarie lacerà, nudiʃque adʃtare lacertis,
     Et Gemitu permiʃta loqui————   Lucan. Lib. 1.
Amidʃt the duʃky horrors of the night,
A wondrous viʃion ʃtood confeʃt to ʃight;
Her awful head *Rome*'s rev'rend image rear'd,
Trembling and ʃad the Matron form appear'd;
A tow'ry crown her hoary temples bound,
And her torn treʃʃes rudely hung around:
Her naked arms uplifted e're ʃhe ʃpoke,
Then groaning thus the mournful ʃilence broke.
          Mr. *Rowe.*
She holds a ʃcepter in her other hand, and ʃits on a
globe of the heavens, to ʃhew that ʃhe is the Sovereign
of nations, and that all the influences of the Sun and
                              Stars.

Stars fall on her dominions. *Claudian* makes the same compliment to *Rome.*

Ipsa triumphatis quæ possidet æthera regnis.

          - Claud. in Prob. et Olyb. Conf.

Jupiter arce suâ totum dum spectat in orbem,
Nil nisi Romanum quod tueatur habet.

          Ov. de fast. lib. 1

Jove finds no realm, when he the globe surveys,
But what to *Rome* submissive homage pays.

Orbem jam totum victor Romanus habebat,
Quà mare, quà tellus, quà sidus currit utrumque. Pet.

Now *Rome*, sole Empress, reigns from pole to pole,
Where ever earth extends, or oceans roll.

Fig. 9. The picture that *Claudian* makes of *Rome* one would think was copied from the next Medal.

———*innuptæ ritus imitata Minervæ:*
Nam neque cæsarium crinali stringere cultu,
Colla nec ornatu patitur mollire retorto:
Dextrum nuda latus, niveos exerta lacertos,
Audacem retegit mammam, laxumque coërcens
Mordet gemma sinum————
Clipeus Titana lucessit
Lumine, quem totà variarat Mulciber arte;
Hîc patrius, Mavortis amor, fœtusque notantur
Romulei, post amnis inest, et bellua nutrix.

          Claud. in Prob. et Olyb. Conf.

No costly fillets knot her hair behind,
Nor female trinkets round her neck are twin'd.
Bold on the right her naked arm she shows,
And half the bosom's unpolluted snows;
Whilst on the left is buckled o'er her breast,
In diamond clasps the military vest,
The Sun was dazled as her shield she rear'd,
Where, varied o'er by *Mulciber*, appear'd
The loves of *Mars* her Sire, fair *Ilia*'s joys,
The wolf, the *Tyber*, and the infant boys.

Fig. 10. The next figure is *Achaia.*

I am sorry, says *Cynthio*, to find you running farther off us. I was in hopes you would have shown us our own nation, when you were so near us as *France.*

                                 I

I have here, says *Philander*, one of *Au-gustus's Britania's*.   You see she is not   *Fig.* 11.
drawn like other countries, in a soft
peaceful posture, but is adorned with emblems that
mark out the military genius of her Inhabitants.   This
is, I think the only commendable quality that the old
Poets have touched upon in the description of our country.   I had once made a collection of all the passages
in the *Latin* Poets, that give any account of us, but I
find them so very malicious, that it would look like a
libel on the nation to repeat them to you.   We seldom
meet with our Forefathers, but they are coupled with
some epithet or another to blacken them.   Barbarous,
Cruel and Inhospitable are the best terms they can af-
ford us, which it would be a kind of injustice to publish
since their posterity are become so polite, good-natured,
and kind to strangers.   To mention therefore those parts
only that relate to the present Medal.   She sits on a globe
that stands in water, to denote that she is Mistress of a
new world, separate from that which the *Romans* had
before conquered, by the interposition of the sea.   I
think we cannot doubt of this interpretation, if we
consider how she has been represented by the ancient
Poets.

Et penitus toto divisos, orbe Britannos.   Virg. Ec. 1.
The rest among the *Britons* be confin'd ;
A race of men from all the world disjoin'd. Mr.*Dryden.*
Adspice, confundit populos impervia tellus :
　Conjunctum, est, quod adhuc orbis, et orbis erat.
　　　　　　　Vt. Poet. apud Scalig. Catul.
At nunc oceanus geminos interluit orbes.
　　　　Id. de Britannia et opposito Continente.
———*nostro diducto Britannia mundo.*　　　Claud.
Nec stetit oceano, remisque ingressa profundum,
Vincendos alio quæsivit in orbe Britannos.　　　Id.
The feet of *Britannia* are wash'd by the waves, in the
same Poet.

———*cujus vestigia verrit*
Cærulus, oceanique æstum mentitur, amictus.
　　　　　　　Id. de Laud: Stil. Lib. 2.

She

She bears a *Roman* Ensign in one of her hands, to confess herself a conquered province.

> —————————————*victricia Cæsar*
> *Signa Caledonios transvexit ad usque Britannos.*
>
> Sidon. Apollin.

Fig. 10 But to return to *Achaia,* whom we left upon her knees before the Emperor *Adrian.* She has a pot before her with a sprig of Parsly rising out of it. I will not here trouble you with a dull story of *Hercules's* eating a sallade of Parsly for his refreshment, after his encounter with the *Nemean* Lion. It is certain, there were in *Achaia* the *Nemean* Games, and that a garland of Parsly was the Victor's reward. You have an account of these Games in *Ausonius.*

> *Quatuor antiquos celebravit Achäia Ludos,*
>   *Cælicolum duo sunt, et duo festa hominum.*
> *Sacra Jovis, Phœbique, Palæmonis, Archemorique:*
>   *Serta quibus pinus, malus, oliva, apium.*
>
> Auf. de Lustral. Agon.

Grecee, in four games thy martial youth were train'd;
For Heroes two, and two for Gods ordain'd:
Jove bade the Olive round his Victor wave;
Phœbus to his an Apple-garland gave:
The Pine, *Palæmon*; nor with less renown,
Archemorus conferr'd the Parsly-crown.

> *Archemori Nemeæ colunt funebria Thebæ.* Id de locis Ag.
> —*Alcides Nemeæ sacravit honorem.* de Auct. Agon. Id.
> *Archemori Nemeæ colunt funebria Thebæ.*   Id.

One reason why they chose Parsly for a Garland, was doubtless because it always preserves its verdure, as *Horace* opposes it to the short liv'd Lilly.

> *Neu vivax apium, nec breve lilium.* Lib. 1. Od. 36.

Let fading Lillies and the Rose
Their beauty, and their smell disclose;
Let long-liv'd Parsly grace the feast,
And gently cool the heated guest.   Mr. *Creech.*

Juvenal mentions the Crown that was made of it, and which here surrounds the head of *Achaia.*

> —————*Graiæque apium meruisse coronæ.*   Juv. Sat. 8.

And winning at a Wake their Parsly crown. M. *Stepeny*

She presents herself to the Emperor in the same posture

ſture that the *Germans* and *Engliſh* ſtill ſalute the Imperial and Royal family.

————*jus imperiumque Phraates*
Cæſaris accepit genibus minor.—— Hor.Epiſt.1 2.Lib.1.
The haughty *Parthian* now to *Cæſar* kneels. M.*Creech.*
Ille qui donat diadema fronti
Quem genu nixæ tremuere gentes. Senec.Thyeſt. Act.3.
————*Non ut inflexo genu,*
Regnantem adores, petimus.   Idem.
Te linguis variæ gentes, miſſique rogatum
Fœdera Perſarum proceres cum patre ſedentem,
Hac quondam videre domo poſitaque tiara
Submiſere genu.————   Claud. ad Honorium.
Thy infant Virtue various climes admir'd,
And various tongues to ſound thy praiſe conſpir'd :
Thee next the Sovereign ſeat, the *Perſians* view'd,
When in this Regal Dome for peace they ſu'd :
Each Turban low, in ſign of worſhip, wav'd ;
And every knee confeſt the boon they crav'd.

Fig, 1 2. *Sicily* appears before *Adrian* in the ſame
poſture. She has a bundle of Corn in her hand, and
a Garland of it on her head, as ſhe abounds in wheat,
and was conſecrated to *Ceres.*
Utraque frugiferis eſt Inſula nobilis arvis:
Nec plus Heſperiam longinquis meſſibus ullæ,
Nec Romana magis complerunt horrea terræ.
                    De Sicilia et Sardinia. Lu. Lib. 2.
Sardinia too, renown'd for yellow fields,
With *Sicily* her bounteous tribute yields ?
No lands a glebe of richer tillage boaſt,
Nor waft more plenty to the *Roman* coaſt. Mr. *Rowe.*
Terra tribus ſcopulis vatum procurrit in æquor
    Trinacris, à poſitu nomen adepta loci,
Grata domus Cereri, multas ibi poſſidet urbes :
    In quibus eſt culto fertilis Henna ſolo. Ov.deFaſt.li.4.
To *Ceres* dear, the fruitful land is fam'd
For three tall Capes, and thence *Trinacria* nam'd :
There *Henna* well rewards the tiller's toil,
The faireſt Champian of the faireſt Iſle.

Fig. 1 3. We find *Judæa* on ſeveral coins of *Veſpa-*
ſian and *Titus,* in a poſture that denotes ſorrow and
                            captivity.

captivity. The first figure of her is drawn to the life, in a picture that *Seneca* has given us of the *Trojan* matrons bewailing their captivity.

—————*paret exertos*
Turba lacertos. Veste remissâ
Substringe sinus, uteroque tenus
Pateant artus———————

—————*cadat ex humeris*
Vestis apertis: imumque tegat
Suffulta latas, jam nuda vocant
Pectora dextras, nunc nunc vires
Exprome, Dolor, tuas.
  Hecuba ad Trojanarum chorum. Sen. Troas. Act. 1.
—————————————Bare
Your arms, your vestures slackly ty'd
Beneath your naked bosoms, slide
Down to your wastes———————
—————————————Let
From your divested shoulders slide
Your garments, down on either side.
Now bared bosoms call for blows,
Now, Sorrow, all thy pow'rs disclose. Sir *Ed. Sherburn.*
—————*apertæ pectora matres*
Significant luctum——————   Ov. Met. Li. 13.
Who bar'd their breasts, and gave their hair to flow:
The signs of grief, and mark of publick woe.
The head is veil'd in both figures, as another expression of grief.

—————*ipsa tristi vestis obtentu caput*
Velata, juxta præsides astat Deos. Sen. Herc. Act. 2.
Sic ubi fata, caput ferali obducit amictu,
Decrevitque pati tenebras, puppisque cavernis
Delituit: sævumque arctè complexa dolorem
Perfruitur lacrymis, et amat pro conjuge luctum.
                    Luc. Li. 9. de Corneliâ.
 So said the Matron; and about her head
 Her veil she draws, her mournful eyes to shade;
 Resolv'd to shroud in thickest shades her woe,
 She seeks the ship's deep darksome Hold below:

                              There

There lonely left, at leifure to complain,
She hugs her forrows, and enjoys her pain;
Still with frefh tears the living grief wou'd feed,
And fondly loves it, in her hufband's ftead. Mr. *Rowe.*

I need not mention her fitting on the ground, becaufe
we have already fpoken of the aptnefs of fuch a pofture
to reprefent an extreme affliction.   I fancy, fays *Eu-genius,* the *Romans* might have an eye on the cuftoms
of the *Jewifh* nation, as well as of thofe of their coun-try; in the feveral marks of forrow they have fet on
this figure.   The Pfalmift defcribes the *Jews* lamen-ting their captivity in the fame penfive pofture.   *By
the waters of* Babylon *we fat down and wept, when
we remembred thee, O* Sion.   But what is more remark-able, we find *Judæa* reprefented as a woman in for-row fitting on the ground, in a paffage of the Prophet,
that foretells the very captivity recorded on this Me-dal.   The covering of the head, and the rending of
garments, we find very often in Holy Scripture, as the
expreffions of a raging grief.   But what is the tree we
fee on both thefe Medals? We find, fays *Philander,*
not only on thefe, but on feveral other coins that re-late to *Judæa,* the figure of a Palm-tree, to fhow us
that Palms are the growth of the country.   Thus *Si-lius Italicus,* fpeaking of *Vefpafian's* conqueft, that is
the fubject of this Medal.

Palmiferamque fenex bello domitabit Idumen. Sil.It.li.3.

Martial feems to have hinted at the many pieces of
painting and fculpture that were occafioned by this
conqueft of *Judæa,* and had generally fomething of
the Palm-tree in them.   It begins an Epigram on the
death of *Scorpus* a chariot-driver, which in thofe de-generate times of the Empire was look'd upon as a pub-lic calamity.

Triftis Idumæas frangat Victoria palmas;
　　Plange Favour fæva pectora nuda manu.

　　　　　　　　Mart. Lib. 10. Epig. 50.

The man by the Palm-tree in the firft of thefe Medals,
is fuppofed to be a *Jew* with his hands bound behind
him.

Fig. 14. I need not tell you that the winged figure on the other Medal is a *Victory*. She is reprefented here as on many other coins, writing fomething on a fhield. We find this way of regiftring a *Victory* touched upon in *Virgil,* and *Silius Italicus.*

Ære cavo clypeum, magni gestamen Abantis,
Postibus adverfis figo, et rem carmine figno ;
Æneas hæc de Danaïs victoribus arma. Vir. Æn.Li.3.

I fix'd upon the Temple's lofty door
The brazen fheld, which vanquifh'd *Abas* bore:
The verfe beneath my name and actions fpeaks,
" Thefe arms *Æneas* took from conqu'ring *Greeks.*

Mr. Dryden.

Pyrenes tumulo clypeum cum carmine figunt ;
Hafdrubalis fpolium Gradivo Scipio victor.

Sil. Ital. Lib. 15.

High on *Pyrene's* airy top they plac'd,
The captive Shield, with this infcription grac'd :
" Sacred to *Mars,* thefe votive fpoils proclaim
" The fate of *Afdrubal,* and *Scipio's* fame.

Fig. 15. *Parthia* has on one fide of her the Bow and Quiver which are fo much talked of by the Poets. *Lucan's* account of the *Parthians* is very pretty and poetical.

——*Parthoque fequente*
Murus erit, quodcunque poteft obstare fagittæ——
Illita tela dolis, nec Martem comminus unquam
Aufa pati virtus, fed longè tendere nervos,
Et, quo ferre, velint, permittere vulnera ventis.

Luc. 1. 8.

Each fence, that can their winged fhafts endure,
Stands, like a fort, impregñable, fecure——
To taint their coward darts is all their care,
And then to truft them to the flitting air. Mr. *Rowe.*

——*Sagittiferofque Parthos.* Catul.

The Crown fhe holds in her hand, refers to the crown of gold that *Parthio,* as well as other provinces, prefented to the Emperor *Antonine.* The prefenting a Crown, was the giving up the fovereignty into his hands.

Ipfe oratores ad me, regnique coronam,
Cum fceptro mifit—— Vir. Æn. Li. 8.

Tarchon

Tarchon the *Tuscan* Chief to me has sent
Their Crown, and ev'ry regal ornament. Mr. *Dryden.*

Fig. 16. *Antioch* has an Anchor by her, in memory of her founder *Seleucus,* whose race was all born
with this mark upon them, if you'll believe Historians.
Ausonius has taken notice of it in his verses on this
city.

——————————*Illa Seleucum*
Nuncupat ingenuum, cujus fuit Anchora signum,
Qualis inusta solet ; generis nota certa, per omnem
Nam sobolis seriem nativa cucurrit imago.
Auf. Ordo Nobil Urbium.

Thee, great *Seleucus,* bright in *Grecian* fame !
The tow'rs of *Antioch* for their founder claim :
Thee *Phœbus* at thy birth his son confest,
By the fair Anchor on the babe imprest ;
Which all thy genuine off-spring wont to grace,
From thigh to thigh transmissive thro' the race.

Fig. 17. *Smyrna* is always represented by an *A-
mazon,* that is said to have been her first foundress. You
see her here entring into a league with *Thyatira.* Each
of them holds her tutelar Deity in her hand.

Jus ille, et icti fœderis testes Deos
Invocat———————— Sen. Phæniffæ. Act. 1.

On the left arm of *Smyrna,* the *Pelta* or Buckler of
the *Amazons,* as the long weapon by her is the *Bipennis*
or *Securis.*

Non tibi Amazonia est pro me sumenda securis,
Aut excisa levi pelta gerenda manu.
Ov. Li. 3. Epist. 1. ex Pont.

Lunatis agmina peltis. Virg.
In their right hands a pointed Dart they wield ;
The left, for ward, sustains the lunar Shield.
Mr. *Dryden.*

Videre Rhœti bella sub Alpibus
Drusum gerentem, et Vindelici quibus ;
 Mos unde deductus per omne
  Tempus Amazonia securi
Dextras obarmet quærere distuli. Hor. Od. 4. Li 4.

K 2
Such

Such *Drusus* did in arms appear,
When near the *Alps* he urg'd the war;
In vain the *Rhæti* did their axes wield,
Like *Amazons* they fought, like women fled the
    field:
But why thofe favage troops this weapon chufe,
Confirm'd by long eftablifh'd ufe,
Hiftorians would in vain difclofe.

Fig. 18. The drefs.that *Arabia* appears in, brings to
my mind the defcription *Lucan* has made of thofe eaftern nations.

> *Quicquid ad Eoos tractus, mundique teporem*
> *Labitur, emollit gentes clementia cœli.*
> *Illic et laxas veftes, et fluxa virorum*
> *Velamenta vides.———*   Luc. Lib. 8.

While *Afia*'s fofter climate, form'd to pleafe,
Diffolves her fons in indolence and eafe.
Her filken robes inveft unmanly limbs,
And in long trains the flowing Purple ftreams.

                         Mr. *Rowe.*

She bears in one hand a fprig of frankincenfe.

> ———*folis eft thurea virga Sabeis.*   Virg.

And od'rous frankincenfe on the *Sabæan* bough.

                        Mr. *Dryden.*

Thuriferos Arabum faltus. Claud. de 3. Conf. Honor.
Thurilegos Arabas———   Ov. de Faf. Lib. 4.

In the other hand you fee the perfumed reed, as the garland on her head may be fuppofed to be woven out of
fome other part of her fragrant productions.

> *Nec procul in molles Arabas terramque ferentem*
> *Delicias, variæque novos radicis honores;*
> *Leniter adfundit gemmantia littora pontus,*
> *Et terræ mare nomen habet———*

        De finu Arabico. Manil. Lib. 4.

More weft the other foft *Arabia* beats,
Where incenfe grows, and pleafing odour fweats:
The Bay is call'd th' *Arabian* gulf; the name
The country gives it, and 'tis great in fame.

                        Mr. *Creech.*

Urantur

Urantur pia thura focis, urantur odores,
Quos tener à terrâ divite mittit Arabs. ·
Tibul. Lib. 2. El. 2.

——————————*fit dives amomo,*
Cinnamaque, coſtumque ſuam, ſudataque ligno
Thura ferat, floreſque alios Panchaïa tellus,
Dum ferat et Myrrham.
Ov. Met. Lib. 10.

Let *Araby* extol her happy coaſt,
Her Cinamon, and ſweet *Amomum* boaſt,
Her fragrant flowers, her trees with precious tears,
Her ſecond harveſts, and her double Years:
How can the land be call'd ſo bleſs'd, that *Myrrha*
    bears?
Mr. Dryden.

——*Odoratæ ſpirant medicamina Sylvæ.*   Manil.
The trees drop balſam, and on all the boughs
Health ſits, and makes it ſovereign as it flows.
Mr. Creech.

Cinnami ſylvas Arabes beatos
 Vidit.——
Sen. OEdip. Act. 1.

What a delicious country is this, ſays *Cynthio?* a man
almoſt ſmells it in the deſcriptions that are made of it.
The Camel is in *Arabia*, I ſuppoſe, a beaſt of burden,
that helps to carry off its ſpices. We find the Camel,
ſays *Philander*, mentioned in *Perſius* on the ſame account.

 Tolle recens primus piper è ſitiente Camelo. Perſ. Sat. 5.
——————The precious weight
Of pepper, and *Sabæan* incenſe, take
With thy own hands, from the tir'd Camel's back.
Mr. Dryden.

He loads the Camel with pepper, becauſe the animal
and its cargo are both the productions of the ſame
country.

 Mercibus hic Italis mutat ſub ſole recenti
 Rugoſum piper   ·
Id. Sat. 5.
The greedy Merchants, led by lucre run
To the parch'd *Indies* and the riſing Sun.

K 3
From

From thence hot pepper, and rich drugs they bear,
Bart'ring for spices their *Italian* ware.   Mr. *Dryden*.

You have given us some quotations out of *Persius* this morning, says *Eugenius*, that in my opinion have a great deal of poetry in them. I have often wondered at Mr. *Dryden* for passing so severe a censure on this Author. He fancies the description of a Wreck that you have already cited, is too good for *Persius*, and that he might be helpt in it by *Lucan*, who was one of his contemporaries. For my part, says *Cynthio*, I am so far from Mr. *Dryden*'s opinion in this particular, that I fancy *Persius* a better Poet than *Lucan*: and that had he been engaged on the same subject, he would at least in his Expressions and Descriptions have out-writ the *Pharsalia*. He was indeed employ'd on subjects that seldom led him into any thing like Description, but where he has an occasion of shewing himself, we find very few of the *Latin* Poets that have given a greater beauty to their Expressions. His obscurities are indeed sometimes affected, but they generally arise from the remoteness of the Customs, Persons and Things he alludes to: as Satyr is for this reason more difficult to be understood by those that are not of the same Age with it, than any other kind of Poetry. Love-verses and Heroics deal in Images that are ever fixed and settled in the nature of things, but a thousand ideas enter into Satyr, that are as changeable and unsteady as the mode or the humours of mankind.

Our three friends had passed away the whole morning among their Medals and *Latin* Poets. *Philander* told them it was now too late to enter on another Series, but if they would take up with such a Dinner as he could meet with at his Lodgings he would afterwards lay the rest of his Medals before them. *Cynthio* and *Eugenius* were both of them so well pleased with the novelty of the subject, that they would not refuse the offer *Philander* made them.

DIA-

DIALOGUE III.

—*caufa eft difcriminis hujus
Concifum Argentum in titulos faciefque
minutas.* Juv. Sat. 14.

A PARALLEL between the Ancient and Modern MEDALS.

PHILANDER ufed every morning to take a
walk in the neighbouring wood, that ftood on the
borders of the *Thames.* It was cut through by abundance
of beautiful alleys, which terminating on the water,
looked like fo many painted views in perfpective. The
banks of the river and the thicknefs of the fhades drew
into them all the birds of the country, that at Sun-
rifing filled the wood with fuch a variety of notes,
as made the prettieft confufion imaginable. I know in
defcriptions of this nature the fcenes are generally
fuppofed to grow out of the Author's imagination;
and if they are not charming in all their parts, the Reader never imputes it to the want of fun or foil, but
to the Writer's barrennefs of invention. It is *Cicero's*
obfervation on the Plane-tree, that makes fo flourifhing a figure in one of *Plato's* Dialogues, that it did
not draw its nourifhment from the fountain that ran
by it and watered its roots, but from the richnefs of

K 4   the

the ftile that defcribes it. For my own part, as I defign only to fix the fcene of the following Dialogue, I
fhall not endeavour to give it any other ornaments than
thofe which nature has beftowed upon it.

Philander was here enjoying the cool of the morning, among the dews that lay on every thing about
him, and that gave the air fuch a frefhnefs as is not
a little agreeable in the hot part of the year. He had
not been here long before he was joined by *Cynthio*
and *Eugenius*. *Cynthio* immediately fell upon *Philander* for breaking his night's reft. You have fo filled
my head, fays he, with old Coins, that I have had
nothing but figures and infcriptions before my eyes.
If I chanced to fall into a little flumber, it was immediately interrupted with the vifion of a *Caduceus* or
a *Cornu-copiæ*. You will make me believe, fays *Philander*, that you begin to be reconciled to Medals. They
fay it is a fure fign a man loves money, when he is
ufed to find it in his dreams. There is certainly, fays
Eugenius, fomething like Avarice in the ftudy of Medals. The more a man knows of them, the more he
defires to know. There is one fubjeft in particular
that *Cynthio*, as well as my felf, has a mind to engage
you in. We would fain know how the Ancient and
Modern Medals differ from one another, and which
of them deferves the preference. You have a mind to
engage me in a fubjeft, fays *Philander*, that is perhaps
of a larger extent than you imagine. To examine it
thoroughly, it would be neceffary to take them in pieces, and to fpeak of the difference that fhews it felf
in their Metals, in the Occafion of ftamping them, in
the Infcriptions, and in the Figures that adorn them.
Since you have divided your fubjeft, fays *Cynthio*, be
fo kind as to enter on it without any further preface.

We fhould firft of all, fays *Philander*, confider the
difference of the Metals that we find in ancient and
modern Coins, but as this fpeculation is more curious
than improving, I believe you will excufe me if I do
not

not dwell long upon it. One may underſtand all the learned part of this ſcience, without knowing whether there were Coins of iron or lead among the old Romans, and if a man is well acquainted with the Device of a Medal, I do not ſee what neceſſity there is of being able to tell whether the Medal it ſelf be of copper or *Corinthian* braſs. There is however ſo great a difference between the antique and modern Medals, that I have ſeen an Antiquary lick an old Coin among other trials, to diſtinguiſh the age of it by its Taſte. I remember when I laught at him for it, he told me with a great deal of vehemence, there was as much difference between the reliſh of ancient and modern braſs, as between an apple and a turnep. It is pity, ſays *Eugenius*, but they found out the Smell too of an ancient Medal. They would then be able to judge of it by all the ſenſes. The touch, I have heard, gives almoſt as good evidence as the Sight, and the Ringing of a Medal is, I know, a very common experiment. But I ſuppoſe this laſt proof you mention relates only to ſuch Coins as are made of your baſer ſorts of metal. And here, ſays *Philander*, we may obſerve the prudence of the Ancients above that of the Moderns, in the care they took to perpetuate the memory of great actions. They knew very well that ſilver and gold might fall into the hands of the covetous or ignorant, who would not reſpect them for the Device they bore, but for the Metal they were made of. Nor were their apprehenſions ill founded; for it is not eaſily imagined how many of theſe noble monuments of hiſtory have periſhed in the goldſmiths hands, before they came to be collected together by the learned men of theſe two or three laſt Centuries. Inſcriptions, Victories, Buildings, and a thouſand other pieces of antiquity were melted down in theſe barbarous Ages, that thought figures and letters only ſerved to ſpoil the gold that was charged with them. Your Medalliſts look on this deſtruction of Coins, as on the burning of the *Alexandrian* Library, and would be con-

K 5

tent to compound for them, with almost the loss of a *Vatican*. To prevent this in some measure, the ancients placed the greatest variety of their devices on their brass and copper Coins, which are in no fear of falling into the clippers hands, nor in any danger of melting till the general conflagration. On the contrary, our modern Medals are most in silver or gold, and often in a very small number of each. I have seen a golden one at *Vienna*, of *Philip* the second, that weighed two and twenty pound, which is probably singular in its kind, and will not be able to keep it self long out of the furnace when it leaves the Emperor's Treasury. I remember another in the King of *Prussia's* collection, that has in it three pound weight of gold. The Princes who struck these Medals, says *Eugenius*, seem to have designed them rather as an ostentation of their Wealth, than of their Virtues. They fancied probably, it was a greater honour to appear in gold than in copper, and that a Medal receives all its value from the rarity of the metal. I think the next subject you proposed to speak of, were the different Occasions that have given birth to ancient and modern Medals.

Before we enter on this particular, says *Philander*, I must tell you by way of preliminary, that formerly there was no difference between Money and Medals. An old *Roman* had his purse full of the same pieces that we now preserve in Cabinets. As soon as an Emperor had done any thing remarkable, it was immediately stampt on a Coin, and became current through his whole Dominions. It was a pretty contrivance, says *Cynthio*, to spread abroad the virtues of an Emperor, and make his actions circulate. A fresh Coin was a kind of a *Gazette*, that published the latest news of the Empire. I should fancy your *Roman* Bankers were very good Historians. It is certain, says *Eugenius*, they might find their profit and instruction mixed together. I have often wondered that no nation among the moderns has imitated the ancient *Romans* in in this particular. I know no other way of securing these kinds of monuments, and making them numerous enough to be handed down to future ages. But where Statesmen are ruled by a spirit of faction and interest, they can have no passion for the glory of their country, nor any concern for the figure it will make among posterity. A man that talks of his nation's honour a thousand years hence, is in very great danger of being laught at. We shall think, says *Cynthio*, you have a mind to fall out with the Government, because it does not encourage Medals. But were all your ancient Coins that are now in Cabinets once current money? It is the most probable opinion, says *Philander*, that they were all of them such excepting those we call Medalions. These in respect of the other Coins were the same as modern Medals, in respect of modern money. They were exempted from all commerce, and had no other value but what was set upon them by the fancy of the owner. They are supposed to have been struck by Emperors for presents to their Friends, foreign Princes, or Ambassadors. However, that the smallness of their number might not endanger the loss of the devices they bore, the *Romans* took care generally to stamp the subject of their medalions on their ordinary Coins that were the running cash of the nation. As if in *England* we should see on our half-penny and farthing pieces, the several designs that shew themselves in their perfection on our Medals.

If we now consider, continued *Philander*, the different Occasions or Subjects of ancient and modern Medals, we shall find they both agree in recording the great actions and successes in war, allowing still for the different ways of making it, and the circumstances that attended it in past ages, and in the present. I shall instance one. I do not remember in any old Coin to have seen the taking of a town mentioned: as indeed there were few conquerors could signalize themselves that way before the invention of powder and fortifications

cations, a fingle battle often deciding the fate of whole kingdoms. Our modern Medals give us feveral fieges and plans of fortified towns, that fhow themfelves in all their parts to a great advantage on the reverfe of a Coin. It is indeed, a kind of juftice, fays *Euge-nius*, that a Prince owes to pofterity, after he has ruined or defaced a ftrong place to deliver down to them a model of it as it ftood whole and entire. The Coin repairs in fome meafure the mifchiefs of his Bombs and Cannons. In the next place, fays *Phi-lander*, we fee both on the ancient and modern Me-dals the feveral noble pieces of Architecture that were finifhed at the time when the Medals were ftamped. I muft obferve however, to the honour of the latter, that they have reprefented their buildings according to the rules of perfpective. This I remember to have feen but in very few of the plans on ancient Coins, which makes them appear much lefs beautiful than the modern, efpecially to a mathematical eye. Thus far our two fetts of Medals agree as to their Subject. But old Coins go farther in their compliments to their Emperor, as they take occafion to celebrate his diftin-guifhing Virtues; not as they fhowed themfelves in any particular action, but as they fhone out in the general view of his character. This humour went fo far, that we fee *Nero*'s fidling, and *Commodus*'s fkill in fencing, on feveral of their Medals. At prefent, you never meet with the King of *France*'s generofity, nor the Emperor's devotion recorded after this man-ner. Again, the *Romans* ufed to regifter the great actions of Peace that turned to the good of the people, as well as thofe of War. The remiffion of a Debt, the taking off a Duty, the giving up a Tax, the mend-ing a Port, or the making a Highway, were not looked upon as improper fubjects for a Coin. They were glad of any opportunity to encourage their Em-perors in the humour of doing good, and knew very well, that many of thefe acts of beneficence had a wider and more lafting influence on the happinefs and welfare of a people, than the gaining a Victory, or the

Conqueft

Conqueſt of a nation. In *England* perhaps it would have looked a little odd, to have ſtamped a Medal on the aboliſhing of Chimney-money in the laſt Reign, or on the giving a hundred thouſand pound a year towards the carrying on a war, in this. I find, ſays *Eugenius*, had we ſtruck in with the practice of the ancient *Romans*, we ſhould have had Medals on the fitting up our ſeveral Docks, on the making of our rivers navigable, on the building our men of War, and the like ſubjects, that have certainly very well deſerved them. The reaſon why it has been neglected, ſays *Philander*, may poſſibly be this. Our Princes have the coining of their own Medals, and perhaps may think it would look like vanity to erect ſo many Trophies and Monuments of praiſe to their own merit; whereas among the ancient *Romans*, the Senate had ſtill a watchful eye on their Emperor, and if they found any thing in his life and actions that might furniſh out a Medal, they did not fail of making him ſo acceptable an offering. 'Tis true, their flatteries betray often ſuch a baſeneſs of ſpirit, as one would little expect to find among ſuch an order of men. And here by the way we may obſerve, that you never find any thing like Satyr or Raillery on old Coins.

Whatever victories were got on foreign enemies, or the ſeveral pretenders to the Empire obtained over one another, they are recorded on Coins without the leaſt bitterneſs or reflection. The Emperors often jeſted on their rivals or predeceſſors, but their Mints ſtill maintained their gravity. They might publiſh invectives againſt one another in their diſcourſes or writings, but never on their Coins. Had we no other hiſtories of the *Roman* Emperors, but thoſe we find on their money, we ſhould take them for the moſt virtuous race of Princes that mankind were ever bleſſed with: whereas, if we look into their lives, they appear many of them ſuch monſters of luſt and cruelty, as are almoſt a reproach to human nature. Medals are therefore ſo many compliments to an Emperor, that aſcribe to him all the Virtues and victories he he himself pretended to. Were you to take from hence all your informations, you would fancy *Claudius* as great a Conqueror as *Julius Cæsar*, and *Domitian* a wiser Prince than his brother *Titus*. *Tiberius* on his Coins is all Mercy and Moderation, *Caligula* and *Nero* are Fathers of their Country, *Galba* the patron of public Liberty, and *Vitellius* the restorer of the city of *Rome*. In short, if you have a mind to see the religious *Commodus*, the pious *Caracalla*, and the devout *Heliogabalus*, you may find them either in the inscription or device of their Medals. On the contrary, those of a modern make are often charged with Irony and Satyr. Our Kings no sooner fall out, but their mints make war upon one another, and their malice appears on their Medals. One meets sometimes with very nice touches of Raillery, but as we have no instance of it among the ancient Coins, I shall leave you to determine, whether or no it ought to find a place there. I must confess, says *Cynthio*, I believe we are generally in the wrong, when we deviate from the ancients: because their practice is for the most part grounded upon reason. But if our fore-fathers have thought fit to be grave and serious, I hope their posterity may laugh without offence. For my part, I cannot but look on this kind of Raillery as a refinement on Medals : and do not see why there may not be some for diversion, at the same time that there are others of a more solemn and majestic nature, as a Victory may be celebrated in an Epigram as well as in an Heroic Poem. Had the ancients given place to Raillery on any of their Coins, I question not but they would have been the most valued parts of a collection. Besides the entertainment we should have found in them, they would have shown us the different state of Wit, as it flourished or decayed in the several ages of the *Roman* Empire. There is no doubt, says *Philander*, but our fore-fathers, if they had pleased, could have been as witty as their posterity. But I am of opinion, they industriously avoided it on their Coins, that they might not give us

occasion

occaſion to ſuſpeċt their ſincerity. Had they run into mirth or ſatyr we ſhould not have thought they
had deſigned ſo much to inſtruċt as to divert us. I
have heard, ſays *Eugenius,* that the *Romans* ſtamped
ſeveral Coins on the ſame occaſion. If we follow
their example, there will be no danger of deceiving
poſterity : ſince the more ſerious ſort of Medals may
ſerve as Comments on thoſe of a lighter charaċter.
However it is, the railery of the Moderns cannot be
worſe than the flattery of the Ancients. But hitherto you have only mentioned ſuch Coins as were made
on the Emperor, I have ſeen ſeveral of our own time
that have been made as a compliment to private perſons. There are pieces of money, ſays *Philander,* that
during the time of the *Roman* Emperors, were coined in honour of the Senate, Army or People. I do
not remember to have ſeen in the upper Empire the
face of any private perſon that was not ſome way related to the Imperial family. *Sejanus* has indeed his
Conſulſhip mentioned on a Coin of *Tiberius,* as he has
the honour to give a name to the year in which our
Saviour was crucified. We are now come to the Legend or Inſcription of our Medals, which as it is
one of the more eſſential parts of them, it may deſerve to be examined more at length. You have choſen a very ſhort Text to enlarge upon, ſays *Cynthio :*
I ſhould as ſoon expeċt to ſee a Critique on the Poſie of
a Ring, as on the Inſcription of a Medal.

I have ſeen ſeveral modern Coins, ſays *Philander,*
that have had part of the Legend running round the
edges, like the *Decus et Tutamen* in our milled money ;
ſo that a few years will probably wear out the aċtion
that the Coin was deſigned to perpetuate. The ancients were too wiſe to regiſter their exploits on ſo nice
a ſurface. I ſhould fancy, ſays *Eugenius,* the moderns
may have choſen this part of the Medal for the inſcription, that the figures on each ſide might appear
to a greater advantage. I have obſerved in ſeveral
old Coins a kind of confuſion between the legend and
the device. The figures and letters were ſo mingled
together,

together, that one would think the Coiner was hard
put to it on what part of the money to bestow the
several words of his inscription. You have found
out something like an excuse, says *Philander*, for your
milled Medals, if they carried the whole legend on
their edges. But at the same time that they are let-
tered on the edges, they have other inscriptions on
the face and the reverse. Your modern Designers
cannot contract the occasion of the Medal into an inscription that is proper to the Volume they write upon : so that having scribbled over both sides, they are
forced, as it were, to write upon the margin. The
first fault therefore that I shall find with a modern
legend, is its Diffusiveness. You have sometimes the
whole side of a Medal over-run with it. One would
fancy the Author had a design of being *Ciceronian* in
his *Latin,* and of making a round period. I will give
you only the reverse of a Coin stampt by the present
Emperor of *Germany,* on the raising of the siege of
Vienna. VIENNA AVSTRIÆ ¼ IVLII AB ACHMETE
II. OBSESSA ½ SEPT. EX INSPERATO AB EO DESER-
TA EST. I should take this, says *Cynthio,* for the para-
graph of a *Gazette,* rather than the inscription of a
Medal. I remember you represented your ancient
Coins as abridgments of history ; but your modern,
if there are many of them like this, should themselves
be epitomized. Compare with this, says *Philander,*
the brevity and comprehensiveness of those legends that
appear on ancient Coins.

*Salus Generis humani. Tellus stabilita. Gloria Orbis
Terræ. Pacator Orbis. Restitutor Orbis Terrarum. Gau-
dium Reipublicæ. Hilaritas populi Romani. Bono Rei-
pub. nati. Roma renascens. Libertas restituta. Sæcu-
lum Aureum. Pullæ Faustinianæ. Rex Parthis datus.
Victoria Germanica. Fides Mutua. Asia Subacta. Judæa capta. Amor mutuus. Genetrix orbis. Sideribus
recepta. Genio Senatûs. Fides exercitûs. Providentia
Senatûs. Restitutori Hispaniæ. Adventui Aug. Bri-
tanniæ.*

taniæ. Regna Adſignata. Adlocutio. Diſcipulina Auguſti. Felicitas publica. Rex Armenis datus.

What a majeſty and force does one meet with in theſe ſhort Inſcriptions! Are not you amazed to ſee ſo much hiſtory gathered into ſo ſmall a compaſs? You have often the ſubject of a Volume in a couple of words.

If our modern Medals are ſo very prolix in their proſe, they are every whit as tedious in their verſe. You have ſometimes a dull Epigram of four lines. This, ſays *Cynthio*, may be of great uſe to immortalize Punns and Quibbles, and to let poſterity ſee their forefathers were a parcel of blockheads. A Coin, I find, may be of great uſe to a bad Poet. If he cannot become immortal by the goodneſs of his verſe, he may by the durableneſs of the Metal that ſupports it. I ſhall give you an inſtance, ſays *Philander*, from a Medal of *Guſtavus Adolphus*, that will ſtand as an eternal monument of Dullneſs and Bravery.

Miles ego Chriſti, Chriſto duce ſterno tyrannos,
  Hæreticos ſimul et calco meis pedibus.
Parcere Chriſticolis me, debellare feroces
  Papicolas Chriſtus dux meus en animat.

It is well, ſays *Cynthio*, you tell us this is a Medal of the Great *Guſtavus*: I ſhould have taken it for ſome one of his *Gothic* Predeceſſors. Does it not bring into your mind *Alexander* the Great's being accompanied with a *Chærilus* in his *Perſian* expedition? If you are offended at the homelineſs of this Inſcription, ſays *Philander*, what would you think of ſuch as have neither ſenſe nor grammar in them. I aſſure you I have ſeen the face of many a great Monarch hemmed in with falſe *Latin*. But it is not only the ſtupidity and tediouſneſs of theſe Inſcriptions that I find fault with; ſuppoſing them of a moderate length and a proper ſenſe why muſt they be in verſe? We ſhould be ſurprized to ſee the title of a ſerious book in rhime, yet is it every whit as ridiculous to give the ſubject of a Medal in a piece of an Hexameter. This however is the

practice

practice of our modern Medallists. If you look into the ancient Inscriptions, you see an air of simplicity in the words, but a great magnificence in the thought; on the contrary, in your modern Medals you have generally a trifling thought wrapt up in the beginning or end of an Heroic verse. Where the sense of an Inscription is low, it is not in the power of *Dactyls* and *Spondees* to raise it, where it is noble, it has no need of such affected ornaments. I remember a Medal of *Philip* the second, on *Charles le Quint*'s resigning to him the Kingdom of *Spain*, with this Inscription, *Ut Quiescat Atlas*. The Device is a *Hercules* with the Sphere on his shoulders. Notwithstanding the thought is poetical, I dare say you would think the beauty of the Inscription very much lost, had it been——*requiescat ut Atlas*. To instance a Medal of our own nation. After the conclusion of the peace with *Holland*, there was one stampt with the following Legend————*Redeant Commercia Flandris*. The thought is here great enough, but in my opinion it would have looked much greater in two or three words of prose. I think truly, says *Eugenius*, it is ridiculous enough to make the Inscription run like a piece of a verse, when it is not taken out of an old Author. But I would fain have your opinion on such Inscriptions as are borrowed from the *Latin* Poets. I have seen several of this sort that have been very prettily applied, and I fancy when they are chosen with art, they should not be thought unworthy of a place in your Medals.

Which ever side I take, says *Philander*, I am like to have a great party against me. Those who have formed their relish on old Coins, will by no means allow of such an innovation; on the contrary, your men of wit will be apt to look on it as an improvement on ancient Medals. You will oblige us however to let us know what kind of rules you would have observed in the choice of your quotations, since you seem to lay a stress on their being chosen with Art. You must know then, says *Eugenius*, I do not think it enough
that

that a quotation tells us plain matter of fact, unlefs it has fome other accidental ornaments to fet it off. Indeed if a great action that feldom happens in the courfe of human affairs, is exactly defcribed in the paffage of an old Poet, it gives the Reader a very a-greeable furprize, and may therefore deferve a place on a Medal.

Again, if there is more than a fingle circumftance of the action fpecified in the quotation, it pleafes a man to fee an old exploit copied out as it were by a Modern, and running parallel with it in feveral of its particulars.

In the next place, when the quotation is not only apt, but has in it a turn of Wit or Satyr, it is ftill the better qualified for a Medal, as it has a double capacity of pleafing.

But there is no Infcription fitter for a Medal, in my opinion, than a quotation that befides its aptnefs has fomething in it lofty and fublime: for fuch a one ftrikes in with the natural greatnefs of the foul, and produces a high idea of the perfon or action it cele-bra es, which is one of the principal defigns of a Medalt

It is certainly very pleafant, fays *Eugenius*, to fee a verfe of an old Poet, revolting as it were from its original fenfe, and fiding with a modern fubject. But then it ought to do it willingly of its own accord, without being forced to it by any change in the words, or the punctuation, for when this happens, it is no longer the verfe of an ancient Poet, but of him that has converted it to his own ufe.

You have, I believe, by this time exhaufted your fubject, fays *Philander*; and I think the criticifms you have made on the poetical quotations that we fo often meet with in our modern Medals, may be very well applied to the Motto's of books, and other Infcriptions of the fame nature. But before we quit the Legends of Medals, I cannot but take notice of a kind of wit that flourifhes very much on many of the modern, efpecially thofe of *Germany*, when they repre-
fent

sent in the Inscription the year in which they were coined. As to mention to you another of *Gustavus Adolphus*. CHRIstVs DVX ErGo TrIVMpVS. If you take the pains to pick out the figures from the several words, and range them in their proper order, you will find they amount to 1627, the year in which the Medal was coined; for do not you observe some of the letters distinguish themselves from the rest, and top it over their fellows? these you must consider in a double capacity, as letters or as cyphers. Your laborious *German* Wits will turn you over a whole Dictionary for one of these ingenious Devices. You would fancy perhaps they were searching after an apt classical term, but instead of that, they are looking out a word that has an L. an M. or a D. in it. When therefore you see any of these Inscriptions, you are not so much to look in them for the thought, as for the year of the Lord. There are foreign Universities where this kind of wit is so much in vogue, that as you praise a man in *England* for being an excellent Philosopher or Poet, it is an ordinary character among them to be a great Chronogrammatist. These are probably, says *Cynthio*, some of those mild provinces of Acrostic land, that Mr. *Dryden* has assigned to his Anagrams, Wings and Altars. We have now done, I suppose, with the Legend of a Medal. I think you promised us in the next place to speak of the Figures.

As we had a great deal of talk on this part of a Coin, replied *Philander*, in our discourse on the Usefulness of ancient Medals, I shall only just touch on the chief heads wherein the Ancient and the Modern differ. In the first place, the *Romans* always appear in the proper Dress of their country, insomuch that you see the little variations of the Mode in the drapery of the Medal. They would have thought it ridiculous to have drawn an Emperor of *Rome* in a *Grecian* Cloak or a *Phrygian* Mitre. On the contrary, our modern Medals are full of *Toga*'s and *Tunica*'s, *Trabea*'s and *Paludamentums*, with a multitude of the like anti-

antiquated garments; that have not been in fashion these thousand years. You see very often a King of *England* or *France* dressed up like a *Julius Cæsar*. One would think they had a mind to pass themselves upon posterity for *Roman* Emperors. The same observation may run through several customs and religions, that appear in our ancient and modern Coins. Nothing is more usual than to see Allusions to *Roman* customs and ceremonies on the Medals of our own nation Nay very often they carry the figure of a heathen god. If posterity takes its notions of us from our Medals, they must fancy one of our Kings paid a great devotion to *Minerva*, that another was a professed Worshipper of *Apollo*, or at best that our whole religion was a mixture of Paganism and Christianity. Had the old *Romans* been guilty of the same extravagance, there would have been so great a confusion in their Antiquities, that their Coins would not have had half the uses we now find in them. We ought to look on Medals as so many monuments consigned over to Eternity, that may possibly last when all other memorials of the same Age are worn out or lost. They are a kind of Present that those who are actually in Being make over to such as lie hid within the depths of Futurity. Were they only designed to instruct the three or four succeeding generations, they are in no great danger of being misunderstood : but as they may pass into the hands of a Posterity, that lie many removes from us, and are like to act their part in the world, when its governments, manners, and religions, may be quite altered; we ought to take a particular care not to make any false reports in them, or to charge them with any Devices that may look doubtful or un-intelligible.

I have lately seen, says *Eugenius*, a Medallic history of the present King of *France*. One might expect, methinks, to see the Medals of that nation in the highest perfection, when there is a society pensioned and set apart on purpose for the designing of them.

We

We will examine them, if you pleafe, fays *Philander*, in the light that our foregoing obfervations have fet them , but on this condition, that you do not look on the faults I find in them any more than my own private opinion. In the firft place then, I think it is impoffible to learn from the *French* Medals either the religion, cuftom, or habits of the *French* nation. You fee on fome of them the Crofs of our Saviour, and on others *Hercules*'s Club. In one you have an Angel, and in another a *Mercury*. I fancy, fays *Cynthio*, pofterity would be as much puzzled on the religion of *Louis le Grand*, were they to learn it from his Medals, as we are at prefent on that of *Conftantine* the Great. It is certain, fays *Philander*, there is the fame mixture of Chriftian and Pagan in their Coins ; nor is there a lefs confufion in their cuftoms. For example, what relation is there between the figure of a Bull, and the planting of a *French* colony in *America?* The *Romans* made ufe of this type in allufion to one of their own cuftoms at the fending out of a colony. But for the *French*, a Ram, a Hog, or an Elephant, would have been every whit as fignificant an emblem. Then can any thing be more unnatural than to fee a King of *France* dreffed like an Emperor of *Rome*, with his arms ftripped up to the elbows, a Laurel on his head, and a *Chlamys* over his fhoulders? I fancy, fays *Eugenius*, the fociety of Medallifts would give you their reafons for what they have done. You your felf allow the Legend to be *Latin*, and why may not the cuftoms and ornaments be of the fame country as the language? efpecially fince they are all of them fo univerfally underftood by the learned. I own to you, fays *Philander*, if they only defign to deliver down to pofterity the feveral parts of their Great Monarch's hiftory, it is no matter for the other circumftances of a Medal : but I fancy it would be as great a pleafure and inftruction for future ages, to fee the Dreffes and Cuftoms of their anceftors, as their Buildings and Victories. Befides, I do not think they have always chofen a proper Occafion

afion for a Medal. There is one ftruck, for example, on the *Englifh* failing in their attempts on *Dun-
irk:* when in the laft reign they endeavoured to blow
up a Fort, and bombard the town. What have the
French here done to boaft of? A Medal however you
have with this infcription, DUNKIRKA ILLÆSA. Not
to cavil at the two K's in *Dunkirka,* or the impropriety
of the word *Illæfa,* the whole Medal, in my opinion,
tends not fo much to the honour of the *French* as of the
Englifh,

>———————*quos opimus*
>*Fallere et effugere eft triumphus.*

I could mention a few other faults, or at leaft what
I take for fuch. But at the fame time muft be forced
to allow, that this Series of Medals is the moft perfect of any among the moderns in the beauty of the
Work, the aptnefs of the Device, and the propriety
of the Legend. In thefe and other particulars, the
French Medals come nearer the ancients than thofe
of any other country, as indeed it is to this nation
we are indebted for the beft lights that have been given to the whole fcience in general.

I muft not here forget to mention the Medallic
hiftory of the Popes, where there are many Coins of
an excellent workmanfhip, as I think they have none
of thofe faults that I have fpoken of in the preceding
fett. They are always *Roman*-Catholic in the Device
and in the Legend, which are both of them many
times taken out of the holy Scriptures, and therefore
not unfuitable to the character of the Prince they reprefent. Thus when *Innocent* XI. lay under terrible
apprehenfions of the *French* King, he put out a Coin,
that on the reverfe of it had a fhip toffed on the waves
to reprefent the Church. Before it, was the figure
of our Saviour walking on the waters, and St. *Peter*
ready to fink at his feet. The Infcription, if I remember, was in *Latin. Help Lord, or elfe I perifh.*
This puts me in mind, fays *Cynthio,* of a Pafquinade,
that at the fame time was fixed up at *Rome. Ad Gal-
li cantum Petrus flet.* But methinks, under this head
of

of the figures on ancient and modern Coins, we might expect to hear your opinion on the difference that appears in the Workmanship of each. You muſt know then, ſays *Philander*, that till about the end of the third Century, when there was a general decay in all the arts of deſigning, I do not remember to have ſeen the head of a *Roman* Emperor drawn with a full face. They always appear in *profil*, to uſe a *French* term of art, which gives us the view of a head, that, in my opinion, has ſomething in it very majeſtic, and at the ſame time ſuits beſt with the dimenſions of a Medal. Beſides that it ſhows the noſe and eyebrows, with the ſeveral prominencies and fallings in of the features, much more diſtinctly than any other kind of figure. In the lower Empire you have abundance of broad *Gothic* faces, like ſo many full Moons on the ſide of a Coin. Among the moderns too, we have of both ſorts, though the fineſt are made after the antique. In the next place, you find the figures of many ancient Coins riſing up in a much more beautiful *relief* than thoſe on the modern. This too is a beauty that fell with the grandeur of the *Roman* Emperors, ſo that you ſee the face ſinking by degrees in the ſeveral declenſions of the Empire, till about *Conſtantine*'s time it lies almoſt even with the ſurface of the Medal. After this it appears ſo very plain and uniform, that one would think the Coiner look'd on the flatneſs of a figure as one of the greateſt beauties in Sculpture. I fancy, ſays *Eugenius*, the Sculptors of that age had the ſame reliſh as a *Greek* Prieſt that was buying ſome religious pictures at *Venice*. Among others he was ſhown a noble piece of *Titian*. The Prieſt having well ſurvey'd it, was very much ſcandalized at the extravagance of the *relief*, as he termed it. You know, ſays he, our religion forbids all idolatry: We admit of no Images, but ſuch as are drawn on a ſmooth ſurface: The figure you have here ſhown me, ſtands ſo much out to the eye, that I would no ſooner ſuffer it in my Church than a Statue. I could recommend your *Greek* Prieſt, ſays *Philander*, to abundance

of

of celebrated. Painters on this fide of the *Alps* that would not fail to pleafe him. We muft own however, that the figures on feveral of our modern Medals are raifed and rounded to a very great perfection. But if you compare them in this particular with the moft finifhed among the ancients, your men of art declare univerfally for the latter.

Cynthio and *Eugenius*, though they were well pleaf-ed with *Philander*'s difcourfe, were glad however to find it at an end: for the Sun began to gather ftrength upon them, and had pierced the fhelter of their walks in feveral places. *Philander* had no fooner done talk-ing, but he grew fenfible of the heat himfelf, and im-mediately propofed to his friends the retiring to his lodgings, and getting a thicker fhade over their heads. They both of them very readily clofed with the pro-pofal, and by that means give me an opportunity of finifhing my Dialogue.

THREE SETTS OF

MEDALS

Illuftrated by the

ANTIENT POETS,

In the foregoing DIALOGUES.

————decipit
Frons prima multos ; rara mens intelligit
Interiori condidit quæ cura angulo.
PHÆDR.
Multa poetarum veniet manus, Auxilio quæ
Sit mihi————◄
HOR.

Printed in the Year, 1735.

THE

FIRST SERIES.

1. VIRTVTI AVGVSTI. S. C. Reverfe of *Domitian.*

2. HONOSET VIRTVS. Reverfe of *Galba.*

3. CONCORDIA AVG. S. C. Reverfe of *Sabina.*

4. PAX ORBIS TERRARVM. Reverfe of *Otho.*

5. ABVNDANTIA AVG. S. C. Reverfe of *Gordianus Pius.*

6, 7. FIDES EXERCITVS. Reverfe of *Heliogabalus.*

8. SPES AVGVSTA. Reverfe of *Claudius.*

9. SECVRITAS PVBLICA. S. C. Reverfe of *Antoninus Pius.*

10. PVDICITIA. S. C. Reverfe of *Fauftina Junior.*

11. PIETAS AVG. S. C. Reverfe of *Fauftina Senior.*

12. AEQVITAS AVGVSTI. S. C. Reverfe of *Vitellius*

13. AETERNITAS. S. C. Reverfe of *Antoninus Pius.*

14. SAECVLVM AVREVM. Reverfe of *Adrian.*

15. FELIX TEMPORUM REPARATIO. Reverfe of *Conftantine.*

16. AETERNITAS AVGVSTI. S. C. Reverfe of *Adrian.*

17. AETERNITAS. S. C. Reverfe of *Antonine.*

18. VICTORIA AVGVSTI. S. C. Reverfe of *Nero.*

19. SARMATIA DEVICTA. A Victory. Reverfe of *Conftantine.*

20. LIBER TAS PVBLICA. S. C. Reverfe of *Galba.*

THE

SECOND SERIES.

1. FELICITATI AVG. COS. III. P. P. S. C. Reverfe of *Hadrian.*
2. PONTIF. MAX. TR. POT. PP. COS. II.
3. P.N.R.S.C. Reverfe of *Claudius.*
4. S.C. Reverfe of *Augustus.*
5. S.P.Q.R.P.P. OB. CIVES. SERVATOS. Reverfe
of *Caligula.*
6. Reverfe of *Tiberius.*
7. FIDES PVBLICA. Reverfe of *Titus.*
8. PRAETOR RECEPT. Reverfe of *Claudius.*
9. FECVNDITAS. S. C. Reverfe of *Julia Augusta.*
10. NERO CLAV. CAESAR. IMP. ET OCTAVIA
AVGVST. F. Reverfe of *Claudius.*
11. ORIENS. AVG. Reverfe of *Aurelian.*
12. Reverfe of *Commodus.*
13. GLORIA EXERCI-⎫
TVS. E. S. I. S. ⎬ Reverfe of *Constantine.*
14. PRINCIPI IVVEN-⎭
TVTIS. S. C.
15. M. CATO. L. VETTIACVS. II. VIR. LEG.
IV. LEG. VI. LEG. X. C. C. A. Reverfe of
Tiberius.
16. TR. P. VII. IMP. III. COS. V. P. P.S. C. Reverfe of *Trajan.*
17. TR. POT. V. IMP. III. COS. II. S. C. Reverfe
of *Lucius Verus.*
18. PAX AVG. S. C. Reverfe of *Vefpafian.*
19. IMP. VIII. COS. III. P. P.⎫
S. C. DE GERMANIS. ⎬ Reverfe of *Marcus*
20. IMP. VIII. COS. III. P. P.⎭ *Aurelius*
S. C. DE SARMATIS
21. Reverfe of *Trajan.*
22. TR. POT. XIIII. P. P. COS. II. Reverfe of *M.
Aurelius.*
23. DIVVS AVGVSTVS PATER. coin'd under *Tiberius.*
24. COS. IIII. S. C. Reverfe of *Antoninus Pius.*

THE
THIRD SERIES.

L 5

1. FELIX ADVENT. AVG. G. NN. PEN. Reverse of *Dioclesian.*

2. AFRICA. S. C. Reverse of *Septimius Severus.*

3. AFRICA. S. C. Reverse of *Adrian.*

4. ÆGYPTOS. S. C. Reverse of *Adrian.*

5. MAVRETANIA. S. C. Reverse of *Adrian.*

6. HISPANIA. S. C. Reverse of *Adrian.*

7. ADVENTVI AVG. GALLIAE. S. C. Reverse of *Adrian.*

8. ITALIA. S. C. Reverse of *Marcus Antoninus.*

9. ROMA. S. C. Reverse of *Nero.*

10. RESTITVTORI ACHAIÆ. Reverse of *Adrian.*

11. BRITANNIA. Reverse of *Antoninus Pius.*

12. RESTITVTORI SICILIAE. S. C. Reverse of *Adrian.*

13. IVDEA CAPTA. S. C.

14. VICTORIA AVGVSTI. S. C. } Reverse of *Vespasian.*

15. PARTHIA. S. C. COS. II. Reverse of *Antoninus Pius.*

16. ANTIOCHIA.

17. ΟΥΑΤΕΙΡΗΝΩΝΚ. CΜΥΡΝ. ΣΤΡ. Τ. ΦΑΒ. ΑΑ. ΑΠΟΑΑΙΝΑΡΙΟΥ. Reverse of *Marcus Aurelius.*

18. ARAB. ADQ. S. P. Q. R. OPTIMO PRINCIPI. S. C. Reverse of *Trajan.*

OF THE

CHRISTIAN

RELIGION.

OF THE
CHRISTIAN RELIGION.

SECTION I.

I. *General division of the following discourse, with regard to* Pagan *and* Jewish *Authors, who mention particulars relating to our Saviour.*

II. *Not probable that any such should be mentioned by* Pagan *writers who lived at the same time, from the nature of such transactions.*

III. *Especially when related by the* Jews.

IV. *And heard at a distance by those who pretended to as great miracles as their own.*

V. *Besides that, no* Pagan *writers of that age lived in* Judæa *or its Confines.*

VI. *And because many books of that age are lost.*

VII. *An Instance of one record proved to be authentick.*

VIII. *A second record of probable, though not undoubted, authority.*

I. THAT

I.

THAT I may lay before you a full ftate of the fubjeﬆ under our confideration, and methodize the feveral particulars that I touched upon in difcourfe with you; I fhall firﬆ take notice of fuch *Pagan* Authors as have given their teﬆimony to the hiﬆory of our Saviour; reduce thefe Authors under their refpeﬆive claffes, and fhew what authority their teﬆimonies carry with them. Secondly, I fhall take notice of *Jewifh* Authors in the fame light.

II. There are many reafons, why you fhould not expeﬆ that matters of fuch a wonderful nature fhould be taken notice of by thofe eminent *Pagan* writers, who were contemporaries with *Jefus Chriﬆ*, or by thofe who lived before his Difciples had perfonally appeared among them; and afcertained the report which had gone abroad concerning a life fo full of miracles.

Suppofing fuch things had happened at this day in *Switzerland*, or among the *Grifons*, who make a greater figure in *Europe* than *Judæa* did in the *Roman* Empire; would they be immediately believed by thofe who live at a great diﬆance from them? or would any certain account of them be tranfmitted into foreign countries, within fo fhort a fpace of time as that of our Saviour's publick miniﬆry? Such kinds of news, though never fo true, feldom gain credit, 'till fome time after they are tranfaﬆed and expofed to the examination of the curious, who by laying together circumﬆances, atteﬆations, and charaﬆers of thofe who are concerned in them, either receive, or rejeﬆ what at firﬆ none but eye-witneffes could abfolutely believe or difbelieve In a cafe of this fort, it was natural for men of fenfe and learning to treat the whole account as fabulous, or at fartheﬆ to fufpend their belief of it, until all things ﬆood together in their full light.

III. Be-

III. Besides, the *Jews* were branded not only for superstitions different from all the religions of the *Pagan* world, but in a particular manner ridiculed for being a credulous people; so that whatever reports of such a nature came out of that country, were looked upon by the heathen world as false, frivolous, and improbable.

IV. We may further observe that the ordinary practice of Magic in those times, with the many pretended Prodigies, Divinations, Apparitions, and local Miracles among the Heathens, made them less attentive to such news from *Judæa*, 'till they had time to consider the nature, the occasion, and the end of our Saviour's miracles, and were awakened by many surprizing events to allow them any consideration at all.

V. We are indeed told by St. *Matthew*, that the fame of our Saviour, during his life, went throughout all *Syria*, and that there followed him great multitudes of people from *Galilee*, *Judæa*, *Decapolis*, *Idumæa*, from beyond *Jordan*, and from *Tyre* and *Sidon*. Now had there been any historians of those times and places, we might have expected to have seen in them some account of those wonderful transactions in *Judæa*; but there is not any single Author extant, in any kind, of that age, in any of those countries.

VI. How many books have perished in which possibly there might have been mention of our Saviour? Look among the *Romans*, how few of their writings are come down to our times? In the space of two hundred years from our Saviour's birth, when there was such a multitude of writers in all kinds, how small is the number of Authors that have made their way to the present age?

VII. One authentick Record, and that the most authentick heathen Record, we are pretty sure is lost. I mean the account sent by the Governor of *Judæa*, under whom our Saviour was judged, condemned, and crucified. It was the custom in the *Roman* Empire, as it is to this day in all the governments of the world, for the præfects and vice-roys of distant provinces to transtranfmit to their Sovereign a fummary relation of every thing remarkable in their adminiftration. That *Pontius Pilate*, in his account, would have touched on fo extraordinary an event in *Judæa*, is not to be doubted; and that he actually did, we learn from *Juftin Martyr*, who lived about a hundred years after our Saviour's death, refided, made Converts, and fuffered martyrdom at *Rome*, where he was engaged with Philofophers, and in a particular manner with *Crefcens* the *Cynick*, who could eafily have detected, and would not fail to have expofed him, had he quoted a Record not in being, or made any falfe citation out of it. Would the great Apologift have challenged *Crefcens* to difpute the caufe of Chriftianity with him before the *Roman* Senate, had he forged fuch an evidence ; or would *Crefcens* have refufed the challenge, could he have triumphed over him in the detection of fuch a forgery ? To which we muft add, that the Apology which appeals to this Record, was prefented to a learned Emperor, and to the whole body of the *Roman* Senate. This father in his apology, fpeaking of the death and fuffering of our Saviour, refers the Emperor for the truth of what he fays to the acts of *Pontius Pilate*, which I have here mentioned. *Tertullian*, who wrote his Apology about fifty years after *Juftin*, doubtlefs referred to the fame Record, when he tells the Governor of *Rome*, that the Emperor *Tiberius* having received an account out of *Paleftine* in *Syria* of the Divine perfon, who had appeared in that country, paid him a particular regard, and threatned to punifh any who fhould accufe the Chriftians; nay, that the Emperor would have adopted him among the Deities whom they worfhipped, had not the Senate refufed to come into his propofal. *Tertullian*, who gives us this hiftory, was not only one of the moft learned men of his age, but what adds a greater weight to his authority in this cafe, was eminently fkilful and well read in the laws of the *Roman* Empire... Nor can it be faid, that *Tertullian* grounded his quotation upon the authority of *Juftin Martyr*, becaufe we find he mixes it with matters of fact which are not related by that Author. *Eufebius* mentions

mentions the fame ancient Record, but as it was not extant in his time, I fhall not infift upon his authority in this point. If it be objected, that this particular is not mentioned in any *Roman* Hiftorian, I fhall ufe the fame argument in a parallel cafe, and fee whether it will carry any force with it. *Ulpian* the great *Roman* Lawyer gathered together all the Imperial Edicts that had been made againft the Chriftians. But did any one ever fay that there had been no fuch Edicts, becaufe they were not mentioned in the hiftories of thofe Emperors? Befides, who knows but this circumftance of *Tiberius* was mentioned in other hiftorians that have been loft, though not to be found in any ftill extant ? Has not *Suetonius* many particulars of this Emperor omitted by *Tacitus*, and *Herodian* many that are not fo much as hinted at by either? As for the fpurious *Acts* of *Pilate*, now extant, we know the occafion and time of their writing, and that had there not been a true and authentick Record of this nature, they would never have been forged.

VIII. The ftory of *Agbarus* King of *Edeffa*, relating to the letter which he fent to our Saviour, and to that which he received from him, is a record of great authority ; and though I will not infift upon it, may venture to fay, that had we fuch an evidence for any fact in *Pagan* hiftory, an Author would be thought very unreafonable who fhould reject it. I believe you will be of my opinion, if you will perufe, with other Authors, who have appeared in vindication of thefe letters as genuine, the additional arguments which have been made ufe of by the late famous and learned Dr. *Grabe*, in the fecond volume of his *Spicilegium*.

SECTION

SECTION II.

I. *What facts in the history of our Saviour might be taken notice of by* Pagan *Authors.*

II. *What particular facts are taken notice of, and by what* Pagan *Authors.*

III. *How* Celsus *represented our Saviour's miracles.*

IV. *The same representation made of them by other unbelievers, and proved unreasonable.*

V. *What facts in our Saviour's history not to be expected from* Pagan *writers.*

I. WE now come to consider what undoubted authorities are extant among *Pagan* writers ; and here we must premise, that some parts of our Saviour's history may be reasonably expected from *Pagans*. I mean such parts as might be known to those who lived at a distance from *Judæa*, as well as to those who were the followers and eye witnesses of *Christ*.

II. Such particulars are most of these which follow, and which are all attested by some one or other of those heathen Authors, who lived in or near the age of our Saviour and his disciples. *That* Augustus Cæsar *had ordered the whole empire to be censed or taxed,* which brought ourSaviour's reputed parents to*Bethlehem.*This is mentioned by several Roman historians, as *Tacitus, Suetonius,* and *Dion. That a great light, or a new star appeared in the east, which directed the wise men to our Saviour :* This is recorded by *Chalcidius. That* Herod *the King of* Palestine, *so often mentioned in the* Roman *history, made a great slaughter of innocent children,* being so jealous of his successor, that he put to death his own sons on that account : This character of him is given by several historians, and this cruel fact mentioned by *Macrobius,* a heathen Author, who tells it as a known thing, without any mark or doubt upon it.

That

That our Saviour had been in Egypt : This *Celsus,* though he raises a monstrous story upon it, is so far from denying, that he tells us our Saviour learned the arts of magic in that country. *That* Pontius Pilate *was Governor of* Judæa ; *that our Saviour was brought in judgment before him, and by him condemned and crucified :* This is recorded by *Tacitus. That many miraculous cures and works out of the ordinary course of nature were wrought by him :* This is confessed by *Julian* the Apostate, *Porphyry,* and *Hierocles,* all of them not only Pagans, but professed enemies and persecutors of Christianity. *That our Saviour foretold several things which came to pass according to his predictions :* This was attested by *Phlegon* in his annals, as we are assured by the learned *Origen* against *Celsus. That at the time when our Saviour died, there was a miraculous darkness and a great earthquake :* This is recorded by the same *Phlegon* the *Trallian,* who was likewise a *Pagan* and Freeman to *Adrian* the Emperor. We may here observe, that a native of *Trallium,* which was not situate at so great a distance from *Palestine,* might very probably be informed of such remarkable events as had passed among the *Jews* in the age immediately preceding his own times, since several of his countrymen with whom he had conversed, might have received a confused report of our Saviour before his crucifixion, and probably lived within the Shake of the earthquake, and the shadow of the eclipse, which are recorded by this Author. *That* Christ *was worshipped as a God among the* Christians; *that they would rather suffer death than blaspheme him : that they received a sacrament, and by it entred into a vow of abstaining from sin and wickedness,* conformable to the advice given by St. *Paul; that they had private assemblies of worship, and used to join together in Hymns :* This is the account which *Pliny* the younger gives of Christianity in his days, about seventy years after the death of *Christ,* and which agrees in all its circumstances with the accounts we have in holy writ, of the first state of Christianity after the crucifixion of our Blessed Saviour. *That* St. Peter,

whose

whose miracles are many of them recorded in holy writ, did many wonderful works, is owned by *Julian* the apostate, who therefore represents him as a great Magician, and one who had in his possession a book of magical secrets left him by our Saviour. *That the devils or evil spirits were subject to them*, we may learn from *Porphyry*, who objects to Christianity, that since *Jesus* had begun to be worshipped, *Æsculapius* and the rest of the gods did no more converse with men. Nay, *Celsus* himself affirms the same thing in effect, when he says, that the power which seemed to reside in Christians, proceeded from the use of certain names, and the invocation of certain dæmons. *Origen* remarks on this passage, that the Author doubtless hints at those Christians who put to flight evil spirits, and healed those who were possessed with them; a fact which had been often seen, and which he himself had seen, as he declares in another part of his discourse against *Celsus*. But at the same time he assures us, that this miraculous power was exerted by the use of no other name but that of *Jesus*, to which were added several passages in his history, but nothing like any invocation to *Dæmons*.

III. *Celsus* was so hard set with the report of our Saviour's miracles, and the confident attestations concerning him, that though he often intimates he did not believe them to be true, yet knowing he might be silenced in such an answer, provides himself with another retreat, when beaten out of this; namely, that our Saviour was a magician. Thus he compares the feeding of so many thousands at two different times with a few loaves and fishes, to the magical feasts of those *Egyptian* impostors, who would present their spectators with visionary entertainments that had in them neither substance nor reality: which, by the way, is to suppose, that a hungry and fainting multitude were filled by an apparition, or strengthned and refreshed with shadows. He knew very well that there were so many witnesses and actors, if I may call them such, in these two miracles, that it was impossible to refute such.

such multitudes, who had doubtless sufficiently spread the fame of them, and was therefore in this place forced to resort to the other solution, that it was done by magic. It was not enough to say that a miracle which appeared to so many thousand eye-witnesses was a forgery of *Christ*'s disciples, and therefore supposing them to be eye-witnesses, he endeavours to shew how they might be deceived.

IV. The unconverted heathens, who were pressed by the many authorities that confirmed our Saviour's miracles, as well as the unbelieving *Jews*, who had actually seen them, were driven to account for them after the same manner: For to work by magic in the heathen way of speaking, was in the language of the *Jews* to cast out devils by *Beelzebub* the Prince of the devils. Our Saviour, who knew that unbelievers in all ages would put this perverse interpretation on his miracles, has branded the malignity of those men, who contrary to the dictates of their own hearts started such an unreasonable objection, as a blasphemy against the Holy Ghost, and declared not only the guilt, but the punishment of so black a crime. At the same time he condescended to shew the vanity and emptiness of this objection against his miracles, by representing that they evidently tended to the destruction of those powers, to whose assistance the enemies of his doctrine then ascribed them. An argument, which, if duly weighed, renders the objection so very frivolous and groundless, that we may venture to call it even blasphemy against common sense. Would Magic endeavour to draw off the minds of men from the worship which was paid to stocks and stones, to give them an abhorrence of those evil spirits who rejoiced in the most cruel sacrifices, and in offerings of the greatest impurity; and in short to call upon mankind to exert their whole strength in the love and adoration of that one Being, from whom they derived their existence, and on whom only they were taught to depend every moment for the happiness and continuance of it ? Was it the business of Magic to humanize our natures with compassion, forgive-

ness,

nefs, and all the inftances of the moft extenfive charity? Would evil fpirits contribute to make men fober, chafte, and temperate, and in a word to produce that reformation, which was wrought in the moral world by thofe doctrines of our Saviour, that received their fanction from his miracles? Nor is it poffible to imagine, that evil fpirits would enter into a combination with our Saviour to cut off all their correfpondence and intercourfe with mankind, and to prevent any for the future from addicting themfelves to thofe rites and ceremonies, which had done them fo much honour. We fee the early effect which Chriftianity had on the minds of men in this particular, by that number of books, which were filled with the fecrets of magic, and made a facrifice to Chriftianity by the converts mentioned in the *Acts* of the Apoftles. We have likewife an eminent inftance of the inconfiftency of our Religion with magic, in the hiftory of the famous *Aquila*. This perfon, who was a kinfman of the Emperor *Trajan*, and likewife a man of great learning, notwithftanding he had embraced Chriftianity, could not be brought off from the ftudies of magic, by the repeated admonitions of his fellow-chriftians: fo that at length they expelled him their fociety, as rather chufing to lofe the reputation of fo confiderable a Profelyte, than communicate with one who dealt in fuch dark and infernal practices. Befides, we may obferve, that all the favourers of magic were the moft profeft and bitter enemies to the chriftian religion. Not to mention *Simon Magus* and many others, I fhall only take notice of thofe two great profecutors of Chriftianity, the Emperors *Adrian* and *Julian* the Apoftate, both of them initiated in the myfteries of divination, and fkilled in all the depths of magic. I fhall only add, that evil fpirits cannot be fuppofed to have concurred in the eftablifhment of a religion which triumphed over them, drove them out of the places they poffeft, and divefted them of their influence on mankind; nor would I mention this particular, though it be unanimoufly reported by all the ancient chriftian Authors: did it not appear from the authorities above cited,

ted, that it was a fact confest by the Heathens themselves.

V. We now see what a multitude of *Pagan* testimonies may be produced for all those remarkable passages, which might have been expected from them: and indeed of several, that, I believe, do more than answer your expectation, as they were not subjects in their own nature so exposed to publick notoriety. It cannot be expected they should mention particulars, which were transacted amongst the Disciples only, or among some few even of the Disciples themselves; such as the transfiguration, the agony in the garden, the appearance of *Christ* after his resurrection, and others of the like nature. It was impossible for a heathen Author to relate these things; because if he had believed them, he would no longer have been a heathen, and by that means his testimony would not have been thought of so much validity. Besides, his very report of facts so favourable to Christianity would have prompted men to say that he was probably tainted with their doctrine. We have a parallel case in *Hecatæus*, a famous *Greek* Historian, who had several passages in his book conformable to the history of the *Jewish* writers, which when quoted by *Josephus*, as a confirmation of the *Jewish* history, when his heathen adversaries could give no other answer to it, they would need suppose that *Hecatæus* was a *Jew* in his heart, though they hd no other reason for it, but because his history gave greater authority to the *Jewish* than the *Egyptian* Records.

SECTION III.

IV. *Of another* Athenian *Philosopher converted to Chri-*
stianity.

V. *Why their conversion, instead of weakning, strength-*
ens their evidence in defence of Christianity.

VI. *Their belief in our Saviour's history founded at first*
upon the principles of historical faith.

VII. *Their testimonies extended to all the particulars of*
our Saviour's history.

VIII. *As related by the four Evangelists.*

I. TO this list of heathen writers who make mention of our Saviour, or touch upon any particulars of his life, I shall add those Authors who were at
first heathens, and afterwards converted to Christianity; upon which account, as I shall here shew, their
testimonies are to be looked upon as the more authentick. And in this list of evidences, I shall confine my
self to such learned *Pagans* as came over to Christianity
in the three first centuries, because those were the times
in which men had the best means of informing themselves
of the truth of our Saviour's history, and because among
the great number of Philosophers who came in afterwards, under the reigns of christian Emperors, there
might be several who did it partly out of worldly motives.

II. Let us now suppose, that a learned heathen writer who lived within 60 years of our Saviour's crucifixion, after having shewn that false miracles were generally wrought in obscurity, and before few or no witnesses, speaking of those which were wrought by our
Saviour, has the following passage. " But his works
" were always seen, because they were true, they were
" seen by those who were healed, and by those who
" were raised from the dead. Nay, these persons who
" were thus healed, and raised, were seen not only at
" the time of their being healed, and raised, but long
" afterwards. Nay they were seen not only all the while
" our Saviour was upon earth, but survived after his
" departure out of this world, nay some of them were
" living in our days.

III.

III. I dare fay you would look upon this as a glorious atteftation for the caufe of Chriftianity, had it come from the hand of a famous *Athenian* Philofopher. Thefe forementioned words however are actually the words of one who lived about fixty years after our Saviour's crucifixion, and was a famous Philofopher in *Athens:* but it will be faid, he was a convert to Chriftianity. Now confider this matter impartially, and fee if his teftimony is not much more valid for that reafon. Had he continued a *Pagan* Philofopher, would not the world have faid that he was not fincere in what he writ, or did not believe it; for, if fo, would not they have told us he would have embraced Chriftianity? This was indeed the cafe of this excellent man : he had fo thoroughly examined the truth of our Saviour's hiftory, and the excellency of that religion which he taught, and was fo entirely convinced of both, that he became a Profelyte, and died a Martyr.

IV. *Ariftides* was an *Athenian* Philofopher, at the fame time, famed for his learning and wifdom, but converted to chriftianity. As it cannot be queftioned that he perufed and approved the apology of *Quadratus*, in which is the paffage juft now cited, he joined with him in an apology of his own, to the fame Emperor, on the fame fubject. This apology, tho' now loft, was extant in the time of *Ado Viennenfis, A. D* 870. and highly efteemed by the moft learned *Athenians*, as that Author witnefses. It muft have contained great arguments for the truth of our Saviour's hiftory, becaufe in it he afferted the divinity of our Saviour, which could not but engage him in the proof of his miracles.

V. I do allow that, generally fpeaking, a man is not fo acceptable and unqueftioned an evidence in facts, which make for the advancement of his own party. But we muft confider that, in the cafe before us, the perfons, to whom we appeal, were of an oppofite party, till they were perfuaded of the truth of

M thofe

those very facts, which they report. They bear evidence to a history in defence of Christianity, the truth of which history was their motive to embrace Christianity. They attest facts which they had heard while they were yet heathens, and had they not found reason to believe them, they would still have continued heathens, and have made no mention of them in their writings.

VI. When a man is born under christian Parents, and trained up in the profession of that religion from a child, he generally guides himself by the rules of *Christian Faith* in believing what is delivered by the Evangelists; but the learned *Pagans* of antiquity, before they became Christians, were only guided by the common rules of *Historical Faith:* That is, they examined the nature of the evidence which was to be met with in common fame, tradition, and the writings of those persons who related them, together with the number, concurrence, veracity, and private characters of those persons; and being convinced upon all accounts that they had the same reason to believe the history of our Saviour, as that of any other person to which they themselves were not actually eye-witnesses, they were bound by all the rules of historical faith, and of right reason, to give credit to this history. This they did accordingly, and in consequence of it published the same truths themselves, suffered many afflictions, and very often death it self, in the assertion of them. When I say, that an historical belief of the acts of our Saviour induced these learned *Pagans* to embrace this doctrine, I do not deny that there were many other motives which conduced to it, as the excellency of his precepts, the fulfilling of prophecies, the miracles of his Disciples, the irreproachable lives and magnanimous sufferings of their followers, with other considerations of the same nature: but whatever other collateral arguments wrought more or less with Philosophers of that age, it is certain that a belief in the history of our Saviour was one motive with every new convert, and that upon which all others turned, as being the very basis and foundation of Christianity.

VII.

VII. To this I muſt further add, that as we have already ſeen many particular facts which are recorded in holy writ, atteſted by particular *Pagan* Authors: the teſtimony of thoſe I am now going to produce, extends to the whole hiſtory of our Saviour, and to that continued ſeries of actions, which are related of him and his Diſciples in the books of the *New Teſtament.*

VIII. This evidently appears from their quotations out of the Evangeliſts, for the confirmation of any doctrine or account of our bleſſed Saviour. Nay a learned man of our nation, who examined the writings of the moſt ancient Fathers in another view, refers to ſeveral paſſages in *Irenæus, Tertullian, Clemens* of *Alexandria, Origen,* and *Cyprian,* by which he plainly ſhows that each of theſe early writers aſcribe to the four Evangeliſts by name their reſpective hiſtories; ſo that there is not the leaſt room for doubting of their belief in the hiſtory of our Saviour, as recorded in the Goſpels. I ſhall only add, that three of the five Fathers here mentioned, and probably four, were *Pagans* converted to Chriſtianity, as they were all of them very inquiſitive and deep in the knowledge of heathen learning and philoſophy.

SECTION IV.

I. *Character of the times in which the Chriſtian religion was propagated:*

II. *And of many who embraced it.*

III. *Three eminent and early inſtances.*

IV. *Multitudes of learned men who came over to it.*

V. *Belief in our Saviour's hiſtory, the firſt motive to their converſion.*

VI. *The names of ſeveral* Pagan *Philoſophers, who were Chriſtian converts.*

I. IT happened very providentially to the honour of the Chriſtian religion, that it did not take its riſe

in

in the dark illiterate ages of the world, but at a time when arts and fciences were at their height, and when there were men who made it the bufinefs of their lives to fearch after truth, and fift the feveral opinions of Philofophers and wife men, concerning the duty, the end, and chief happinefs of reafonable creatures.

II. Several of thefe therefore, when they had informed themfelves of our Saviour's hiftory, and examined with unprejudiced minds the doctrines and manners of his difciples and followers, were fo ftruck and convinced, that they profeffed themfelves of that fect; notwithftanding, by this profeffion in that juncture of time, they bid farewel to all the pleafures of this life, renounced all the views of ambition, engaged in an uninterrupted courfe of feverities, and expofed themfelves to publick hatred and contempt, to fufferings of all kinds, and to death it felf.

III. Of this fort we may reckon thofe three early converts to Chriftianity, who each of them was a member of a Senate famous for its wifdom and learning. . *Jofeph* the *Arimathean* was of the *Jewifh Sanhedrim*, *Dionyfius* of the *Athenian Areopagus*, and *Flavius* *Clemens*, of the *Roman* Senate; nay at the time of his death Conful of *Rome*. Thefe three were fo tho-roughly fatisfied of the truth of the Chriftian religion, that the firft of them, according to all the reports of antiquity, died a martyr for it; as did the fecond, unlefs we difbelieve *Ariftides*, his fellow-citizen and contemporary; and the third, as we are informed both by *Roman* and Chriftian Authors.

IV. Among thofe innumerable multitudes, who in moft of the known nations of the world came over to Chriftianity at its firft appearance, we may be fure there were great numbers of wife and learned men, befides thofe whofe names are in the Chriftian records, who without doubt took care to examine the truth of our Saviour's hiftory, before they would leave the religion of their country and of their forefathers, for the fake of one that would not only cut them off from

from the allurements of this world, but subject them to every thing terrible or disagreeable in it *Tertullian* tells the *Roman* Governors, that their corporations, councils, armies, tribes, companies, the palace, senate, and courts of judicature were filled with Christians; as *Arnobius* asserts, that men of the finest parts and learning, Orators, Grammarians, Rhetoricians, Lawyers, Physicians, Philosophers, despising the sentiments they had been once fond of, took up their rest in the Christian religion.

V. Who can imagine that men of this character did not thoroughly inform themselves of the history of that person, whose doctrines they embraced? for however consonant to reason his precepts appeared, how good soever were the effects which they produced in the world, nothing could have tempted men to acknowledge him as their God and Saviour, but their being firmly persuaded of the miracles he wrought, and the many attestations of his divine mission, which were to be met with in the history of his life. This was the ground work of the Christian religion, and, if this failed, the whole superstructure sunk with it. This point therefore, of the truth of our Saviour's history, as recorded by the Evangelists, is every where taken for granted in the writings of those, who from *Pagan* Philosophers became Christian Authors, and who, by reason of their conversion, are to be looked upon as of the strongest collateral testimony for the truth of what is delivered concerning our Saviour.

VI. Besides innumerable Authors that are lost, we have the undoubted names, works or fragments of several *Pagan* Philosophers, which shew them to have been as learned as any unconverted heathen Authors of the age in which they lived. If we look into the greatest nurseries of learning in those ages of the world, we find in *Athens, Dionysius, Quadratus, Aristides, Athenagoras*; and in *Alexandria, Dionysius, Clemens, Ammonius, Arnobius*, and *Anatolius*, to whom we may add *Origen*; for though his father was a Christian martyr, he became, without all controversy,

M 3 ·the

the moſt learned and able Philoſopher of his age, by his education at *Alexandria,* in that famous ſeminary of arts and ſciences.

SECTION V.

I. *The learned* Pagans *had means and opportunities of informing themſelves of the truth of our Saviour's hiſtory;*

II. *From the proceedings,*

III. *The characters, ſufferings,*

IV. *And miracles of the perſons who publiſhed it.*

V. *How theſe firſt Apoſtles perpetuated their tradition, by ordaining perſons to ſucceed them.*

VI. *How their ſucceſſors in the three firſt centuries preſerved their tradition.*

VII. *That five generations might derive this tradition from* Chriſt, *to the end of the third century.*

VIII. *Four eminent Chriſtians that delivered it down ſucceſſively to the year of our Lord* 254.

IX. *The faith of the four above-mentioned perſons, the ſame with that of the Churches of the Eaſt, of the Weſt, and of* Egypt.

X. *Another perſon added to them, who brings us to the year* 343, *and that many other liſts might be added in as direct and ſhort a ſucceſſion.*

XI. *Why the tradition of the three firſt centuries, more authentick than that of any other age, proved from the converſation of the primitive Chriſtians.*

XII. *From the manner of initiating men into their religion.*

XIII. *From the correſpondence between the Churches.*

XIV. *From the long lives of ſeveral of* Chriſt's *Diſciples, of which two inſtances.*

I. IT now therefore only remains to conſider, whether theſe learned men had means and opportunities

of

of informing themselves of the truth of our Saviour's history; for unless this point can be made out, their testimonies will appear invalid, and their enquiries ineffectual.

. II. As to this point, we must confider, that many thousands had seen the transactions of our Saviour in *Judæa*, and that many hundred thousands had received an account of them from the mouths of those who were actually eye-witnesses. I shall only mention among these eye witnesses the twelve Apostles, to whom we must add St. *Paul*, who had a particular call to this high office, though many other disciples and followers of *Christ* had also their share in the publishing this wonderful history. We learn from the ancient records of Christianity, that many of the Apostles and Disciples made it the express business of their lives, travelled into the remotest parts of the world, and in all places gathered multitudes about them, to acquaint them with the history and doctrines of their crucified Master. And indeed, were all Christian records of these proceedings entirely lost, as many have been, the effect plainly evinces the truth of them; for how else during the Apostles lives, could Christianity have spread it self with such an amazing progress through the several nations of the *Roman* empire? how could it fly like lightning, and carry conviction with it, from one end of the earth to the other?

III. Heathens therefore of every age, sex, and quality, born in the most different climates, and bred up under the most different institutions, when they saw men of plain sense, without the help of learning, armed with patience and courage, instead of wealth, pomp, or power, expressing in their lives those excellent doctrines of Morality, which they taught as delivered to them from our Saviour, averring that they had seen his miracles during his life, and conversed with him after his death; when, I say, they saw no suspicion of falshood, treachery, or worldly interest, in their behaviour and conversation, and that they submitted to the most ignominious and cruel deaths,

deaths, rather than retract their testimony, or even be silent in matters which they were to publish by their Saviour's especial command, there was no reason to doubt of the veracity of those facts which they related, or of the Divine Mission in which they were employed.

IV. But even these motives to Faith in our Saviour would not have been sufficient to have brought about in so few years such an incredible number of conversions, had not the Apostles been able to exhibit still greater proofs of the truths which they taught. A few persons of an odious and despised country could not have filled the world with Believers, had they not shown undoubted credentials from the divine person who sent them on such a message. Accordingly we are assured, that they were invested with the power of working miracles, which was the most short and the most convincing argument that could be produced, and the only one that was adapted to the reason of all mankind, to the capacities of the wise and ignorant, and could overcome every cavil and every prejudice. Who would not believe that our Saviour healed the sick, and raised the dead, when it was published by those who themselves often did the same miracles, in their presence, and in his name! Could any reasonable person imagine, that God Almighty would arm men with such powers to authorize a lye, and establish a religion in the world which was displeasing to him, or that evil spirits would lend them such an effectual assistance to beat down vice and idolatry?

V. When the Apostles had formed many assemblies in several parts of the *Pagan* world, who gave credit to the glad tidings of the Gospel, that, upon their departure, the memory of what they had related might not perish, they appointed out of these new converts, men of the best sense, and of the most unblemished lives, to preside over these several assemblies, and to inculcate without ceasing what they had heard from the mouths of these eye-witnesses.

VI. Upon

VI. Upon the death of any of thofe fubftitutes to the Apoftles and Difciples of *Chrift*, his place was filled up with fome other perfon of eminence for his piety and learning, and generally a member of the fame Church, who after his deceafe was followed by another in the fame manner, by which means the fucceffion was continued in an uninterrupted line. *Irenæus* informs us, that every church preferved a catalogue of its Bifhops in the order that they fucceeded one another, and (for an example) produces the catalogue of thofe who govern'd the church of *Rome* in that character, which contains eight or nine perfons, though but at a very fmall remove from the times of the Apoftles.

Indeed the lifts of Bifhops, which are come down to us in other churches, are generally filled with greater numbers than one would expect. But the fucceffion was quick in the three firft centuries, becaufe the Bifhop very often ended in the Martyr: for when a perfecution arofe in any place, the firft fury of it fell upon this Order of holy men, who abundantly teftified by their deaths and fufferings that they did not undertake thefe offices out of any temporal views, that they were fincere and fatisfied in the belief of what they taught, and that they firmly adhered to what they had received from the Apoftles, as laying down their lives in the fame hope, and upon the fame principles. None can be fuppofed fo utterly regardlefs of their own happinefs as to expire in torment, and hazard their Eternity, to fupport any fables and inventions of their own, or any forgeries of their predeceffors who had prefided in the fame church, and which might have been eafily detected by the tradition of that particular church, as well as by the concurring teftimony of others. To this purpofe, I think it is very remarkable, that there was not a fingle Martyr among thofe many Hereticks, who difagreed with the Apoftolical church, and introduced feveral wild and abfurd notions into the doctrines of Chriftianity. They durft not ftake their prefent and future happi-

nefs

neſs on their own chimerical imaginations, and did not only ſhun perſecution, but affirmed that it was unneceſſary for their followers to bear their religion through ſuch fiery tryals.

VII. We may fairly reckon, that this firſt age of Apoſtles and Diſciples, with that ſecond generation of many who were their immediate converts, extended it ſelf to the middle of the ſecond Century, and that ſeveral of the third generation from theſe laſt mentioned, which was but the fifth from *Chriſt*, continued to the end of the third Century. Did we know the ages and numbers of the members in every particular church, which was planted by the Apoſtles, I doubt not but in moſt of them there might be found five perſons who in a continued ſeries would reach through theſe three centuries of years, that is, till the 265th from the death of our Saviour.

VIII. Among the accounts of thoſe very few out of innumerable multitudes, who had embraced Chriſtianity, I ſhall ſingle out four perſons eminent for their lives, their writings and their ſufferings, that were ſucceſſively contemporaries, and bring us down as far as to the year of our Lord 254. St: *John*, who was the beloved Diſciple, and converſed the moſt intimately with our Saviour, lived till *Anno Dom.* 100; *Polycarp*, who was the Diſciple of St. *John*, and had converſed with others of the Apoſtles and Diſciples of our Lord, lived till *Anno Dom.* 167, though his life was ſhortened by martyrdom. *Irenæus*, who was the Diſciple of *Polycarp*, and had converſed with many of the immediate Diſciples of the Apoſtles, lived, at the loweſt computation of his age, till the year 202; when he was likewiſe cut off by martyrdom; in which year the great *Origen* was appointed Regent of the Catechetick ſchool in *Alexandria*, and as he was the miracle of that age, for induſtry, learning, and philoſophy, he was looked upon as the champion of Chriſtianity, till the year 254, when, if he did not ſuffer martyrdom, as ſome think he did, he was certainly actuated by the ſpirit of it, as appears in the whole courſe of his life and writings; nay, he had often been put to the

the torture, and had undergone tryals worfe than death. As he converfed with the moft eminent Chriftians of his time in *Egypt*, and in the Eaft, brought over multitudes both from herefy and heathenifm, and left behind him feveral Difciples of great fame and learning, there is no queftion but there were confiderable numbers of thofe who knew him, and had been his hearers, fcholars, or profelytes, that lived till the end of the third century, and to the reign of *Conftantine* the Great.

IX. It is evident to thofe, who read the lives and writings of *Polycarp*, *Irenæus*, and *Origen*, that thefe three Fathers believed the accounts which are given of our Saviour in the four Evangelifts, and had undoubted arguments that not only St. *John*, but many others of our Saviour's difciples, publifhed the fame accounts of him. To which we muft fubjoin this fur-ther remark, that what was believed by thefe Fathers on this fubject, was likewife the belief of the main body of Chriftians in thofe fucceffive ages when they flourifhed; fince *Polycarp* cannot but be looked upon, if we confider the refpect that was paid him, as the reprefentative of the Eaftern Churches in this particular, *Irenæus* of the Weftern upon the fame account, and *Origen*, of thofe eftablifhed in *Egypt*.

X. To thefe I might add *Paul* the famous hermite, who retired from the *Decian* perfecution five or fix years before *Origen*'s death, and lived till the year 343. I have only difcovered one of thofe channels by which the hiftory of our Saviour might be conveyed pure and unadulterated, through thofe feveral ages that produced thofe *Pagan* Philofophers, whofe teftimonies I make ufe of for the truth of our Saviour's hiftory. Some or other of thefe Philofophers came into the Chriftian faith during its infancy, in the feveral periods of thefe three firft centuries, when they had fuch means of informing themfelves in all the particulars of our Saviour's hiftory. I muft further add, that though I have here only chofen this fingle link of martyrs, I might find out others among thofe those names which are still extant, that delivered down this account of our Saviour in a succeffive tradition, till the whole *Roman* empire became Chriftian; as there is no queftion but numberlefs feries of witneffes might follow one another in the fame order, and in as fhort a chain, and that perhaps in every fingle-Church, had the names and ages of the moft eminent primitive Chriftians been tranfmitted to us with the like certainty.

XI. But to give this confideration more force, we muft take notice, that the tradition of the firft ages of Chriftianity had feveral circumftances peculiar to it, which made it more authentick than any other tradition in any other age of the world. The Chriftians, who carried their religion through fo many general and particular perfecutions, were inceffantly comforting and fupporting one another, with the example and hiftory of our Saviour and his Apoftles. It was the fubject not only of their folemn affemblies, but of their private vifits and converfations. *Our virgins*, fays *Tatian*, who liv'd in the fecond century, *difcourfe over their diftaffs on divine fubjects*. Indeed, when religion was woven into the civil government, and flourifhed under the protection of the Emperors, men's thoughts and difcourfes were, as they are now, full of fecular affairs; but in the three firft centuries of Chriftianity, men, who embraced this religion, had given up all their interefts in this world, and lived in a perpetual preparation for the next, as not knowing how foon they might be called to it: fo that they had little elfe to talk of but the life and doctrines of that divine perfon, which was their hope, their encouragement, and their glory. We cannot therefore imagine, that there was a fingle perfon arrived at any degree of age or confideration, who had not heard and repeated above a thoufand times in his life, all the particulars of our Saviour's birth, life, death, refurrection, and afcenfion.

XII. Efpecially if we confider, that they could not then be received as Chriftians, till they had undergone
feveral

feveral examinations. Perfons of riper years, who flocked daily into the Church during the three firft centuries, were obliged to pafs through many repeated inftructions, and give a ftrict account of their proficiency, before they were admitted to Baptifm. And as for thofe who were born of Chriftian parents, and had been baptifed in their infancy, they were with the like care prepared and difciplined for confirmation, which they could not arrive at, till they were found upon examination to have made a fufficient progrefs in the knowledge of Chriftianity.

XIII. We muft further obferve, that there was not only in thofe times this religious converfation among private Chriftians, but a conftant correfpondence between the Churches that were eftablifhed by the Apoftles or their fucceffors, in the feveral parts of the world. If any new doctrine was ftarted, or any fact reported of our Saviour, a ftrict enquiry was made among the Churches, efpecially thofe planted by the Apoftles themfelves, whether they had received any fuch doctrine or account of our Saviour, from the mouths of the Apoftles, or the tradition of thofe Chriftians, who had preceded the prefent members of the Churches which were thus confulted. By this means, when any novelty was publifhed, it was immediately detected and cenfured.

XIV. St. *John*, who lived fo many years after our Saviour, was appealed to in thefe emergencies as the living Oracle of the Church ; and as his oral teftimony lafted the firft century, many have obferved that by a particular providence of God, feveral of our Saviour's Difciples, and of the early converts of his religion, lived to a very great age, that they might perfonally convey the truth of the Gofpel to thofe times, which were very remote from the firft publication of it. Of thefe, befides St. *John*, we have a remarkable inftance in *Simeon*, who was one of the feventy fent forth by our Saviour to publifh the Gofpel befor his crucifixion, and a near kinfman of the Lord. This venerable perfon, who had probably heard with his own ears our Saviour's prophecy of the deftruction of *Jerufalem,*

rufalem, prefided over the Church eftablifhed in that city, during the time of its memorable fiege, and drew his congregation out of thofe dreadful and unparallel'd calamities which befel his countrymen, by following the advice our Saviour had given, when they fhould fee *Jerufalem* encompaffed with armies, and the *Roman* ftandards, or abomination of defolation, fet up. He lived till the year of our Lord 107, when he was martyred under the Emperor *Trajan.*

SECTION VI.

I. *The tradition of the Apoftles fecured by other excellent inftitutions* ;

II. *But chiefly by the writings of the Evangelifts.*

III. *The diligence of the Difciples and firft Chriftian converts, to fend abroad thefe writings.*

IV. *That the written account of our Saviour was the fame with that delivered by tradition :*

V. *Proved from the reception of the Gofpel by thofe Churches which were eftablifhed before it was written* ;

VI. *From the uniformity of what was believed in the feveral Churches* ;

VII. *From a remarkable paffage in* Irenæus.

VIII. *Records which are now loft, of ufe to the three firft centuries, for confirming the hiftory of our Saviour.*

IX. *Inftances of fuch records.*

I. THUS far we fee how the learned *Pagans* might apprize themfelves from oral information of the particulars of our Saviour's biftory. They could hear, in every Church planted in every diftant part of the earth, the account which was there received and preferved among them, of the hiftory of our Saviour. They could learn the names and characters of thofe firft miffionaries that brought to them thefe accounts, and the miracles by which God Almighty attefted their reports. But the Apoftles and Difciples of *Chrift*, to preferve the hiftory of his life, and to fecure their accounts of him from

error

error and oblivion, did not only set aside certain persons for that purpose, as has been already shown, but appropriated certain days to the commemoration of those facts which they had related concerning him. The first day of the week was in all its returns a perpetual memorial of his resurrection, as the devotional exercises adapted to *Friday* and *Saturday,* were to denote to all ages that he was crucified on the one of those days, and that he rested in the grave on the other. You may apply the same remark to several of the annual festivals instituted by the Apostles themselves, or at furthest by their immediate Successors, in memory of the most important particulars in our Saviour's history ; to which we must add the Sacraments instituted by our Lord himself, and many of those rites and ceremonies which obtained in the most early times of the Church. These are to be regarded as standing marks of such facts as were delivered by those, who were eye-witnesses to them, and which were contrived with great wisdom to last till time should be no more. These, without any other means, might have, in some measure, convey'd to posterity, the memory of several transactions in the history of our Saviour, as they were related by his Disciples. At least, the reason of these institutions, though they might be forgotten, and obscured by a long course of years, could not but be very well known by those who lived in the three first Centuries, and a means of informing the inquisitive *Pagans* in the truth of our Saviour's history, that being the view in which I am to consider them.

II. But lest such a tradition, though guarded by so many expedients, should wear out by the length of time, the four Evangelists within about fifty, or, as *Theodoret* affirms, thirty years, after our Saviour's death, while the memory of his actions was fresh among them, consigned to writing that history, which for some years had been published only by the mouth of the Apostles and Disciples. The further consideration of these holy penmen will fall under another part of this discourse.

III. It

III. It will be fufficient to obferve here, that in the age which fucceeded the Apoftles, many of their immediate Difciples fent or carried in perfon the books of the four Evangelifts, which had been written by Apoftles, or at leaft approved by them, to moft of the Churches which they had planted in the different parts of the world. This was done with fo much diligence, that when *Pantænus*, a man of great learning and piety, had travelled into *India* for the propagation of Chriftianity, about the year of our Lord 200, he found among that remote people the Gófpel of·St. *Matthew*, which upon his return from that country he brought with him to *Alexandria*. This gofpel is generally fuppofed to have been left in thofe parts by St. *Bartholomew* the Apoftle of the *Indies*, who probably carried it with him before the writings of the three other Evangelifts were publifh'd.

IV. That the hiftory of our Saviour, as recorded by the Evangelifts, was the fame with that which had been before delivered by the Apoftles and Difciples, will further appear in the profecution of this difcourfe, and may be gathered from the following confiderations.

V. Had thefe writings differed from the fermons of the firft planters of Chriftianity, either in hiftory or doctrine, there is no queftion but they would have been rejected by thofe Churches which they had already formed. But fo confiftent and uniform was the relation of the Apoftles, that thefe hiftories appeared to be nothing elfe but their tradition and oral atteftations made fixt and permanent. Thus was the fame of our Saviour, which in fo few years had gone through the whole earth, confirmed and perpetuated by fuch records, as would preferve the traditionary account of him to after-ages; and rectifie it, if at any time, by paffing through feveral generations, it might drop any part that was material, or contradict any thing that was falfe or fictitious.

VI. Accordingly we find the fame *Jefus Chrift*, who was born of a Virgin, who had wrought many

miracles

miracles in *Palestine*, who was crucified, rose again, and ascended into Heaven ; I say, the same *Jesus Christ* had been preached, and was worshipped, in *Germany,* *France*, *Spain*, and *Great-Britain,* in *Parthia*, *Media,* *Mesopotamia*, *Armenia*, *Phrygia*, *Asia* and *Pamphylia!* in *Italy*, *Egypt*, *Afric*, and beyond *Cyrene*, *India* and *Persia*, and, in short, in all the Islands and Provinces that are visited by the rising or setting sun. The same account of our Saviour's life and doctrine was delivered by thousands of Preachers, and believed in thousands of places, who all, as fast as it could be conveyed to them, received the same account in writing from the four Evangelists.

VII. *Irenæus* to this purpose very aptly remarks, that those barbarous nations, who in his time were not possest of the written gospels, and had only learned the history of our Saviour from those who had converted them to Christianity before the Gospels were written, had among them the same accounts of our Saviour, which are to be met with in the four Evangelists. An uncontestable proof of the harmony and concurrence between the holy scripture and the tradition of the Churches in those early times of Christianity.

VIII. Thus we see what opportunities the learned and inquisitive heathens had of informing themselves of the truth of our Saviour's history, during the three first Centuries, especially as they lay nearer one than another to the fountain-head : beside which there were many incontroverted traditions, records of Christianity, and particular histories, that then threw light into these matters, but are now entirely lost, by which, at that time, any appearance of contradiction, or seeming difficulties, in the history of the Evangelists, were fully cleared up and explained : though we meet with fewer appearances of this nature in the history of our Saviour, as related by the four Evangelists, than in the accounts of ony other person, published by such a number of different historians who lived at so great a distance from the present age,

IX. Among

IX. Among thofe records which are loft, and were of great ufe to the primitive Chriftians, is the letter to *Tiberius*, which I have already mentioned ; that of *Marcus Aurelius*, which I fhall take notice of hereafter ; the writings of *Hegefippus*, who had drawn down the hiftory of Chriftianity to his own time, which was not beyond the middle of the fecond Century ; the genuine *Sibylline* oracles, which in the firft ages of the Church were eafily diftinguifhed from the fpurious ; the records preferved in particular Churches, with many other of the fame nature.

SECTION VII.

I. THERE were other means, which I find had a great influence on the learned of the three firft Centuries, to create and confirm in them the belief of our bleffed Saviour's hiftory, which ought not to be paffed over in filence. The firft was, the opportunity they enjoyed of examining thole miracles, which were on feveral occafions performed by Chriftians, and appeared in the Church more or lefs, during thefe firft ages of Chriftianity. Thefe had great weight with the men I am now fpeaking of, who, from learned *Pagans*, became fathers of the Church ; for they frequently boaft of them in their writings, as atteftations given by God himfelf to the truth of their religion.

II. At

II. At the fame time, that thefe learned men declare
ow difingenuous, bafe and wicked it would be, how
uch beneath the dignity of Philofophy, and contrary
 the precepts of Chriftianity, to utter falfhoods or for-
:ries in the fupport of a caufe, though never fo juft in
felf, they confidently affert this miraculous power,
hich then fubfifted in the Church, nay tell us that they
emfelves had been eye-witneffes of it at feveral times,
d in feveral inftances; nay appeal to the heathens
emfelves for the truth of feveral facts they relate, nay
iallenge them to be prefent at their affemblies, and fa-
fie themfelves, if they doubt of it; nay we find that
agan Authors have in fome inftances confeffed this mi-
culous power.

III. The letter of *Marcus Aurelius*, whofe army was
eferved by a refrefhing fhower, at the fame time
at his enemies were difcomfited by a ftorm of light-
ng, and which the heathen hiftorians themfelves al-
w to have been fupernatural and the effect of magic:
fay, this letter, which afcribed this unexpected affif-
nce to the prayers of the Chriftians, who then ferved
 the army, would have been thought an unquefti-
able teftimony of the miraculous power I am fpeak-
g of, had it been ftill preferved. It is fufficient for
e in this place to take notice, that this was one of
ofe miracles which had its influence on the learned
onverts, becaufe it is related by *Tertullian*, and the
ry letter appealed to. When thefe learned men faw
knefs and frenzy cured, the dead raifed, the ora-
:s put to filence, the *Dæmons* and evil fpirits forced
 confefs themfelves no Gods, by perfons who only
ade ufe of prayer and adjurations in the name of
:ir crucified Saviour; how could they doubt of their
viour's power on the like occafions, as reprefented to
:m by the traditions of the Church, and the writings
 the Evangelifts?

IV. Under this head, I cannot omit that which ap-
:ars to me a ftanding miracle in the three firft Cen-
:ies, I mean that amazing and fupernatural courage
 patience, which was fhewn by innumerable multitudes

tudes of Martyrs, in thofe flow and painful torments that were inflicted on them. I cannot conceive a man placed in the burning iron chair at *Lyons*, amid the infults and mockeries of a crowded Amphitheatre, and ftill keeping his feat; or ftretched upon a grate of iron, over coals of fire, and breathing out his foul among the exquifite fufferings of fuch a tedious execution, rather than renounce his religion, or blafpheme his Saviour. Such tryals feem to me above the ftrength of human nature, and able to over-bear duty, reafon, faith, conviction, nay, and the moft abfolute certainty of a future ftate. Humanity, unaffifted in an extraordinary manner, muft have fhaken off the prefent preffure, and have delivered it felf out of fuch a dreadful diftrefs, by any means that could have been fuggefted to it. We can eafily imagine, that many perfons, in fo good a caufe, might have laid down their lives at the gibbet, the ftake, or the block: but to expire leifurely among the moft exquifite tortures, when they might come out of them, even by a mental refervation, or an hypocrify which was not without a poffibility of being followed by repentance and forgivenefs, has fomething in it, fo far beyond the force and natural ftrength of mortals, that one cannot but think there was fome miraculous power to fupport the fufferer.

V. We find the Church of *Smyrna*, in that admirable Letter which gives an account of the death of *Polycarp* their beloved Bifhop, mentioning the cruel torments of other early Martyrs for Chriftianity, are of opinion, that our Saviour ftood by them in a vifion, and perfonally converfed with them, to give them ftrength and comfort during the bitternefs of their long continued agonies; and we have the ftory of a young man, who, having fuffered many tortures, efcaped with life, and told his fellow-chriftians, that the pain of them had been rendred tolerable, by the prefence of an Angel who ftood by him, and wiped off the tears and fweat, which ran down his face whilft he lay under his fufferings. We are affured at

: that the firft Martyr for Chriftianity was encouraged
iis laft moments, by a vifion of that divine perfon,
whom he fuffered, and into whofe prefence he was
a haftening.

VI. Let any man calmly lay his hand upon his
rt, and after reading thefe terrible conflicts in which
ancient Martyrs and Confeffors were engaged, when
y paffed through fuch new inventions and varieties
pain, as tired their tormentors; and afk himfelf,
vever zealous and fincere he is in his religion, whe-
r under fuch acute and lingring tortures he could
l have held faft his integrity, and have profeffed
faith to the laft, without a fupernatural affiftance of
ne kind or other. For my part, when I confider
t it was not an unaccountacle obftinacy in a fingle
in, or in any particular fett -of men, in fome ex-
ordinary juncture; but that there were multitudes
each fex, of every age, of different countries and
iditions, who for near 300 years together made
s glorious confeffion of their faith, in the midft of
tures, and in the hour of death: I muft conclude,
t they were either of another make than men are
prefent, or that they had fuch miraculous fupports
were peculiar to thofe times of Chriftianity, when
thout them perhaps the very name of it might have
n extinguifhed.

VII. It is certain, that the deaths and fufferings of
: primitive Chriftians had a great fhare in the con-
fion of thofe learned *Pagans*, who lived in the ages
perfecution, which with fome intervals and abate-
nts lafted near 300 years after our Saviour. *Juftin
irtyr, Tertullian, Lactantius, Arnobius,* and others,
us, that this firft of all alarmed their curiofity,
fed their attention, and made them ferioufly inqui-
ve into the nature of that religion, which could en-
: the mind with fo much ftrength, and overcome
fear of death, nay raife an earneft defire of it,
ugh it appeared in all its terrors. This they found
l not been effected by all the doctrines of thofe
lofophers, whom they had thoroughly ftudied,
and

and who had been labouring at this great point. The fight of thofe dying and tormented Martyrs engaged them to fearch into the hiftory and doctrines of him for whom they fuffered. The more they fearched, the more they were convinced; till their conviction grew fo ftrong, that they themfelves embraced the fame truths, and either actually laid down their lives, or were always in a readinefs to do it, rather than depart from them.

SECTION VIII.

I. *The completion of our Saviour's prophecies confirmed* Pagans *in their belief of the Gofpel.*
II. Origen's *obfervation on that of his Difciples being brought before Kings and Governours;*
III. *On their being perfecuted for their religion;*
IV. *On their preaching the Gofpel to all nations;*
V. *On the deftruction of* Jerufalem, *and ruine of the* Jewifh *œconomy.*
VI. *Thefe arguments ftrengthened by what has happened fince* Origen's *time.*

I. THE fecond of thofe extraordinary means, of great ufe to the learned and inquifitive *Pagans* of the three firft Centuries, for evincing the truth of the hiftory of our Saviour, was the completion of fuch prophecies as are recorded of him in the Evanvangelifts. They could not indeed form any arguments from what he foretold, and was fulfilled during his life, becaufe both the prophecy and the completion were over before they were publifhed by the Evangelifts; though, as *Origen* obferves, what end could there be in forging fome of thefe predictions, as that of St. *Peter's* denying his mafter, and all his Difciples forfaking him in the greateft extremity, which

reflects

reflects fo much fhame on the great Apoftle, and on all his companions? Nothing but a ftrict adherence to truth, and to matters of fact, could have prompted the Evangelifts to relate a circumftance fo difadvantageous to their own reputation; as that Father has well obferved.

II. But to purfue his reflections on this fubject. There are predictions of our Saviour recorded by the Evangelifts, which were not completed till after their deaths, and had no likelihood of being fo, when they were pronounced by our bleffed Saviour. Such was that wonderful notice he gave them, that they fhould be brought before Governours and Kings for his fake, for a teftimony againft them and the *Gentiles, Mat. x 28.* with the other like prophecies, by which he foretold that his Difciples were to be perfecuted. Is there any other doctrine in the world, fays this Father, whofe followers are punifhed? Can the enemies of *Chrift* fay, that he knew his opinions were falfe and impious, and that therefore he might well conjecture and foretell what would be the treatment of thofe perfons who fhould embrace them? Suppofing his doctrines were really fuch, why fhould this be the confequence? what likelihood that men fhould be brought before Kings and Governors for opinions and tenets of any kind, when this never happened even to the *Epicureans,* who abfolutely denied a Providence; nor to the *Peripateticks* themfelves, who laughed at the prayers and facrifices which were made to the Divinity? Are there any but the Chriftians who, according to this Prediction of our Saviour, being brought before Kings and Governors for his fake, are preffed to their lateft gafp of breath, by their refpective judges, to renounce Chriftianity, and to procure their liberty and reft, by offering the fame facrifices. and taking the fame oaths that others did?

III. Confider the time when our Saviour pronounced thofe words, *Matt. x. 32. Whofoever fhall confefs me before men, him will I confefs alfo before my Father which is in heaven: but whofoever fhall deny me before*

men,

men, him will I also deny before my Father which is in heaven. Had you heard him speak after this manner, when as yet his Disciples were under no such tryals, you would certainly have said within your self, If these speeches of *Jesus* are true, and if, according to his prediction, Governors and Kings undertake to ruine and destroy those who shall profess themselves his Disciples, we will believe (not only that he is a Prophet, but) that he has received power from God sufficient to preserve and propagate his religion; and that he would never talk in such a peremptory and discouraging manner, were he not assured that he was able to subdue the most powerful opposition, that could be made against the faith and doctrine which he taught.

IV. Who is not struck with admiration, when he represents to himself our Saviour at that time foretelling that his Gospel should be preached in all the world, for a witness unto all nations, or as St. *Origen* (who rather quotes the sense than the words) to serve for a conviction to Kings and people, when at the same time he finds that his Gospel has accordingly been preached to *Greeks* and *Barbarians*, to the learned and to the ignorant, and that there is no quality or condition of life able to exempt men from submitting to the doctrine of *Christ*? As for us, says this great Author, in another part of his book against *Celsus*, " When " we see every day those events exactly accomplished " which our Saviour foretold at so great a distance: " that his Gospel is preached in all the world, *Matt-* " *thew* xxiv. 14. That his Disciples go and teach all na- " tions, *Matthew* xxviii. 19. And that those, who have " received his doctrine, are brought for his sake be- " fore Governors, and before Kings, *Matthew* x. 18. " we are filled with admiration, and our faith in him " is confirmed more and more. What clearer and " stronger proofs can *Celsus* ask for the truth of what " he spoke?

V. *Origen* insists likewise with great strength on that wonderful prediction of our Saviour, concerning the destruction of *Jerusalem*, pronounced at a time, as he ob-

obferves, when there was no likelihood nor appearance of it. This has been taken notice of and inculcated by fo many others, that I fhall refer you to what this Father has faid on the fubject in the firft book againft *Celfus.* And as to the accomplifhment of this remarkable prophecy, fhall only obferve, that whoever reads the account given us by *Jofephus,* without knowing his character, and compares it with what our Saviour foretold, would think the hiftorian had been a Chriftian, and that he had nothing elfe in view but to adjuft the event to the prediction.

VI I cannot quit this head without taking notice, that *Origen* would ftill have triumphed more in the foregoing arguments, had he liv'd an age longer, to have feen the *Roman* Emperors, and all their Governors and provinces, fubmitting themfelves to the Chriftian religion, and glorying in its profeffion, as fo many Kings and Sovereigns ftill place their relation to *Chrift* at the head of their titles.

How much greater confirmation of his faith would he have received, had he feen our Saviour's prophecy ftand good in the deftruction of the temple, and the diffolution of the *Jewifh* œconomy, when *Jews* and *Pagans* united all their endeavours under *Julian* the Apoftate, to baffle and falfifie the prediction? The great preparations that were made for re-building the temple, with the hurricane, earthquake, and eruptions of fire, that deftroyed the work, and terrified thofe employed in the attempt from proceeding in it, are related by many hiftorians of the fame age, and the fubftance of the ftory teftified both by *Pagan* and *Jewifh* writers, as *Ammianus Marcellinus* and *Zemath-David.* The learned *Chryfoftom,* in a fermon againft the *Jews,* tells them this fact was then frefh in the memories even of their young men, that it happened but twenty years ago, and that it was attefted by all the inhabitants of *Jerufalem,* where they might ftill fee the marks of it in the rubbifh of that work, from which the *Jews* defifted in fo great a fright, and which even *Julian* had not the courage to carry on.

This fact, which is in it self so miraculous, and so in-disputable, brought over many of the *Jews* to Christianity; and shows us, that after our Saviour's prophecy against it, the temple could not be preserved from the plough passing over it, by all the care of *Titus*, who would fain have prevented its destruction, and that in stead of being re-edified by *Julian*, all his endeavours towards it did but still more literally accomplish our Saviour's prediction, that, not one stone should be left upon another.

The ancient Christians were so intirely perfuaded of the force of our Saviour's prophecies, and of the punishment which the *Jews* had drawn upon themselves, and upon their children, for the treatment which the *Messiah* had received at their hands, that they did not doubt but they would always remain an abandoned and disperfed people, an hissing and an astonishment among the nations, as they are to this day. In short, that they had lost their peculiarity of being God's people, which was now transferred to the body of Christians, and which preserved the Church of *Christ* among all the conflicts, difficulties and persecutions, in which it was engaged, as it had preserved the *Jewish* government and œconomy for so many ages, whilst it had the same truth and vital principle in it, notwithstanding it was so frequently in danger of being utterly abolished and destroyed. *Origen*, in his fourth book against *Celsus*, mentioning their being cast out of *Jerusalem*, the place to which their worship was annexed, deprived of their temple and sacrifice, their religious rites and solemnities, and scattered over the face of the earth, ventures to assure them with a face of confidence, that they would never be re-established, since they had committed that horrid crime against the Saviour of the world. This was a bold assertion in the good man, who knew how this people had been so wonderfully re-established in former times, when they were almost swallowed up, and in the most desperate state of desolation, as in their deliverance out of the *Babylonish* captivity, and the

the oppreſſions of *Antiochus Epiphanes*. Nay, he knew that within leſs than a hundred years before his own time, the *Jews* had made ſuch a powerful effort for their re-eſtabliſhment under *Barchocab*, in the reign of *Adrian*, as ſhook the whole *Roman* empire. But he founded his opinion on a ſure word of prophecy, and on the puniſhment they had ſo juſtly incurred; and we find, by a long experience of 1500 years, that he was not miſtaken, nay, that his opinion gathers ſtrength daily, ſince the *Jews* are now at a greater diſtance from any probability of ſuch a re-eſtabliſhment, than they were when *Origen* wrote.

SECTION IX.

I. *The lives of primitive Chriſtians, another means of bringing learned* Pagans *into their religion.*
II. *The change and reformation of their manners.*
III. *This looked upon as ſupernatural by the learned* Pagans,
IV. *And ſtrengthened the accounts given of our Saviour's life and hiſtory.*
V. *The* Jewiſh *prophecies of our Saviour, an argument for the heathens belief:*
VI. *Purſued:*
VII. *Purſued.*

I. THere was one other means enjoyed by the learned *Pagans* of the three firſt centuries, for ſatisfying them in the truth of our Saviour's hiſtory, which I might have flung under one of the foregoing heads; but as it is ſo ſhining a particular, and does ſo much honour to our religion, I ſhall make a diſtinct article of it, and only conſider it with regard to the ſubject I am upon: I mean the lives and manners of thoſe holy men, who believ'd in *Chriſt* during the firſt ages of Chriſtianity. I ſhould be thought to ad-

vance

vance a paradox, fhould I affirm that there were more Chriftians in the world during thofe times of perfe. cution, than there are at prefent in thefe which we call the flourifhing times of Chriftianity. But this will be found an indifputable truth, if we form our calculation upon the opinions which prevailed in thofe days, that every one who lives in the habitual practice of any voluntary fin, actually cuts himfelf off from the benefits and profeffion of Chriftianity, and whatever he may call himfelf, is in reality no Chriftian, nor ought to be-efteemed as fuch.

II. In the times we are now furveying, the Chriftian religion fhowed its full force and efficacy on the minds of men, and by many examples demonftrated what great and generous fouls it was capable of producing. It exalted and refined its profelytes to a very high degree of perfection, and fet them far above the pleafures, and even the pains of this life. It ftrengthened the infirmity, and broke the fiercenefs of human nature. It lifted up the minds of the ignorant to the knowledge and worfhip of him that made them, and infpired the vicious with a rational devotion, a ftrict purity of heart, and an unbounded love to their fellow-creatures. In proportion as it fpread through the world, it feemed to change mankind into another fpecies of Beings. No fooner was a convert initiated into it, but by an eafy figure he became a New Man, and both acted and looked upon himfelf as one regenerated and born a fecond time into another ftate of exiftence.

III. It is not my bufinefs to be more particular in the accounts of primitive Chriftianity, which have been exhibited fo well by others, but rather to obferve, that the *Pagan* converts, of whom I am now fpeaking, mention this great reformation of thofe who had been the greateft finners, with that fudden and furprizing change which it made in the lives of the moft profligate, as having fomething in it fupernatural, miraculous, and more than human. *Origen* reprefents this power in the Chriftian religion, as

no

no lefs wonderful than that of curing the lame and blind, or cleanfing the leper. Many others reprefent it in the fame light, and looked upon it as an argument that there was a certain divinity in that religion, which fhewed itfelf in fuch ftrange and glorious effects.

IV. This therefore was a great means not only of recommending Chriftianity to honeft and learned heathens, but of conforming them in the belief of our Saviour's hiftory, when they faw multitudes of virtuous men daily forming themfelves upon his example, animated by his precepts, and actuated by that Spirit which he had promifed to fend among his Difciples.

V. But I find no argument made a ftronger impreffion on the minds of thefe eminent *Pagan* converts, for ftrengthening their faith in the hiftory of our Saviour, than the predictions relating to him in thofe old prophetick writings, which were depofited among the hands of the greateft enemies to Chriftianity, and owned by them to have been extant many ages before his appearance. The learned heathen converts were aftonifhed to fee the whole hiftory of their Saviour's life publifhed before he was born, and to find that the Evangelifts and Prophets, in their accounts of the *Meffiah*, differ'd only in point of time, the one foretelling what fhould happen to him, and the other defcribing thofe very particulars as what had actually happened. This our Saviour himfelf was pleafed to make ufe of as the ftrongeft argument of his being the promifed *Meffiah*, and without it would hardly have reconciled his Difciples to the ignominy of his death, as in that remarkable paffage which mentions his converfation with the two Difciples, on the day of his refurrection. St. *Luke*, chap. 24. verfe 13, to the end.

VI. The heathen converts, after having travelled through all human learning, and fortified their minds with the knowledge of arts and fciences, were particularly qualified to examine thefe prophecies with great

care

care and impartiality, and without prejudice or pre-
poffeffion. If the *Jews* on the one fide put an unnatural interpretation on thefe prophecies, to evade the
force of them in their controverfies with the Chriftians; or if the Chriftians on the other fide over-
ftrained feveral paffages in their applications of them,
as it often happens among men of the beft underftanding, when their minds are heated with any confideration that bears a more than an ordinary weight with
it: the learned heathens may be looked upon as neu-
ters in the matter, when all thefe prophecies were
new to them, and their education had left the interpretation of them free and indifferent. Befides, thefe
learned men among the primitive Chriftians, knew
how the *Jews*, who had preceded our Saviour, interpreted thefe predictions, and the feveral marks by
which they acknowledged the *Meffiah* would be difcovered, and how thofe of the *Jewifh* Doctors who
fucceeded him, had deviated from the interpretations
and doctrines of their forefathers, on purpofe to ftifle
their own conviction.

VII. This fett of arguments had therefore an invin-
cible force with thofe *Pagan* Philofophers who became Chriftians, as we find in moft of their writings.
They could not disbelieve our Saviour's hiftory, which
fo exactly agreed with every thing that had been
written of him many ages before his birth, nor doubt
of thofe circumftances being fulfilled in him, which
could not be true of any perfon that lived in the world
befides himfelf. This wrought the greateft confufion
in the unbelieving *Jews*, and the greateft conviction,
in the *Gentiles*, who every where fpeak with aftonifh-
ment of thefe truths they met with in this new magazine of learning, which was opened to them, and
carry the point fo far as to think whatever excellent
doctrine they had met with among *Pagan* writers,
had been ftole from their converfation with the *Jews*,
or from the perufal of thefe writings which they had
in their cuftody.

T H E

THE PRESENT

STATE *of the* WAR,

AND THE

Neceſſity of an AUGMENTATION,
conſidered.

PREFACE.

THE *Author of the following Essay has endeavoured to draw into one continued scheme the whole state of the present war, and the methods that appear to him the most proper for bringing it to a happy conclusion.*

After having considered that the French *are the constant and most dangerous enemies to the* British *nation, and that the danger from them is now greater than ever, and will still increase till their present union with* Spain *be broken, he sets forth the several advantages which this Union has already given* France, *and taken from* Great-Britain, *in relation to the* West-Indies, *the woollen manufacture, the trade of the* Levant, *and the naval power of the two nations.*

He shews how these advantages will still rise higher after a peace, notwithstanding our present conquests, with new additions, should be confirmed to us; as well because the monarchy of Spain *would not be weakened by such concessions, as because no Guarrantee could be found sufficient to secure them to us. For which reasons he lays it down as a fixt Rule, that no peace is to be made without an entire disunion of the* French *and* Spanish *Monarchies.*

That

P R E F A C E.

That this may be brought about, he endeavours to prove from the progress we have already made towards it, and the successes we have purchased in the present war, which are very considerable, if well pursued, but of no effect if we acquiesce in them.

In order to complete this disunion in which we have gone so far, he would not have us rely upon exhausting the French Treasury, attempts on the Spanish Indies, descents on France, but chiefly upon out-numbring them in troops, France being already drained of her best supplies, and the confederates masters of much greater forces for multitude and strength, both in men and horse, and provided with Generals of greater fame and abilities.

He then considers the wrong measures we have hitherto taken in making too small levies after a successful campaign, in regulating their number by that of the enemies forces, and hiring them of our confederates; shewing at the same time the inconveniencies we suffer from such hired troops, and several advantages we might receive from employing those of our own nation.

He further recommends this augmentation of our forces, to prevent the keeping up a standing body of them in times of peace, to enable us to make an impression on the enemy in the present posture of the war, and to secure our selves against a Prince, who is now at the head of a powerful army, and has not yet declared himself.

In the last place, he answers by several considerations those two popular objections, That we furnish more towards the war than the rest of the Allies, and That we are not able to contribute more than we do already.

These are the most material heads of the following Essay, in which there are many other subordinate reflections that naturally grow out of so copious a subject.

November, 1707.

THE

THE PRESENT

STATE *of the* WAR,

AND THE

Neceſſity of an Augmentation, *conſidered.*

THE *French* are certainly the moſt implacable, and the moſt dangerous enemies of the *Britiſh* nation. Their form of government, their religion, their jealouſy of the *Britiſh* power, as well as their proſecutions of commerce, and purſuits of univerſal Monarchy, will fix them for ever in their animoſities and averſion towards us, and make them catch at all opportunities of ſubverting our conſtitution, deſtroying our religion, ruining our trade, and ſinking the figure which we make among the nations of *Europe:* Not to mention the particularities of honour, that lie on their preſent King to impoſe on us a Prince, who muſt prove fatal to our country, if he ever reigns over us.

As we are thus in a natural ſtate of war, if I may ſo call it, with the *French* nation; it is our misfortune, that they are not only the moſt inveterate, but moſt formidable of our enemies; and have the greateſt power, as well as the ſtrongeſt inclination, to ruin us. No other ſtate equals them in the force of their fleets and armies, in the nearneſs and conveniency of their ſituation, and in the number of friends and well-wiſhers, which, it is to be feared, they have among us.

For

For these reasons our wars with *France* have always affected us in our most tender interests, and concerned us more than those we have had with any other nation ; but I may venture to say, this Kingdom was never yet engaged in a war of so great consequence, as that which now lies upon our hands. Our all is at stake, and irretrievably lost, if we fail of success. At other times, if a war ended in a dishonourable peace, or, with equal loss, we could comfort our selves with the hopes of a more favourable juncture, that might set the balance right, or turn it to our advantage. We had still the prospect of forming the same alliance, or perhaps strengthning it with new confederacies, and by that means of trying our fortune a second time, in case the injustice or ambition of the enemy forced us into the field. At present, if we make a drawn game of it, or procure but moderate advantages, we are in a condition which every *British* heart must tremble at the thought of. There are no second tryals, no wars in reserve, no new schemes of alliance to which we can have recourse. Should the *French* King be able to bear down such an united force as now makes head against him, at a time when *Spain* affords him no greater assistance ; what will he do, when the trade of the *Levant* lies at his mercy ; when the whole Kingdom of *Spain* is supplied with his manufactures, and the wealth of the *Indies* flows into his coffers ; and, what is yet worse, when this additional strength must arise in all its particulars from a proportionable decay in the States that now make war upon him ? It is no wonder therefore that our late King of glorious memory, who, by the confession of his greatest enemies, was a prince that perfectly understood the interests of *Europe*, should in his last speech recommend to his parliament the declaring war against *France* in those memorable words : *You have yet an opportunity, by God's blessing, to secure to you and your posterity the quiet enjoyment of your religion and liberties, if you are not wanting to your selves, but will exert the ancient vigour of the* English *nation : but I tell you plainly, my opinion is, if you do not lay hold on this occasion, you have no reason to hope for another.*

We

We have already a dreadful proof of the increase of power that accrues to *France* from its conjunction with *Spain.* So expensive a war as that which the *French* Monarchy hath been carrying on in so many and so remote parts at once, must long since have drained and exhausted all its substance, had there not been several secret springs, that swelled their treasury from time to time, in proportion as the war has sunk it. The King's coffers have been often reduced to their lowest ebb, but have still been seasonably refreshed by frequent and unexpected supplies from the *Spanish America.* We hear indeed of the arrival but of very few ships from those parts; but as in every vessel there is stowage for immense treasures, when the cargo is pure Bullion, or merchandise of as great a value; so we find by experience they have had such prodigious sums of money conveyed to them by those secret channels, that they have been enabled to pay more numerous armies, than they ever had on foot before; and that at a time when their trade fails in all its other branches, and is distressed by all the arts and contrivances of their neighbouring nations. During the last four years, by a modest computation, there have been brought into *Brest* above six millions of pounds sterling in bullion. What then shall we suppose wou'd be the effect of this correspondence with *America*, might the wealth of those parts come to them on squadrons of men of war, and fleets of galeons? If these little by-currents, that creep into the country by stealth, have so great a force, how shall we stem the whole torrent, when it breaks in upon us with its full violence; and this certainly will be our case, unless we find a means to dissolve the union between *France* and *Spain.* I have dwelt the longer on this consideration, because the present war hath already furnished us with the experiment, and sensibly convinced us of the increase of power, which *France* has received from its intercourse with the *Spanish West-Indies.*

As there are many who look upon every thing which they do not actually see and feel as bare probability

and

and ſpeculation, I ſhall only touch on' thoſe other reaſons of which we have already had ſome experience, for our preventing this coalition of intereſts and deſigns in the two monarchies.

The Woollen manufacture is the *Britiſh* ſtrength, the ſtaple commodity and proper growth of our country ; if this fails us, our trade and eſtates muſt ſink together, and all the caſh of the nation be conſumed on foreign merchandize. The *French* at preſent gain very much upon us in this great article of our trade, and ſince 'the acceſſion of the *Spaniſh* monarchy, ſupply with cloth, of their own making, the very beſt mart we had in Europe. And what a melancholy proſpect have we, if ever a peace gives them leave to enrich their manufacture with mixtures of *Spaniſh* wool, to multiply the hands employed in it, to improve themſelves in all the niceties of the art, and to vend their wares in thoſe places, where was the greateſt conſumption of our woollen works, and the moſt conſiderable gain for the *Britiſh* merchant. Notwithſtanding our many ſeaſonable recruits from *Portugal,* and our plantations, we already complain of our want of bullion, and muſt at laſt be reduced to the greateſt exigencies; if this great ſource be dryed up, and our traffick with *Spain* continue under its preſent diſcouragement.

The trade of the *Levant* muſt likewiſe flouriſh, or decay in our hands, as we are friends or enemies of the *Spaniſh* monarchy. The late conqueſt of *Naples* will very little alter the caſe, though *Sicily* ſhould follow the fate of her ſiſter kingdom. The *Streight's* mouth is the key of the *Levant,* and will be always in the poſſeſſion of thoſe who are Kings of *Spain.* We may only add, that the ſame cauſes which ſtraiten the *Britiſh* commerce, will naturally enlarge the *French* ; and that the naval force of either nation will thrive or languiſh in the ſame degree as their commerce gathers or loſes ſtrength. And if ſo powerful and populous a nation as that of *France* become ſuperior to us by ſea, our whole is loſt, and we are no more a people. The conſideration of ſo narrow a channel

betwixt.

betwixt us, of ſuch numbers of regular troops on the enemy's ſide, of ſo ſmall a ſtanding force on our own, and that too in a country deſtitute of all ſuch forts and ſtrong places as might ſtop the progreſs of a victorious army, hath ſomething in it ſo terrifying, that one does not care for ſetting it in its proper light. Let it not therefore enter into the heart of any one that hath the leaſt zeal for his religion, or love of liberty, that hath any regard either to the honour or ſafety of his country, or a well-wiſh for his friends or poſterity, to think of a peace with *France* till the *Spaniſh* monarchy be entirely torn from it, and the houſe of *Bourbon* diſabled from ever giving the law to *Europe*.

Let us ſuppoſe that the *French* King would grant us the moſt advantageous terms we can deſire ; without the ſeparation of the two monarchies they muſt infallibly end in our deſtruction. Should he ſecure to us all our preſent acquiſitions ; ſhould he add two or three frontier-towns to what we have already in *Flanders* ; ſhould he join the kingdoms of *Sicily* and *Sardinia* to *Milan* and *Naples* ; ſhould he leave King *Charles* in the peaceable poſſeſſion of *Catalonia* ; ſhould he make over to *Great Britain* the town and harbour of *Cadiz*, as well as that of *Gibraltar*; and at the ſame time reſign his conqueſts in *Portugal* ; it would all be of no effect towards the common ſafety of *Europe*, while the bulk of the *Spaniſh* continent and the riches of *America* remain in the poſſeſſion of the *Bourbon* family.

Boccalini when he weighs the States of *Europe* in his political balance, after having laid *France* in one ſcale, throws *Spain* into the other, which wanted but very little of being a counter-poiſe. The *Spaniards* upon this, ſays he, begun to promiſe themſelves the honour of the balance: reckoning that if *Spain* of it ſelf weighed ſo well, they could not fail of ſucceſs when the ſeveral parts of the monarchy were lumped in the ſame ſcale. Their ſurpriſe was very great when upon the throwing in of *Naples* they ſaw the ſcale

riſe,

rise, and was greater still when they found that. *Milan* and *Flanders* had the same effect. The truth of it is, these parts of the *Spanish* monarchy are rather for ornament than strength. They furnish out Vice-royalties for the Grandees, and posts of honour for the noble families; but in a time of war are incumbrances to the main body of the kingdom, and leave it naked and exposed by the great number of hands they draw from it to their defence. Should we therefore continue in the possession of what we have already made ourselves masters with such additions as have been mentioned, we should have little more than the excrescencies of the *Spanish* monarchy. The strength of it will still join it self to *France*, and grow the closer to it by its disunion from the rest. And in this case the advantages which must arise to that people from their intimate alliance with the remaining part of the *Spanish* dominions, would in a very few years not only repair all the damages they have sustained in the present war, but fill the kingdom with more riches than it hath yet had in its most flourishing periods.

The *French* King hath often entred on several expensive projects, on purpose to dissipate the wealth that is continually gathering in his coffers in times of peace. He hath employed immense sums on architecture, gardening, water-works, painting, statuary, and the like, to distribute his treasures among his people, as well as to humour his pleasures and his ambition; but if he once engrosses the commerce of the *Spanish* *Indies*, whatever quantities of gold and silver stagnate in his private coffers, there will be still enough to carry on the circulation among his subjects. By this means in a short space of time he may heap up greater wealth than all the Princes of *Europe* joined together; and in the present constitution of the world, wealth and power are but different names for the same thing. Let us therefore suppose that after eight or ten years of peace, he hath a mind to infringe any of his treaties, or invade a neighbouring State; to revive the pretensions of *Spain* upon *Portugal*, or attempt the

thè taking thoſe places which were granted us for our
ſecurity; what reſiſtance, what oppoſition can we
make to ſo formidable an enemy? Should the ſame alliance riſe againſt him that is now in war with him,
what could we hope for from it, at a time when the
States engaged in it will be comparatively weakened,
and the enemy who is now able to keep them at a
ſtand, will have received ſo many new acceſſions of
ſtrength?

But I think it is not to be imagined that in ſuch a
conjunƈture as we here ſuppoſe, the ſame confederates,
or any other of equal force, could be prevailed upon to
join their arms, and endeavour at the pulling down
ſo exorbitant a power. Some might be bought into his
intereſts by money, others drawn over by fear, and
thoſe that are liable to neither of theſe impreſſions, might
not think their own intereſt ſo much concerned as in
the preſent war; or if any appeared in a diſpoſition to
enter into ſuch a confederacy, they might be cruſhed ſe-
parately before they could concert meaſures for their mu-
tual defence.

The keeping together of the preſent alliance can be
aſcribed to nothing elſe but the clear and evident con-
viƈtion, which every member of it is under, that if it
ſhould once break without having had its effeƈt, they
can never hope for another opportunity of re-uniting, or
of prevailing by all the joint efforts of ſuch an union.
Let us therefore agree on this as a fixt rule, and an in-
violable maxim, never to lay down our arms againſt
France, till we have utterly disjoyned her from the *Spaniſh* monarchy. Let this be the firſt ſtep of a publick
treaty, the baſis of a general peace.

Had the preſent war indeed run againſt us, and all
our attacks upon the enemy been vain, it might look
like a degree of frenzy, or a mixture of obſtinacy and
deſpair; to be determined on ſo impraƈticable an undertaking. But on the contrary, we have already done
a great part of our work, and are come within view
of the end that we have been ſo long driving at. We
remain viƈtorious in all the ſeats of war. In *Flanders*
we

we have gotten into our hands several open countries, rich towns, and fortified places. We have driven the enemy out of all his alliances, dispossessed him of his strong holds, and ruined his allies in *Germany*. We have not only recovered what the beginning of the war had taken from us, but possessed ourselves of the kingdom of *Naples*, the dutchy of *Milan*, and the avenue of *France* in *Italy*. The *Spanish* war hath given us a haven for our ships, and the most populous and wealthy province of that kingdom. In short, we have taken all the outlying parts of the *Spanish* monarchy, and made impressions upon the very heart of it. We have beaten the *French* from all their advanced posts in *Europe*, and driven them into their last entrenchments. One vigorous push on all sides, one general assault will force the enemy to cry out for quarter, and surrender themselves at discretion. Another *Blenheim* or *Ramillies* will make the confederates masters of their own terms, and arbitrators of a peace.

But notwithstanding the advantages already gained are very considerable if we pursue them, they will be of no effect unless we improve them towards the carrying of our main point. The enemy staggers ; if you follow your blow, he falls at your feet; but if you allow him respite, he will recover his strength, and come upon you with greater fury. We have given him several repeated wounds that have enfeebled him, and brought him low ; but they are such as time will heal, unless you take advantage from his present weakness to redouble your attacks upon him. It was a celebrated part in *Cæsar*'s character, and what comes home to our present purpose, that he thought nothing at all was done, while any thing remained undone. In short, we have been tugging a great while against the stream, and have almost weathered our point; a stretch or two more will do the work; but if instead of that we slacken our arms, and drop our oars, we shall be hurried back in a moment to the place from whence we first set out.

After

After having feen the neceffity of an entire feparation of the kingdoms of *France* and *Spain*, our fubject naturally leads us into the confideration of the moſt proper means for effecting it.

We have a great while flattered ourfelves with the profpect of reducing *France* to our own terms by the want of money among the people, and the exigencies of the publick treafury ; but have been ſtill difappointed by the great fums imported from *America*, and the many new expedients which the Court hath found out for its relief. A long confumptive war is more likely to break the grand alliance, than difable *France* from maintaining fufficient armies to oppofe it. An arbitrary govern‧ ment will never want money, fo long as the people have it; and fo active a people will always have it, whilſt they can fend what merchandiſes they pleafe to *Mexico* and *Peru.* The *French* fince their alliance with *Spain* keep thirty fhips in conſtant motion between the weſtern ports of *France* and the fouth feas of *America.* The King himfelf is an adventurer in this traffick, and befides the fhare that he receives out of the gains of his fubjects, has immenfe fums that come directly from it into his own hands.

We may further confider, that the *French* fince their abandoning *Bavaria* and *Italy* have very much retrenched the expence of the war, and lay out among themfelves all the money that is confumed in it.

Many are of opinion, that the moſt probable way of bringing *France* to reafon would be by the making an attempt upon the *Spaniſh Weſt-Indies*, and by that means to cut off all communication with this great fource of riches, or turn the current of it into our own country. This I muſt confefs carries fo promi‧ fing an appearance, that I would by no means difcourage the attempt : but at the fame time I think it fhould be a collateral project, rather than our principal defign. Such an undertaking (if well concerted, and put into good hands) would be of infinite advantage to the common caufe : but certainly an enterprife that carries in it the fate of *Europe,* fhould not turn

upon

upon the uncertainty of winds and waves, and be liable to all the accidents that may befal a naval expedition.

Others there are that have long deceived themselves with the hopes of an insurrection in *France*, and are therefore for laying out all our strength on a descent. These, I think, do not enough consider the natural love which the gross of mankind have for the constitution of their fathers. A man that is not enlightened by travel or reflection, grows as fond of arbitrary power, to which he hath been used from his infancy, as of cold climates or barren countries, in which he hath been born and bred. Besides there is a kind of sluggish resignation, as well as poorness and degeneracy of spirit, in a state of slavery that we meet with but very few who will be at the pains or danger of recovering themselves out of it; as we find in history instances of persons who after their prisons have been flung open, and their fetters struck off, have chosen rather to languish in their dungeons, than stake their miserable lives and fortunes upon the success of a revolution. I need not instance the general fate of descents, the difficulty of supplying men and provisions by sea against an enemy that hath both at hand, and without which it is impossible to secure those conquests that are often made in the first onsets of an invasion. For these and other reasons I can never approve the nursing up commotions and insurrections in the enemy's country, which for want of the necessary support are likely to end in the massacre of our friends, and the ruine of their families.

The only means therefore for bringing *France* to our conditions, and what appears to m , in all human probability, a sure and infallible expedient, is to throw in multitudes upon them, and overpower them with numbers. Would the confederacy exert itself as much to annoy the enemy, as they themselves do for their defence, we might bear them down with the weight of our armies, and in one summer overset the whole power of *France*.

The

The *French* monarchy is already exhausted of its best and bravest subjects. The flower of the nation is consumed in its wars: the strength of their armies consists at present of such as have saved themselves by flight: from some or other of the victorious confederates; and the only proper persons to recruit them are but the refuse of those who have been already picked out for the service. Mareschal *de Vauban,* though infinitely partial in his calculations of the power of *France,* reckons that the number of its inhabitants was two millions less at the peace of *Ryswick,* than in the beginning of the war that was there concluded: and though that war continued nine years, and this hath as yet lasted but six, yet considering that their armies are more strong and numerous; that there hath been much more action in the present war; and that their losses sustained in it have been very extraordinary; we may, by a moderate computation, suppose that the present war hath not been less prejudicial than the foregoing one in the ravage which it has made among the people. There is in *France* so great a disproportion between the number of males and females; and among the former, between those who are capable of bearing arms, and such as are too young, sickly, or decrepit for the service; and at the same time such vast numbers of Ecclesiasticks, secular and religious, who live upon the labours of others, that when the several trades and professions are supplied, you will find most of those that are proper for war absolutely necessary for filling up the laborious part of life, and carrying on the underwork of the nation. They have already contributed all their superfluous hands, and every new levy they make must be at the expence of their farms and vineyards, their manufactures and commerce.

On the contrary, the grand Alliance have innumerable sources of recruits, not only in *Britain* and *Ireland,* the *United Provinces,* and *Flanders;* but in all the populous parts of *Germany* that have little trade or manufactures, in proportion to the number of their inha-

inhabitants. We may add that the *French* have only *Switzerland*, befides their own country, to recruit in; and we know the difficulties they meet with in getting thence a fingle regiment : whereas the Allies have not only the fame refource, but may be fupplied for money from *Denmark* and other neutral States. In fhort, the Confederates may bring to the field what forces they pleafe, if they will be at the charge of them : but *France*, let her wealth be what it will, muft content herfelf with the product of her own country.

The *French* are ftill in greater ftreights for fupplies of horfe than men. The breed of their country is neither fo good nor numerous as what are to be found in moft of the countries of the Allies. They had laft fummer about threefcore thoufand in their feveral armies, and could not perhaps bring into the field thirty thoufand more, if they were difpofed to make fuch an augmentation.

The *French* horfe are not only few, but weak in comparifon of ours. Their cavalry in the battle of *Blenheim* could not fuftain the fhock of the *Britifh* horfe. For this reafon our late way of attacking their troops fword in hand is very much to the advantage of our nation, as our men are more robuft, and our horfes of a ftronger make than the *French* ; and in fuch attacks it is the weight of the forces, fuppofing equal courage and conduct, that will always carry it. The *Englifh* ftrength turned very much to account in our wars againft the *French* of old, when we ufed to gall them with our long bows, at a greater diftance than they could fhoot their arrows : this advantage we loft upon the invention of fire arms, but by the prefent method our ftrength as well as bravery may again be of ufe to us in the day of battle.

We have very great encouragement to fend what numbers we are able into the field, becaufe our Generals at prefent are fuch as are likely to make the beft ufe of them, without throwing them away on any frefh attempts or ill concerted projects. The Confederate armies have the happinefs of being commanded

by

by perſons who are eſteemed the greateſt leaders of the preſent age, and are perhaps equal to any that have preceded them. There is a ſort of reſemblance in their characters; a particular ſedateneſs in their converſation and behaviour, that qualifies them for council, with a great intrepidity and reſolution that fits them, for action. They are all of them men of concealed fire, that doth not break out with noiſe and heat in the ordinary circumſtances of life; but ſhews it ſelf ſufficiently in all great enterpriſes that require it. It is true, the General upon the *Rhine* hath not had the ſame occaſions as the others to ſignalize himſelf; but if we conſider the great vigilance, activity and courage, with the conſummate prudence, and the nice ſenſe of honour which appears in that Prince's character, we have great reaſon to hope, that as he purchaſed the firſt ſucceſs in the preſent war, by forcing into the ſervice of the Confederates an army that was raiſed againſt them in the very heart of the Empire, he will give one of the finiſhing ſtrokes to it, and help to conclude the great work which he ſo happily begun. The ſudden check that he gave to the *French* army the laſt campaign, and the good order he eſtabliſhed in that of the *Germans*, look like happy preſages of what we may expect from his conduct. I ſhall not pretend to give any character of the Generals on the enemies ſide; but I think we may ſay this, that in the eyes of their own nation they are inferior to ſeveral that have formerly commanded the *French* armies. If then we have greater numbers than the *French*, and at the ſame time better Generals, it muſt be our own fault if we will not reap the fruit of ſuch advantages.

It would be loſs of time to explain any further our ſuperiority to the enemy in numbers of men and horſe. We ſee plainly that we have the means in our hands, and that nothing but the application of them is wanting. Let us only conſider what uſe the enemy would make of the advantage we have mentioned, if it fell on their ſide; and is it not very ſtrange that we ſhould not be as active and induſtrious for our ſecurity, as

they

they would certainly be for our destruction? But before we consider more distinctly the method we ought to take in the prosecution of the war, under this particular view, let us reflect a little upon those we have already taken in the course of it for these six years past.

The Allies after a successful summer, are too apt, upon the strength of it, to neglect their preparations for the ensuing campaign, while the *French* leave no art nor stratagem untried to fill up the empty spaces of their armies, and swell them to an equal bulk with those of the Confederates. By this means our advantage is lost, and the fate of *Europe* brought to a second decision. It is now become an observation, that we are to expect a very indifferent year after a very successful one. *Blenheim* was followed by a summer that makes no noise in the war. *Ramillies*, *Turin*, and *Barcelona*, were the parents of our last campaign. So many dreadful blows alarmed the enemy, and raised their whole country up in arms. Had we on our side made proportionable preparations, the war by this time had been brought to a happy issue. If after having gained the great victories of *Blenheim* and *Ramillies*, we had made the same efforts as we should have done had we lost them, the power of *France* could not have withstood us.

In the beginning of the winter we usually get what intelligence we can of the force which the enemy intends to employ in the campaigns of the succeeding year, and immediately cast about for a sufficient number of troops to face them in the field of battle. This, I must confess, would be a good method if we were engaged in a defensive war. We might maintain our ground with an equal number of forces; but our business is not only to secure what we are already in possession of; we are to wrest the whole *Spanish* Monarchy out of the hands of the enemy; and in order to it, to work our way into the heart of his country by dint of arms. We should therefore put forth all our strength, and without having an eye to his preparations, make the greatest push that we are able on our own side. We are told that the enemy

at

at present thinks of raising threescore thousand men for the next summer; if we regulate our navies in that view we do nothing; let us perform our utmost, as they do, and we shall overwhelm them with our multitudes. We have it in our power at least to be four times as strong as the *French*, but if ten men are in war with forty, and the latter detach only an equal number to the engagement, what benefit do they receive from their superiority?

It seems therefore to be the business of the Confederates to turn to their advantage their apparent odds in men and horse; and by that means to out-number the enemy in all recounters and engagements. For the same reason it must be for the interest of the Allies to seek all opportunities of battle, because all losses on the opposite side are made up with infinitely more difficulty than on ours; besides that the *French* do their business by lying still, and have no other concern in the war than to hold fast what they have already got into their hands.

The miscarriage of the noblest project that ever was formed in *Europe*, can be ascribed to nothing else but our want of numbers in the several quarters of the war. If our armies on all sides had begun to busie and insult the enemy, at the same time that the forces marched out of *Piemont*, *Toulon* had been at present in the hands of the Duke of *Savoy*. But could that Prince ever have imagined that the *French* would have been at liberty to detach whole armies against him? or will it appear credible to posterity, that in a war carried on by the joint force of so many populous and powerful nations, *France* could send so great a part of its troops to one seat of the war, without suffering in any of the rest? Whereas it is well known, that if the Duke of *Savoy* had continued before *Toulon* eight days longer, he had been attacked by an army of sixty thousand men, which was more than double the number of his own; and yet the enemy was strong enough every where else to prevent the Confederates from making any impreſſion upon them. However, let us fall into the right meaſures, and we may hope that the ſtroke is only deferred. The Duke of *Savoy* hath ſecured a paſſage into *Dauphiny*, and if the Allies make ſuch efforts in all parts, as we may reaſonably expect from them, that Prince may ſtill make himſelf Maſter of the *French* dominions on the other ſide of the *Rhone*.

There is another part of our conduct which may perhaps deſerve to be conſidered. As ſoon as we have agreed with the States General upon any augmentation of our forces, we immediately negotiate with ſome or other of the *German* Princes, who are in the ſame confederacy, to furniſh out our quota in Mercenaries. This may be doubly prejudicial to the alliance; Firſt, as it may have an ill influence on the reſolutions of theſe Princes in the Diet of the Empire, who may be willing to ſettle as ſmall a quota as they can for themſelves, that they may have more troops to hire out; and in the next place, as it may hinder them from contributing the whole quota which they have ſettled. This actually happened in the laſt campaign, when we are told the *Germans* excuſed themſelves for their want of troops upon the *Rhine*, as having already put moſt of their forces into the *Britiſh* and *Dutch* ſervice. Such an excuſe, indeed, is very unjuſt, but it would be better to give them no occaſion of making it; and on ſuch occaſions to conſider what men are apt to do, as well as what they may do with reaſon.

It might therefore be for our advantage that all the foreign troops in the *Britiſh* pay ſhould be raiſed in neutral countries. *Switzerland* in particular, if timely applied to, might be of great uſe to us; not only in reſpect of the reinforcements which we might draw from thence, but becauſe ſuch a draught of forces would leſſen the number of thoſe that might otherwiſe be employed in the *French* ſervice. The bulk of our levies ſhould nevertheleſs be raiſed in our own country, it being impoſſible for neutral States to furniſh both the *Britiſh* and *Dutch* with a ſufficient num-

ber

ber of effective men; besides that the *British* soldiers will be more at the disposal of their General, and act with greater vigour under the conduct of one for whom they have so just a value, and whom they do not consider only as their leader, but as their country-man. We may likewise suppose that the soldiers of a neutral state, who are not animated by any national interest, cannot fight for pay with the same ardour and alacrity, as men that fight for their Prince and Country, their wives and children.

It may likewise be worth while to consider whether the military Genius of the *English* nation may not fall by degrees, and become inferiour to that of our neighbouring states, if it hath no occasion to exert it self. Minds that are altogether set on trade and profit, often contract a certain narrowness of temper, and at length become uncapable of great and generous resolutions. Should the *French* ever make an unexpected descent upon us, we might want soldiers of our own growth to rise up in our defence; and might not have time to draw a sufficient number of troops to our relief from the remote corners of *Germany*. It is generally said, that if King *Charles* II. had made war upon *France* in the beginning of his reign, he might have conquered it by the many veterans which were scattered up and down this kingdom, and had been inured to service in the civil wars. It is to be hoped we shall never have such another nursery of soldiers; but if the present war gives a more military turn to all other nations of *Europe*, than to our own, it is to be feared we may lose in strength, what we gain in number. We may apply the same consideration nearer home. If all our levies are made in *Scotland* or *Ireland*, may not those two parts of the *British* monarchy, after the disbanding of the present army, be too powerful for the rest, in case of a revolt? though, God be thanked, we are not in any danger of one at present. However, as these considerations do not concern the more essential part of our design, it is sufficient to have mentioned them.

The

The sparing of ourselves in so important a conjuncture, when we have but this single opportunity left or the preserving every thing that is precious amongst us, is the worst sort of management that we can possibly fall into. The good husbandry of one age may intail an endless expence upon all posterity. We must venture the sacrificing a part of our lives and fortunes at present, if we will effectually secure both for the future. The *British* Kingdom is so well stock'd with people, and so much abounds in horse, that we have power enough in our own hands, did we make our utmost use of it, to humble *France*, and in a campaign or two to put an end to the war.

There is not a more disagreeable thought to the people of *Great-Britain*, than that of a standing army. But if a Peace be made before the disunion of *France* and *Spain*, there are few, perhaps, that will not think the maintaining a settled body of numerous forces indispensable for the safety of our country. We have it therefore in our choice to raise such a strong reinforcement of troops as at present may be sufficient, in conjunction with those of the allies, for breaking the strength of the enemy; or when the peace is concluded, to keep on foot such an army as will be necessary for preventing his attempts upon us.

It is to be hoped that those who would be the most zealous against keeping up a constant body of regular troops after a general peace, will the most distinguish themselves for the promoting an augmentation of those which are now on foot; and by that means take care that we shall not stand in need of such an expedient.

We are indeed obliged by the present situation of our affairs to bring more troops into the field than we have yet done. As the *French* are retired within their lines, and have collected all their strength into a narrow compass, we must have greater numbers to charge them in their intrenchments, and force them to a battle. We saw the last campaign that an army of fourscore thousand of the best troops in *Europe*, with the Duke of *Marlborough* at the head of them,

could

could do nothing againſt an enemy that were too numerous to be aſſaulted in their camps, or attacked in
their ſtrong holds.

There is another conſideration which deſerves our
utmoſt attention. We know very well, that there is a
prince at the head of a powerful army, who may give
a turn to the war, in which we are engaged, if he thinks
fit to ſide with either party. I cannot preſume to gueſs
how far our Miniſters may be informed of his deſigns : but unleſs they have very ſtrong aſſurances of
his falling in with the grand alliance, or not oppo-
ſing it; they cannot be too circumſpect and ſpeedy in
taking their precautions againſt any contrary reſolution. We ſhall be unpardonable, if after ſuch an expence or blood and treaſure, we leave it in the power
of any ſingle Prince to command a peace, and make
us accept what conditions he thinks fit. It is certain,
according to the poſture of our affairs in the laſt
campaign, this Prince could have turn'd the ballance
on either ſide; but it is to be hoped the liberties of
Europe will not depend any more on the determination
of one man's will. I do not ſpeak this becauſe I
think there is any appearance of that Prince's uniting
himſelf to *France.* On the contrary, as he hath an
extraordinary zeal for the reformed religion, and great
ſentiments of honour, I think it is not improbable
we ſhould draw him over to the Confederacy, if we
preſs him to it by proper motives. His love for religion, and his ſenſe of glory, will both have their effect on a Prince who hath already diſtinguiſhed himſelf
by being a patron of proteſtants, and guarantee of the
Weſtphalian treaty. And if his intereſt hath any part
in his actions, the Allies may make him greater offers
than the *French* King can do in the preſent conjuncture.
There are large extents of dominion in the forfeited
principalities of the Empire; doubtful ſucceſſions, to
which the King of *Sweden* ſeems to have very juſt pre-
tentions; and at the ſame time a great title not yet diſ-
poſed of, and a ſeat of war on the *Moſelle*, where none
of our Generals have ſignalized themſelves. It would

be

be presumption to be particular in any proposals on such an occasion; it is enough to have shewn in general, that there are fair opportunities, of which the wisdom of the confederates may make use.

Common sense will direct us, when we see so warlike a Prince at the head of so great an army hovering on the borders of our confederates; either to obtain his friendship, or secure our selves against the force of his arms: We are sure whatever numbers of troops we raise, we shall have no hands but what will turn to account. Nay, we are certain, that extraordinary funds and augmentations for one or two campaigns may spare us the expence of many years; and put an end to taxes and levies for a whole age; whereas a long parsimonious war will drain us of more men and money, and in the end may prove ineffectual.

There is still a great popular objection, which will be made to every thing that can be urged on this subject. And indeed it is such a one as falls so much in with the prejudices and little passions of the multitude, that when it is turned and set off to advantage by illdesigning men, it throws a damp on the publick spirit of the nation, and gives a check to all generous resolutions for its honour and safety. In short, we are to be told, that *England* contributes much more than any other of the Allies, and that therefore it is not reasonable she should make any addition to her present efforts. If this were true in fact, I do not see any tolerable colour for such a conclusion. Supposing among a multitude embarqued in the same vessel, there are several that in the fury of a tempest will rather perish than work for their preservation; would it not be madness in the rest to stand idle, and rather chuse to sink together than do more than comes to their share? Since we are engaged in a work so absolutely necessary for our welfare, the remissness of our Allies should be an argument for us to redouble our endeavours rather than slacken them. If we must govern our selves by example, let us rather imitate the vigilance and activity

tivity of the common enemy, than the supineness and negligence of our friends.

We have indeed a much greater share in the war than any other part of the confederacy. The *French* King makes at us directly, keeps a King by him to set over us, and hath very lately augmented the salary of his court, to let us see how much he hath that design at his heart. Few of the nations in war with him, should they ever fall into his hands, would lose their religion or form of government, or interfere at present with him in matters of commerce. The *Dutch*, who are likely to be the greatest losers after the *Britains*, have but little trade to the *Levant* in comparison with ours, have no considerable plantations or commerce in the *West-Indies*, or any woollen manufactures for *Spain*; not to mention the strong barrier they have already purchased between *France* and their own country.

But after all, every nation in the confederacy makes the same complaint, and fancies it self the greatest sufferer by the war. Indeed in so common a pressure, let the weight be never so equally distributed, every one will be most sensible of that part which lies on his own shoulders. We furnish, without dispute, more than any other branch of the alliance: but the question is, whether others do not exert themselves in proportion according to their respective strength. The Emperor, the King of *Prussia*, the Elector of *Hannover*, as well as the States of *Holland* and the Duke of *Savoy*, seem at least to come up to us. The greatest powers in *Germany* are borrowing money where they can get it, in order to maintain their stated Quota's, and go thorough their part of the expence: and if any of the Circles have been negligent, they have paid for it much more in their late contributions, than what would have furnished out their shares in the common charges of the war.

There are others who will object the poverty of the nation, and the difficulties it would find in furnishing greater supplies to the war than it doth at present.

To

To this we might answer, that if the nation were really as poor as this objection makes it, it should be an argument for enforcing rather than diminishing our present efforts against *France*. The finking our taxes for a few years would be only a temporary relief, and in a little time occasion far greater impofitions, than thofe which are now laid upon us. Whereas the feafonable expence of part of our riches, will not only preferve the reft; but by the right ufe of them procure vaft additions to our prefent ftock. It may be neceffary for a perfon languifhing under an ill habit of body to lofe feveral ounces of blood, notwithftanding it will weaken him for a time, in order to put a new ferment into the remaining mafs, and draw into it frefh fupplies.

But we can by no means make this conceffion, to thofe who fo induftrioufly publifh the nation's poverty. Our country is not only rich, but abounds in wealth much more than any other of the fame extent in *Europe*. *France*, notwithftanding the goodnefs of its climate, the fertility of its foil, the multitude of its inhabitants, its convenient harbours, both for the *Ocean* and *Mediterranean*, and its prefent correfpondence with the *Weft-Indies*, is not to compare with *Great-Britain* in this particular. I fhall tranfcribe word for word the paffage of a late celebrated *French* Author, which will lay this matter in its full light; and leave the Reader to make the counter-part of the parallel between the two nations.

" According to all the enquiries that I have been
" able to make during feveral years, in which I have
" applied myfelf to this fort of remarks, I have ob-
" ferved, that about a tenth part of the people of this
" kingdom are reduced to beggary, and are actual
" beggars. That among the nine other parts, five
" are not in a condition to give alms or relief to thofe
" aforementioned, being very near reduced themfelves
" to the fame miferable condition. Of the four other
" remaining parts, three are very uneafy in their cir-
" cumftances, and embaraffed with debts and lawfuits.

, " In-

" In the tenth part, I reckon the Soldiers, Lawyers,
" Ecclefiafticks, Merchants and fubftantial Citizens,
" which cannot make up more than an hundred thou-
" fand families. And I believe I fhould not be miftaken,
" if I fhould fay, that there are not above ten thoufand
" of thefe families, who are very much at their eafe ;
" and if out of thefe ten thoufand we fhould take the
" the men that are employed in publick bufinefs, with
" their dependents and adherents, as alfo thofe whom
" the King fupports by his bounty, with a few Mer-
" chants, the number of thofe who remain will be fur-
" prifingly little. *Dixme Royale.*

What a dreadful account is this of nineteen millions
of people; for fo many the Author reckons in that
kingdom. How can we fee fuch a multitude of fouls
caft under fo many fubdivifions of mifery, without
reflecting on the abfurdity of a form of government
that facrifices the eafe and happinefs of fo many reafonable Beings to the glory of one of their fellow-creatures? But this is not our affair at prefent.

If we run over the other nations of *Europe* that
have any part in the prefent war, we fhall only pafs
through fo many different fcenes of poverty. *Spain,*
Portugal, and *Savoy* are reduced to great extremities.
Germany is exhaufted to the laft degree in many parts
of it, and in others plundered of all fhe had left.
Holland indeed flourifhes above the reft in wealth and
plenty : but if we confider the infinite induftry and
penurioufnefs of that people, the coarfenefs of their
food and raiment, their little indulgences of pleafure
and excefs, it is no wonder that notwithftanding they
furnifh as great taxes as their neighbours, they make
a better figure under them. In a commonwealth there
are not fo many overgrown eftates as in monarchies,
the wealth of the country is fo equally diftributed,
that moft of the community are at their eafe, though
few are placed in extraordinary points of fplendor and
magnificence. But notwithftanding thefe circumftances may very much contribute to the feeming profpe-
rity of the *United Provinces,* we know they are indebted
many

many millions more than their whole republick is worth, and if we confider the variety of taxes and impofitions they groan under at a time when their private diffentions run high, and fome of the wealthieft parts of the government refufe to bear their fhare in the publick expence, we fhall not think the condition of that people fo much to be envied as fome amongft us would willingly reprefent it.

Nor is *Great Britain* only rich as fhe ftands in comparifon with other States, but is really fo in her own intrinfick wealth. She had never more fhips at fea, greater quantities of merchandife in her warehoufes, larger receipts of cuftoms, or more numerous commodities rifing out of her manufactures than fhe has at prefent. In fhort, fhe fits in the midft of a mighty affluence of all the neceffaries and conveniences of life. If our filver and gold diminifhes, our publick credit continues unimpaired, and if we are in want of bullion, it lies in our own power to fupply our felves. The old *Roman* General, when he heard his army complain of of thirft, fhewed them the fprings and rivers that lay behind the enemy's camp. It is our own cafe: the rout of a *Spanifh* army would make us mafters of the *Indies*.

If Prince *Eugene* takes upon him the command of the confederate forces in *Catalonia*, and meets with that fupport from the alliance which they are capable of giving him, we have a fair profpect of reducing *Spain* to the entire obedience of the houfe of *Auftria*. The *Silefian* fund (to the immortal reputation of thofe generous patriots who were concerned in it) enabled that Prince to make a conqueft of *Italy*, at a time when our affairs were more defperate there, than they are at prefent in the kingdom of *Spain*.

When our Parliament has done their utmoft, another publick-fpirited project of the fame nature, which the common enemy could not forefee nor prepare againft, might in all probability fet King *Charles* upon the throne for which he hath fo long contended. One pitched battle would determine the fate of the *Spanifh* continent.

Let us therefore exert the united ſtrength of our whole Iſland, and by that means put a new life and ſpirit into the confederates, who have their eyes fixed upon us, and will abate or increaſe their preparations according to the example that is ſet them. We ſee the neceſſity of an augmentation if we intend to bring the enemy to reaſon, or reſcue our country from the miſeries that may befal it; and we find ourſelves in a condition of making ſuch an augmentation as, by the bleſſing of God, cannot but prove effectual. If we carry it on vigorouſly, we ſhall gain for our ſelves and our poſterity a long, a glorious, and a laſting peace; but if we neglect ſo fair an opportunity, we may be willing to employ all our hands, and all our treaſures, when it will be too late; and ſhall be tormented with one of the moſt melancholy reflections of an afflicted heart, That it was once in our power to have made our ſelves and our children happy.

The End of the Second Volume.

Lightning Source UK Ltd.
Milton Keynes UK
UKHW010004291118
333023UK00013B/1474/P